PERSUASION
AN INTERACTIVE-DEPENDENCY APPROACH

PERSUASION
AN INTERACTIVE-DEPENDENCY APPROACH

VICTORIA O'DONNELL
North Texas State University

JUNE KABLE
Midwestern State University

RANDOM HOUSE  NEW YORK

Library of Congress Cataloging in Publication Data

O'Donnell, Victoria.
Persuasion: an interactive dependency approach.
Bibliography: p. 248
Includes index.
1. Persuasion. (Rhetoric) 2. Persuasion (Psychology)
I. Kable, June. II. Title.
PN4121.03   808   81-11907
ISBN 0-394-32601-6   AACR2

Manufactured in the United States of America by R.R. Donnelley & Sons Company, Harrisonburg, Virginia
Composed by In-House Typesetting
Book design by Dana Kasarsky Design

CREDITS AND ACKNOWLEDGMENTS

ART CREDITS

6—Figure 1.1. Copyright Frank F. X. Dance, Denver, Colorado; 7—Figure 1.2. Copyright © 1975 by Donald Byker and Loren J. Anderson. By permission of Harper & Row, Publishers, Inc; 24—Figure 2.1. Rokeach, M. *Beliefs, Attitudes and Values*. Jossey-Bass, Inc., San Francisco: 1969. By permission; 37—Figure 3.1. Fishbein/Ajzen, *Belief, Attitude, Intention and Behavior: An Introduction-to Theory and Research*, © 1975, chapter 1, page 15, figure 1.1. Reprinted with permission; 43—Figure 3.3. *Attitude Change*: John Wiley, Inc. Permission by John Wiley, Inc.; 86—Figure 4.1. Albert Bandura, *Social Learning Theory*, © 1977, p. 23. Reprinted by permission of Prentice-Hall, Inc., Englewood Cliffs, New Jersey; 117—Figure 6.1. This figure is drawn from "The Judgment of Communicant Acceptability." by Gary Cronkhite and J. R. Liska. Reprinted from *Persuasion: New Directions in Theory and Research*. SAGE Annual Reviews of Communication Research, vol. 8, Michael E. Rologg and Gerald R. Miller, eds., copyright 1980, pp. 101–139. By permission of the publisher, Sage Publications, Beverly Hills, London; 208—Figure 9.1. Page 264, Figure 8, *Society, Media, and Audience: Reciprocal Relationships*. Reprinted by permission.

PHOTO AND CARTOON CREDITS

20—*Andy Capp* by Reggie Smythe. © 1980, Daily Mirror Newspapers, Ltd. Distributed by Field Newspapers Syndicate; 22—Copyright, Time Inc., 1980; 25—Permission granted by "World-Wide Photos"; 28—By permission; 30—The National Bureau of Standards, Washington, D.C.; 61—Reprinted courtesy of Chesebrough-Ponds, Inc.; 79—© Clairol, Inc., 81—Permission by Sam C. Rawls; 85—Reprinted by courtesy of *New Women* Magazine. Copyright © 1980 by NEW WOMEN: 102–103—

Dan Pryor; 108–109—Suzanne Aplin; 123—Boy Scouts of America; 148—Reprinted by Permission; 155—Reprinted by permission from *VFW* Magazine; 156—Johnson and Johnson Baby Products Company. By permission; 188—Reprinted with permission of Old Fashioned Distillery, Inc., division of Somerset Importers, Inc.; 207—Harley Schwadron. Reprinted with Permission from *TV Guide* ® Magazine. Copyright © 1980 by Triangle Publications, Inc, Radnor, Penn.; 242—Copyright by Burke Breathed.

This book is lovingly dedicated to

Browning and Christopher
(Victoria O'Donnell's sons)

and

The late George W. Cowart
(June Kable's father)

PREFACE

Persuasion is a major means of interacting with the people in your world—getting along with your family, dating, working, buying, selling, and obtaining and maintaining rights, respect, and security. You interact with others when you want to persuade them and when they want to persuade you. In order for persuasion to take place, there has to be interaction. Furthermore, when you persuade, you are dependent upon another if the goals of persuasion are to be achieved. In a like manner, if someone is to be persuaded, some need or desire must be fulfilled. There is a mutual dependency inherent in the persuasive interaction. That is why our book is entitled *Persuasion: An Interactive-Dependency Approach*. Throughout it, we have emphasized both the persuader and persuadee; thus, hopefully, it should be useful to you wherever you may find yourself during the persuasion process.

There are professions such as advertising, public relations, politics, marketing, among them, that are entirely devoted to persuasion. Other professions, for example, law, medicine, broadcasting, entertainment, journalism, make extensive use of persuasion as well. In fact, whatever your personal and professional goals and activities, you can benefit from the study of persuasion, for if you are interested in the dynamics of reinforcement and change, there will be something of interest to you within these pages.

The first chapter puts persuasion within the context of communication and highlights the nature of the interactive-dependency approach. Chapter 1 also defines persuasion and presents the authors' model of it. The rest of the book can be divided into four general areas.

The first section is comprised of Chapters 2, 3, and 4 and concerns itself with the "targets of persuasion." The targets are what the persuader wants to change or what may be changed in the persuadee. These are beliefs, attitudes, and behavior. Many theories and reports of research are included in these chapters, for it is necessary to know the nature of belief, attitudes, and behavior as well as the conditions under which they can be changed.

The second section is made up of Chapters 5, 6, 7, and 8 and is about the "stimulants to persuasion." These chapters include an analysis of the facilitating factors that seem to induce persuasion. Facilitating factors are those elements which make possible the reception and possible acceptance of the message by the persuadee. The facilitating factors discussed in these chapters are environment, source credibility, content and strategies of the message, organization, and language.

In persuasive speech, delivery is also a facilitating factor. Therefore, a section on preparing and delivering the persuasive speech is included in the Appendix.

The third section of the book is Chapter 9, which expands the "contexts of persuasion" to include the mass media. A seemingly endless flow of events, issues, ideas, objects, and personalities are brought to the attention of the public by the media. The relationship between the media, its audiences, and society is a complex one. Chapter 9 explores the preeminent media—film and television—according to their persuasive impact.

Chapter 10 represents the fourth area, "the resistance to persuasion," a very important topic for both the persuader and persuadee. It is important to not only know how to persuade and be a critical receptor of persuasion, but it is also critical to know how to purposefully inhibit or resist persuasion. It is also helpful to know why persuasion fails, even when we do not want it to. Sometimes persuasion seems to be successful, but its apparent achievement may have been influenced by the persuadee's desire to please others, and thus the long-term effects are neither real nor lasting.

We have tried to take a realistic approach to persuasion. In this book you will find theories and techniques designed to make you a successful persuader and persuadee, but sometimes persuasion fails in spite of the best efforts. It is useful to understand that it can not always succeed and to know why.

Both authors of this book have done research in persuasion and have taught the subject for many years. In addition, we have reviewed thousands of research reports in scholarly journals. What we have presented to you in this book is not a new theory of persuasion, but an integration of pervious theory and research, some of which is as recent as we could find and some of which is tried and true. Most of the material comes out of the behavioral sciences, for the contents of this book are essentially an attempt to promote applied behavioral science. We have tried our ideas and concepts out on colleagues in our convention papers, but most of all, we have refined and revised them with the help of students in our undergraduate and graduate persuasion classes. To all of our students who helped us, we are immensely grateful.

There are others whom we would like to thank. A long time ago a debate coach at The Pennsylvania State University persuaded Victoria O'Donnell to major in speech communication. She would like to thank Clayton H. Schug for his constant encouragement and belief in her abilities. The speech communication professors at Penn State were all very accomplished and deserve much gratitude, but one in particular stands out for her dedication to her students, Iline Fife. She is a fine role model for the student of persuasion.

The members of the Speech Communication and Theatre Department at Midwestern State University gave June Kable infinite moral support throughout the stages of this book, and she is in their debt. We also want to express our thanks to June's husband, Tim Kable, who for over two years shared many weekends not only with the two authors and their book, but with Browning and his dogs as well.

Since we live one hundred and fifty miles apart, we used to meet halfway between to work together in two small Texas towns, Bowie and Alvord. We want to say a special word of thanks to the waitresses in the Travel Inn and the Alvord Truck Stop who kept our coffee cups filled for hours on end.

Finally, we want to thank Robbie Pemberton for assisting us with the research for this book, Georgette Gerlach for getting books and articles through the interlibrary loan, Dan Pryor, Nancy Keiser, and Suzanne Aplin for taking photographs for Chapter 5, Junellen Simons and Carol Thayer for typing the manuscript, Terrell J. Book for getting the manuscript to the airport on time, Joseph DeVito, Robert Francesconi, David Jabusch, Roberta Ray, and Richard C. Rea, and, especially, Michael Roloff for their suggestions which considerably improved the book, and Richard Garretson and Kathleen Domenig, our editors at Random House, for their professional assistance and cheerful encouragement.

CONTENTS

PERSUASION
AN INTERACTIVE-DEPENDENCY APPROACH

1

PERSUASION
A THEORETICAL
AND
FUNCTIONAL OVERVIEW

OBJECTIVES

Upon completion of this chapter you should be able to:
1. Define *communication* and understand it as a process.
2. Define *persuasion* and understand it as an interactive-dependent process.
3. Understand the role of the variables in the model of persuasion.
4. Appreciate how knowledge of persuasion helps us coexist in society.

Persuasion is an integral and vital part of our daily life. Most of us tend to interact with people throughout the course of each day, and, when we do, we cannot help but engage in persuasion. We attempt to influence others on many levels, and they attempt to influence us with varying degrees of success.

In a free society, persuasive communication is often the only available means of influencing human conduct. We turn to persuasion as a tool to coexist in society, to get along with our fellow human beings, and to deal with our environment. Persuasion as a means of influencing people is part of the democratic way of life. Just as democracy is a complex ideology, persuasion is a complex process of attempts to influence people to change their attitudinal and behavioral responses. Because persuasion is complex, we often are unable to understand it completely. Yet we seem to have faith in it as a tool that we can use and that can be used on us.

Consider some comtemporary problems in which persuasion has been used. Americans experienced considerable frustration as they listened to reports of former President Carter's initially unsuccessful attempts to persuade the Iranians to release the American hostages. Although some people favored the use of force, most Americans hoped for a release which ultimately came about through a peaceful persuasive process. The energy crisis in America is another example that illustrates various means of persuading the public to alter behaviors in order to conserve energy. Some of these means have been successful. We were asked to change our thermostat settings, to drive to work in carpools, and to insulate our homes. Our lawmakers persuaded each other to require lower driving speeds and to regulate the temperatures in public buildings. We have resisted mandatory controls such as gasoline rationing, again with the hope that we could solve our problem through cooperation instead of coercion. In this sense, we have attempted to be dependent on one another, for if the users of energy would comply with voluntary standards of behavior and if they would carry out democratically made laws, then some of their energy would be conserved and they may not have to be forced to comply with undesirable actions such as rationing.

Because it is an adaptive process in which we interact with each other to fulfill personal needs, persuasion is unlikely to involve physical force or coercion. Whether or not persuasion is successful is contingent on the choices people make. One person chooses to attempt to persuade in order to fulfill a perceived need; another chooses to be exposed to persuasion because of the opportunity to have a perceived need fulfilled. The needs may not be the same, but their fulfillment is perceived to be mutually dependent. The act of getting people to perceive a mutual set of needs is a challenge in itself.

Take, for example, another recent and severe problem in America, the alarming increase in teen-age deaths. The 1980 surgeon general's report on the status of health and life span in the United States revealed that, although infant mortality and old-age maladies such as strokes have de-

4

clined, there is a large increase in deaths among teen-age Americans, especially violent deaths from suicide and automobile accidents, many of which appear to be related to a growing consumption of alcohol. The report concluded that steps must be taken to reverse this trend (National Public Radio News, KERA-FM, Dallas, Texas, December 4, 1980). Although medical research will continue to improve treatment of health problems, a different approach will have to be used to reduce teen-age deaths. This is a problem in persuasion, for teen-agers will have to be induced to alter their behavior. Another remarkably complex challenge, it incorporates people interacting with other people on many levels—in the family, at school, in public institutions, and on the highways. Those of us who think we can help will have to convince teen-agers that they need, perhaps, to use mature judgment about their drinking behavior. We will also have to recognize what needs teen-agers have that cause them to behave the way they do in the first place. Again, the focus is on the interactive-dependency of the parties concerned and involved in the process.

Although we engage in persuasion on a daily basis, we often do so without an appreciation of how complex the process is. Futhermore, we engage in persuasion with little knowledge of how to persuade, with frustration when we are unsuccessful in our attempts to persuade or to resist the persuasion of others, and with slight understanding of what happens to us when we are persuaded. Also, people do not always respond in the same way to persuasion, and some may choose not to respond at all. Indeed, certain individuals may respond one way one day and another way on a different day, depending on many variables.

Knowing what these variables are and how they function in the persuasive interaction may not only make us effective persuaders but may also make us enlightened persuadees. Subsequently, this knowledge can make us better participants in the dynamics of change in our society. It is to this end that this book has been written.

INTERACTIVE-DEPENDENCY

Gerald Miller and Michael Burgoon, in a recent overview of persuasion research, stress the need for a view of persuasion as a transaction rather than for a consideration of persuasion as a linear, unidirectional communicative activity that assumes an active persuader attempting to influence a relatively passive persuadee. A transactional view considers persuasion as a reciprocal activity wherein the interdependent participants influence one another (Ruben 1978, pp. 29–47). Miller and Burgoon cite D. Berlo, who characterizes the persuasive relationship as one "in which both users approach the engagement with expectations, plans, and anticipation . . . the contact may better be understood in terms of how both parties use and approach a message-event [rather] than in terms of how one person uses the contact to direct the other" (Ruben 1978, p. 31). In the persuasion process, the participants interact in a mutually dependent way. Such an *interactive-dependency* approach to persuasion is also the focus of this book. The interdependent, reciprocal relationship between the persuader and the persuadee is a dynamic, interactive, developmental, and continuing process. The persuader comes to the persuasion event with goals, needs, desires, and expectations to influence or cause some change in the persuadee. The persuadee comes to the persuasion event with his/her own set of goals, needs, desires, and expectations, which may or may not influence the persuader. Through communication, verbal and nonverbal, the agents affect each other and the outcome. The result may depend on whether or not their individual expectations are met.

It would be naïve, however, to assume that people are overly aware of their beliefs, values, attitudes, and behaviors in all situations. E. Langer (1978) suggests that much of our communication behavior is mindless because we are not consciously aware of many of the variables that are relevant to the successful resolution of a problem. Mindless behavior often occurs because people react in patterned or "scripted" ways to predictable situations and because cognitive activity can be exhausting (Roloff in Roloff and Miller 1980, p. 50).

It may be helpful, at this point, to examine the communication process before going further into the specific characteristics of persuasion.

COMMUNICATION AND PERSUASION

We have adapted Frank Dance's definition of *communication*, "human communication is the eliciting of a response through verbal symbols" (Dance 1967, p. 289), to include nonverbal symbols as well. Dance argues that what is unique about *human* communication is the ability of people to use verbal symbols. While this is true, human communication also relies heavily on nonverbal symbols, most of which have learned meanings. Thus, *communication* is defined as the eliciting of a response through verbal and nonverbal symbols.

Communication is a process that has been described by means of both linear and circular models. Dance offers a three-dimensional model (Figure 1.1) that is patterned after "a spiral that looks like a coiled ladder" and that widens at the top (Dance 1967, p. 295). A helix is three-dimensional and combines the features of the straight line and the circle model. Dance compares the helix to a child's Slinky toy, which tumbles down staircases by coiling in upon itself:

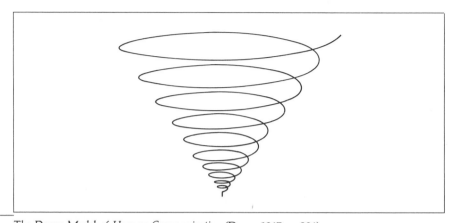

FIGURE
1.1

The Dance Model of Human Communication (Dance 1967, p. 296)

If you extend the spring halfway and then compress just one side of the helix, you can envision a communicative process open in one dimension but closed in another. At any and all times, the helix gives geometrical testimony to the concept that communication while moving forward is at the same moment coming back upon itself and being affected by its past behavior, for the coming curve of the helix is fundamentally affected by the curve from which it emerges. . . . The communication process, like the helix, is constantly moving forward and yet is always to some degree dependent upon the past, which informs the present and the future. (p. 296)

Although Dance applies the helical spiral model to the development of communication in an individual, it beautifully describes the communication process, which also is constantly moving forward but is dependent on the past to inform the present and the future. When two people communicate, they bring their past beliefs, experiences, and needs to the communication experience. Their past influences how and what they communicate as well as the act of communication itself.

Another model that describes the dynamics of communication, but in a two-dimensional, circular fashion, is the Byker-Anderson model (Figure 1.2) (Byker and Anderson 1975, p. 11). This model depicts two overlapping circles which represent two individuals interacting out of their own autonomous pasts and personalities. The area where the circles overlap is where they come together through communication to share or to be consubstantial in their gregariousness, their beliefs, attitudes, and values, and to use language and nonverbal symbols; here they share their ability and willingness to reason together, and here they share their pleasures and pains. The notion of reciprocity and interaction is clear in this model. The arrows depict motion and demonstrate that communication is ongoing, coactive, and developmental. Above all, communication enables us to share our ideas, to coexist in society, and to build a better world.

Hugh D. Duncan, a sociologist whose works stressed the necessity of understanding the significance of communication for social action, said, "Voices are everywhere wanting to be heard, and to be heard in dialogue" (Duncan 1968, p. 248). Another sociologist, Joyce O. Hertzler, reiterated Duncan's belief in communication as essential to society:

Communication is necessary in order to establish all social ties, to conduct action with or against others. Without it—and in sufficient quantity, quality, and range—there can be no inter-stimulation and reciprocal response, no establishment of common meaningful conceptualizations, no . . . provocative invitational, or directive action, no invention, no recording, accumulation, and transmission of knowledge, no social organization, no planning and reorganization. (Hertzler 1965, pp. 26–27)

Because of the importance of communication, especially persuasion, to society, scholars since the beginning of history have been concerned

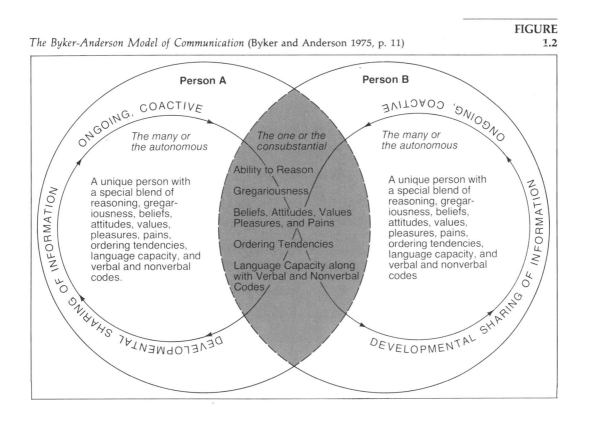

FIGURE
1.2

The Byker-Anderson Model of Communication (Byker and Anderson 1975, p. 11)

Person A

Person B

ONGOING, COACTIVE

ONGOING, COACTIVE

The many or
the autonomous

The one or the
consubstantial

The many or
the autonomous

A unique person with
a special blend of
reasoning, gregar-
iousness, beliefs,
attitudes, values,
pleasures, pains,
ordering tendencies,
language capacity, and
verbal and nonverbal
codes.

Ability to Reason

Gregariousness

Beliefs, Attitudes, Values
Pleasures, and Pains

Ordering Tendencies

Language Capacity along
with Verbal and Nonverbal
Codes

A unique person with
a special blend of
reasoning, gregar-
iousness, beliefs,
attitudes, values,
pleasures, pains,
ordering tendencies,
language capacity, and
verbal and nonverbal
codes

DEVELOPMENTAL SHARING OF INFORMATION

DEVELOPMENTAL SHARING OF INFORMATION

with the understanding and development of theories of rhetoric. In the fifth century B.C., Corax, the rhetorician who along with Tisius wrote the *Art of Rhetoric*, observing the Sicilians striving in the courts to retrieve the property that had been confiscated by tyrants who formerly ruled their land, developed the concept of probability to use in the courtroom. In Athens, when intellectual freedom was in full bloom, persuasion was practiced in the legislature, the courts, and at state ceremonies. In 333 B.C., Aristotle wrote *Rhetoric*, which became the conceptual framework for traditional persuasion theory. Rhetoricians throughout the centuries developed theories to describe, and in some cases prescribe, practices of persuasion. What is interesting is that most of the key works on rhetoric were developed in societies that were in the midst of political and social upheaval, but that allowed discourse in an open and free manner. Few great writings on persuasion have been found in countries where the people's right to speak out has been repressed.

Persuasion has traditionally been thought of as a form of communication designed to bring about change. Perhaps a better word than *change* would be *response*. Miller describes such "response" in three processes (Miller in Roloff and Miller 1980, p. 16).

First, there is the response-shaping process, which is similar to a learning process. Children learn to pick up their toys. The mother who shows them how it is done at first might be thought of as a teacher. Yet, when she is coping with their reluctance to pick up toys, she may be seen in the role of a persuader.

Second, there is the response-reinforcing process. This process does not concern change. It refers to those persuasive efforts that say, "Stay like you are, but more so." Several years ago in the Texas Speech Communication Association, the slogan was "Be loyal members—attend the convention." Recently, even more commitment from members is being requested with the slogan "Contact your state representative concerning the issues which directly affect our professional survival." Likewise, Democrats tell us to be better Democrats. The United Fund pats us on the back for last year's contribution and pleads for more. All of these are examples of persuasive reinforcement.

Third, there is the response-changing process, which is the type of persuasion that is the most familiar to us. In the 1980 election, Republicans were asked to become Democrats, and Democrats were asked to become Republicans. Both were asked to become Independents. Thus, we can say that persuasion is a form of communication designed to create learning responses, to reinforce desirable responses, and to change certain responses.

The study of persuasion is important beyond the person-to-person interaction, especially at the national and international levels. The development of competition in business and politics and the growing influence of the mass media challenge us not only to be effective individual persuaders, but to become astute observers and partakers of the persuasive process on a broad scale.

A DEFINITION AND A MODEL OF PERSUASION

Persuasion is a complex process of human interaction. A process view of the world perceives all of the ingredients of a persuasive act as interacting. To understand this is to comprehend the persuader and persuadee as they respond both to themselves and to forces outside themselves.

Persuasion emphasizes influence over others, influence over their perceptions, ideas, beliefs, attitudes, and behavior. The persuader attempts to influence the response of the persuadee in a way consistent with the persuadee's values and cultural norms. The persuadee is expected to exercise judgment about the persuasive message. Thus, the basis of persuasion is the assumption of reciprocity. The persuader seeks a desired response; the persuadee responds to stimuli that have some meaning or importance to him or her. Kenneth Burke's admonition to identify with the persuadee is an essential guideline for the persuader: "Only those voices from without are effective which can speak in the language of the voice within" (1950, p. 563).

The persuasive process is complex not only because it is reciprocal and dependent on bonds of identification, but also because it involves contexts that may be perceived differently by the involved parties. Furthermore, the process requires symbolic transactions during which the persuader and persuadee alternate their roles.

The key word in defining persuasion is *influence*. A complete definition of persuasion would include the concept of persuasion as a process. *Persuasion* is a complex, continuing, interactive process in which a sender and a receiver are linked by symbols, verbal and nonverbal, through which the persuader attempts to influence the persuadee to adopt a change in a given attitude or behavior because the persuadee has had perceptions enlarged or changed. Briefly, then, a positive response from the persuadee might be, "I never thought of it that way before" or "I never saw it that way before." Messages are related to or contrasted with the persuadee's existing repertoire of information. Consequently, he/she may think about, add to, or challenge the information stated in the message. As a result, his/her perception may be changed (Perloff and Brock in Roloff and Miller 1980, p. 69). Thus, persuasion, when it changes attitudes or behavior, changes perception as an integral part of the process. Our model of persuasion (Figure 1.3), which includes this concept, is shown on page 10.

The persuasion model can be divided into four general categories: (1) reality, (2) persuader and persuadee: autonomous individuals, (3) environment, and (4) message processing, with the process of persuasive communication pulling it altogether.

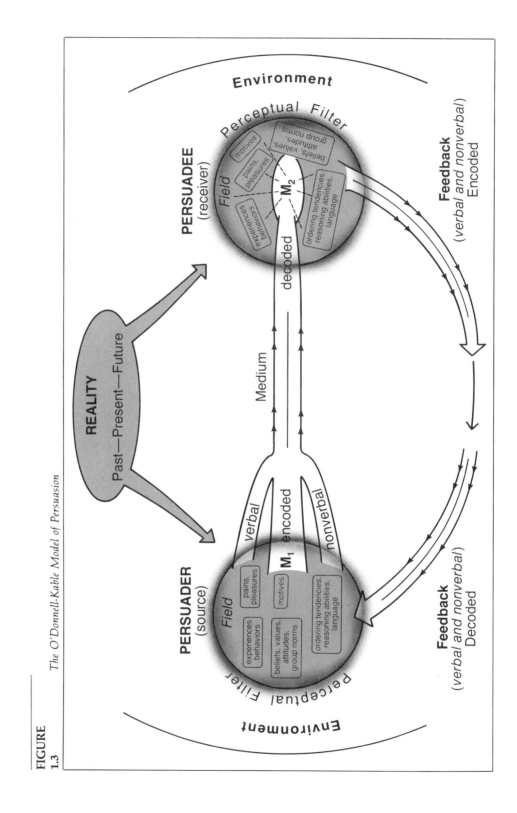

FIGURE
1.3   *The O'Donnell-Kable Model of Persuasion*

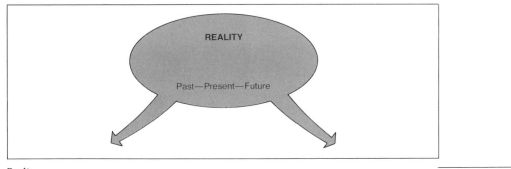

Reality

FIGURE
1.4

Reality

External reality (Figure 1.4) is made up of events from the past, present, and future as perceived by us and others. "The temperature was fifty degrees yesterday," "It is seventy degrees today," and "Since it is snowing heavily right now, it will probably be colder in the morning" are reality statements. Reality is perceived and interpreted according to the people who observe and experience it.

Persuader and Persuadee: Autonomous Individuals

Figure 1.5 represents an autonomous individual. Each individual possesses his/her special blend of values, beliefs, attitudes, group norms, pleasures,

Autonomous Individual

FIGURE
1.5

pains, experiences, behaviors, motives, language, reasoning abilities, and ordering tendencies. These attributes form the individual's *field*, which is comprised of psychological sets and communicative abilities. The "field" concept is borrowed from Kurt Lewin's Field Theory (Hall and Lindzey, 1970). Lewin was interested in the individual's psychological field or life space. The field is not an objective world, but a subjective world. The life space is a complex and fluid field in which a person moves on the basis of the tensions of the moment. The tensions arise because of the physiological and psychological needs of the individual, which are related to perceived goals in a given situation. Perception of reality is tempered by these inner needs and goals. A person selects a behavior according to a desire to satisfy needs and goals. Our beliefs, values, attitudes, experiences, and so on will determine what stimuli in external reality we respond to and how these stimuli are perceived.

Perception is the process of extracting information from the world outside (external reality) as well as from within ourselves. Reality is perceived through our *perceptual filters*, which are determined by the elements within our fields. The persuader perceives reality through perceptual filters in a way that may significantly differ from the way in which the persuadee perceives reality because of differing fields and subsequent different perceptual filters. The process of persuasion is an attempt to create similar perceptions of reality for mutual satisfaction of goals.

Because people are unique and possess individualized experiences, values, group norms, and other characteristics represented in the circles shown in Figure 1.6, a persuader must seek similar experiences, values,

FIGURE
1.6

Overlapping Circles

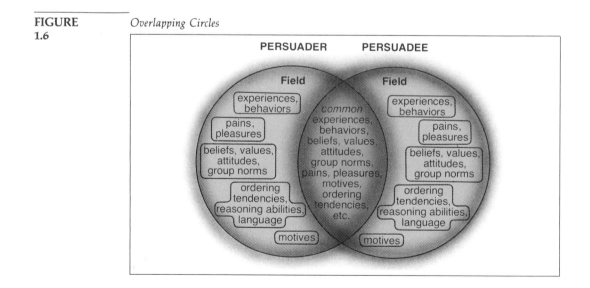

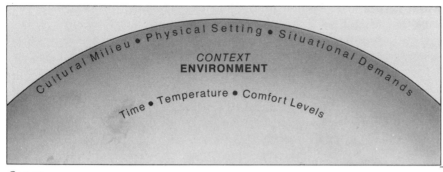

Context

FIGURE
1.7

group norms, and so forth through which he/she can communicate a message. A persuader should never assume that a message sent is automatically received simply because it is spoken or written. A seventy-degree temperature may be perceived and thus spoken of as a "heat wave" by a person from Scotland, whereas a Texan who had endured temperatures over one hundred degrees for weeks during the summer of 1980 may perceive and thus speak of seventy degrees as a "cool spell." In order for the Scot and the Texan to share a perception, they would have to locate a common experience with weather conditions and work from it.

When commonalities are discovered and expressed, the two circles, the persuader and the persuadee, overlap because something is shared. The Byker-Anderson model (p. 7) refers to the two autonomous individuals becoming consubstantial—that is, they come together in substance because they share thoughts, words, and deeds. Consubstantiality unites the two parties because they, through the process of communication, now share something. We have all had the experience of being a stranger in a new place and of meeting someone who may have visited our hometown. Because we shared once having been in a similar location, we feel an affinity for the other person. As people get to know each other and discover that they share similar experiences, values, attitudes, and so on, their circles overlap more and more.

Environment

The persuasion process is depicted in the model by means of the persuader perceiving elements of the external reality through a perceptual filter within a given *environment*. The environment (Figure 1.7) of persuasion includes the cultural milieu, architecture, and other aspects of the physical setting—the time, temperature, conditions of comfort or discomfort, and the demands of

the situation. The psychological sets of the individual's field are often related to the environment of the persuasion setting. The environment itself
can be persuasive and will influence the persuadee's reception of the message. If a persuader is motivated to elicit a response from a persuadee, the
persuader will conceive a message designed to obtain it.

Message Processing

The message is encoded, put into symbols for the transaction, according to
the persuader's verbal and nonverbal encoding abilities (Figure 1.8). This is
represented as M_1(*Message Number One*). The message, in the form of the
verbal language of words and the nonverbal language of the voice and body,
is sent through a *medium*. The medium may be sound and light waves, paper
and pencil, radio, television, music, or anything else that transmits the symbols to someone else. Given the freedom from interference or communication "noise," the message may reach the persuadee.

  If and when the message is received, it will pass through the persuadee's *perceptual filters* much like hot water passes through ground coffee,
and that which survives the passage through the persuadee's *perceptual filters*
becomes M_2 (*Message Number Two*). This message is *decoded* or assigned
meaning according to the field of the persuadee. It will be assigned value on
the basis of the persuadee's psychological sets and communicative response
mechanisms and possibly incorporated into them. The message will also be

**FIGURE
1.8**
 Message Processing

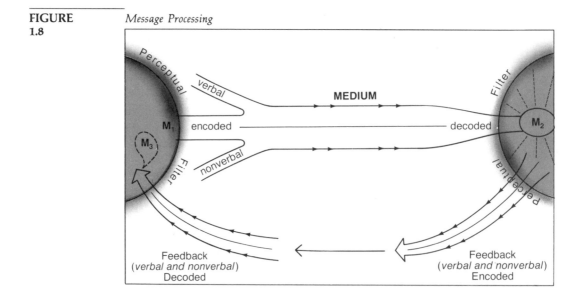

perceived according to the persuadee's own context in the persuasion transaction as well as with the persuadee's own perception of reality.

The persuadee may then choose to react to the message by encoding a response or feedback to the persuader and the message. The feedback will have to be decoded by the persuader, who may respond with a different version of the message (M_3). *Feedback* is a verbal or nonverbal response to the persuader's message (Clement and Frandsen 1976, p. 26). The roles of persuader and persuadee are not static in nature, but can be interchanged throughout a message. Each person can function as both persuader and persuadee by means of a continuous interchange of verbal and nonverbal messages.

For the persuader, feedback provides information about how the persuadee is being affected as well as how the persuadee is perceiving and interpreting the message. For the persuadee, feedback indicates how adaptable and sensitive the persuader is to the persuadee's responses.

As the developmental and interactive process continues, it is possible to have refined messages—M_4, M_5, and so on—until mutual satisfaction is attained or the process of persuasion comes to a standstill.

If the persuader is successful in achieving the desired response, the fulfillment of the persuasive purpose, the new attitude of the persuadee will change the persuadee's perception of reality. It will be a voluntary change because the persuadee has evaluated the message according to the needs and goals within his/her field and thus should feel a sense of satisfaction. Successful persuasion causes the persuadee to feel that agreement has occured because something is to be gained by it and not because the persuader has forced agreement.

A few years ago, the California Heart Association offered tape recordings, to be played at intervals, to smokers desirous of quitting smoking. These recordings evoked responses from smokers who had other needs. For example, one recording said, "Did you know that you can get reduced life and automobile insurance premium rates when you do not smoke? It's true, because nonsmokers are better insurance risks. What a great idea!" If it were successful, this message would have involved changing the smoker's perception by offering the fulfillment of a need, saving money, instead of criticizing smoking behavior. Another tape said, "Kissing a smoker is a little like making love to an ash tray." This could evoke the response "I never thought of it that way before." If the smoker needed to be sexually attractive, the persuasion of the tape offered satisfaction of a vital need.

It is true that people will respond to persuasion that has a goal for them or promises to help them in some way by satisfying a want or need. A persuasive message must arouse and confirm ideas that are consistent with the needs, wants, and desires of the audience. If we are to be successful as persuaders, we must remember what Charles Henry Woolbert said over sixty years ago: "To study persuasion is to study human nature minutely.

Without a guide to men's action probabilities, without appreciating and understanding their action grooves, a speaker or writer works in a vacuum and so has no possible basis for insuring success. . . . More than half of success in winning men [and women] is in understanding how they work" (Woolbert 1920).

In the ensuing chapters of this book, we shall consider how men and women "work." Each of the elements of the individual's "field" are discussed to give you a working knowledge of the variables together with a functional approach to sending and receiving persuasive messages. Whether you desire to be an effective public or private persuader or persuadee or both, if you follow the approach of this book, we think you will enhance those ends. It is important to remember, however, that persuasion does not always succeed. The information in this book may help you understand why it does not, and that is useful information as well.

SUMMARY

Persuasion is a complex communication process that affects us in our daily lives. Because people look to each other to fulfill various needs, they interact through persuasion in a mutually dependent way. The interactive-dependency relationship inherent in persuasion is the focus of this book and of the model of persuasion that has been developed in the chapter. The persuader and persuadee are equally important and attention is given to each one. The forces exerted by external and internal factors on individuals as they engage in persuasion are explored in the subsequent chapters.

KEY WORDS

Interactive-dependency	Perceptual filter
Reciprocity	Field
Communication	Feedback
Helix	Consubstantial
Medium	Environment
Persuasion	Encode
Process	Decode

EXERCISES

1. Describe a dozen times when you have been involved in persuasion in the last twenty-four hours. Were you mainly the persuader or the persuadee? Were you successfully persuasive? Were you easily persuaded?
2. Rate yourself as both a persuader and a persuadee. Make a list of personal objectives that you would like to achieve from taking a course in persuasion.
3. Describe a specific persuasive situation in which interactive-dependency was readily apparent to you. What were the needs and expectations of the persuader? What were the needs and expectations of the persuadee?
4. Develop and draw your own model of communication.
5. Keeping the Byker-Anderson model of communication in mind, try to solve the following problem:

    You are an airplane pilot flying solo somewhere over New Guinea. Your plane is malfunctioning, and you have to bail out. You do not know exactly where you are, but you observe that you are near water and a beach surrounded by a thick jungle. You have been unable to spot any towns, buildings, or roads from the air. All you can see is water and trees. Your parachute opens, and you know that you will land safely on the beach. As you drift toward the sand, you see that you will land about twenty feet from a human being who is walking down the beach. He is naked, dark-skinned, male, and carrying a spear. He looks like the pictures you have seen of aborigines. He appears to be your only source of help. How will you communicate with him? How will you get him to help you find food and shelter and, above all, a means to get back home? How will you get your autonomous circles to overlap?

6. Using the O'Donnell-Kable model of persuasion, describe a persuasive situation in which you have been involved. Identify and describe all of the components in the model.

READINGS

Corbett, E. P. J. "A Survey of Rhetoric." In *Classical Rhetoric for the Modern Student*, New York: Oxford University Press, 1971, pp. 594-630.

Dance, F. E. X., ed. *Human Communication Theory*. New York: Holt, Rinehart, and Winston, 1967.

Duncan, H. D. *Communication and Social Order*. New York: Oxford University Press, 1962.

———. *Symbols and Society*. New York: Oxford University Press, 1968.

Miller, G. R., and Burgoon, M. "Persuasion Research: Review and Commentary." In *Communication Yearbook 2*, edited by B. D. Ruben. New Brunswick, N.J.: International Communication Association, 1978.

ANCHORS FOR PERSUASION
BELIEFS, VALUES, AND GROUP NORMS

OBJECTIVES

Upon completion of this chapter you should be able to:

1. Discover anchors for persuasive propositions.
2. Distinguish among primitive, authority, derived, and inconsequential beliefs.
3. Understand the difference between a belief and a value.
4. Understand the importance of values in making decisions about how to behave in certain situations.
5. Relate membership in groups to the influence of the group's norms upon its members.
6. See how groups that you do not belong to influence you with their norms.

A radio editorial on KQV in Pittsburgh (June 17, 1976) advocated open competition in liquor sales, a radical change since liquor could only be sold by state liquor stores owned and operated by the state of Pennyslvania. The basis for the persuasion in the editorial was that "We believe in and value free enterprise." The belief in free enterprise was an *anchor* to which the specific persuasive proposition (open competition in liquor sales) was tied. An *anchor* is a starting point for a change because it represents something that is already widely accepted by the potential persuadees. This chapter is about anchors—beliefs, values, and group norms—to which individual persuasive goals can be tied. It is based on the premise that a persuader has to use already established beliefs to create new beliefs.

Paul Holtzman tells of an overheard telephone conversation between a professor aspiring to conduct some research and a representative of the Office of Education, which was about to sponsor the research project. There appeared to be some problem over the project budget, and the people involved were trying to find ways to reduce the cost of a proposed survey of graduate programs from the varying points of view of related disciplines. Holtzman reports the conversation as follows:

OE: Why do you have to send four men out to each program? Couldn't one person do the interviewing just as well?

PROFESSOR: We want the study to be interdisciplinary, don't we?

OE: Yes, I guess I wasn't thinking of it in that way. (Holtzman 1970, p. 105)

Potential persuadees are not necessarily "thinking of it in that way" at the outset. The persuader's task is to elicit that response through the establishment of a link between what is already accepted by the persuadees and what the persuader would like them to accept.

BELIEF

A persuader should have some idea of what beliefs his/her potential audience has before attempting to bring about change. A *belief* is an inference that a person makes about the world. It is a cognition about the existence of things, events, ideas, and persons. Milton Rokeach (1960) says that a belief is a simple statement preceded by "I believe that . . ."

Specifically, a belief represents a perceived probability of a relationship between two things or a thing and a characteristic of that thing (Bem 1970, p. 4). In expressing a belief, there is also an inherent judgment about the object of belief. The judgment may be about oneself ("I believe I am intelligent"), another person ("I believe that Kermit is honest"), an idea

(Fort Worth Star Telegram April 26, 1980, p. F5)

("Research is necessary in writing a book"), an event ("It rained yesterday"), a thing ("The soccer ball is round"), or the environment ("The sky is blue"). Thus, beliefs involve the establishment of a link between any two aspects of an individual's world (Fishbein and Ajzen 1975, p. 131). Beliefs are often based on other beliefs *in* something, such as one's perceptual senses ("I believe that what I see with my eyes is really there") or in the existence of something ("I believe in God"). Beliefs are also based on beliefs *about* something that links the belief object to some attribute ("I believe that God is omnipotent"). We have acquired our beliefs from experience, from authority figures in our lives, and from other beliefs. Thus, a belief comes from a trust in one's perceptions, trust in other people, and previous acceptance of other beliefs as true or false.

In order to change old beliefs or create new ones, the persuader will have to build on beliefs that already exist inside the members of the audience. In other words, the persuader has to use anchors of belief to create a new belief. Think of a formula: "*If* you believe in X, *then* you should believe in Y." For example, if you believe "the orange is round," you are indicating first that "my eyes tell me that what I see is there" and, second, that there is a conceptual belief in "roundness" that was learned from some authority figure. Thus, what happens in terms of our formula is this: "*If* my eyes tell me true, *then* I see an orange." "*If* the concept that Mother taught me as 'round' is applied to that orange, *then* the orange is round." You have established a link between your perception and an object, between a concept learned from an authority and an object, and between an object and some attribute of it. This breakdown of characteristics of a simple belief is so central to our thinking that it is seldom questioned. Daryl Bem says that this is usually a nonconscious process, a sort of unawareness of the belief sources of simple beliefs. These kinds of beliefs, which Bem characterizes as "primitive beliefs," are often shared by many people (1970, p. 4).

High-order beliefs represent more of a dimension of probability and thus may vary from person to person. They are beliefs that are derived from other beliefs ("I believe what I read in this book"). This kind of belief depends on the believer's acceptance of the source (the authors and their sources), other sources (the teacher who assigned it, the publishing company, book reviewers), previous knowledge (what one has learned in other books and courses, and from teachers, peers, etc.), and previous experiences. The high-order belief may be generated from just one other belief, or it may be generated from a multitude of other beliefs. The high-order belief can be characterized in the form of a syllogism, and it is differentiated. I may believe that my brand of mattress is the best because *Consumer Reports* says it is. A syllogism would look like this:

Major premise: *Consumer Reports* is a reliable source for finding out what is the best product.
Minor premise: *Consumer Reports* says brand X mattress is the best mattress.
Conclusion: Therefore, Brand X mattress is the best mattress.

You may agree with the belief that brand X mattress is the best mattress, but for a different reason. Your syllogism may look like this:

Major premise: A mattress that gives me a good night's sleep is a good mattress.
Minor premise: Brand X mattress gives me a good night's sleep every night.
Conclusion: Therefore, Brand X mattress is a good mattress.

The point is that people may believe the same things for different reasons, and their reasons may be tested by formal logic or may have little or no basis in logic. The one thing that high-order beliefs have in common is that they are derived from other beliefs that are related to one another on a conscious level.

People have hundreds of thousands of beliefs. Not all are equally important, for they vary according to centrality in one's belief system and in their changeability. Some beliefs are easily changed, and some are nearly totally resistant to change. Rokeach (1969) discusses beliefs within systems that are characterized by levels and intensity of belief.

Systems of Belief

There are five kinds of beliefs resting on three functions:

1. The belief systems are not equal in importance or value.
2. The more important beliefs have a greater resistance to change than the less important ones. The propensity for change has a direct correlation

Everything is relative.

(*Time* March 23, 1978)

with the level of importance of a belief—that is, inconsequential and peripheral beliefs can be changed more readily than primitive beliefs.
3. The more important the belief being changed, the more serious the repercussions to the change.

Rokeach, like Bem, classifies beliefs according to how difficult it would be to change them. The first and most central belief is the primitive belief, which has unanimous concensus or complete agreement in society and to which an individual holds with complete conviction. The second is also a primitive belief, but it has zero consensus, for it is possible that only the individual believes it. It is a belief that is highly personal and that has developed from individual experience. While this belief may not have a consensus in society, it is strongly held by the individual. The third is the authority belief, which tells the individual who or what are trustworthy sources of belief. These sources can be highly credible people or sources of information. The fourth is the derived belief, which stems from the belief in authority. The fifth is the inconsequential belief, which is not of major consequence and tends to be arbitrary. The fourth and fifth beliefs are peripheral, some of which could be traced back to primitive beliefs. Figure 2.1 (see page 24) includes Rokeach's examples of each type of belief.

This hierarchy of beliefs is very important to persuasion, for not only are the central (primitive) beliefs in the system almost impossible to change, but Rokeach has also found that they are more resistant to change than those based on authority (1969, pp. 22–61). The persuader, therefore, would be well advised to not try to change the persuadee's primitive beliefs or even the authority beliefs, but rather to concentrate on peripheral beliefs. Utilizing the concept of anchoring, however, the persuader could link the desired peripheral belief to a primitive or authority belief. For example, *if* a persuadee has a primitive belief in Christian brotherhood, *then* a persuader could ask for a change in a peripheral belief regarding an international food-sharing program. The persuader could also link the desired belief to an authority belief as an anchor. *If* you believe in the president and his goals for international peace, *then* you will support his program for sharing food with other nations.

The more a persuader knows about the beliefs of the persuadees, the more potential for anchoring there is. Beliefs, especially central beliefs, can be used to create peripheral beliefs and to elicit the "I never thought of it that way before" responses.

PERSUADER: You believe in individual freedom, don't you?
PERSUADEE: Of course. I always have.
PERSUADER: Then, you should favor open housing.
PERSUADEE: Well, I never thought of it that way before.

The use of anchors in this manner may not successfully change peripheral beliefs, but it causes the persuadee to at least reassess certain peripheral beliefs to fit them in with the more central beliefs in his/her belief system.

VALUES

Many of our primitive beliefs are values. Rokeach says, "a value is an *enduring* belief that a specific mode of conduct or end-state of existence is personally or socially preferable to an opposite or converse mode of conduct or end-state of existence" (1973, p. 5). Specifically, a *value* is a prescriptive belief that judges whether or not a means or an end is desirable or

---

Type A: Primitive Beliefs, Unanimous Consensus

    1. I was born in (real birthplace).
    2. I am _____ years old.
    3. My name is _____.

Type B: Primitive Beliefs, Zero Consensus

    4. I believe my mother loves me.
    5. Sometimes I have a strong urge to kill myself.
    6. I like myself.

Type C: Authority Beliefs

    7. The philosophy of Adolf Hitler is basically a
       sound one, and I am all for it.
    8. The philosophy of the pope is basically a sound one.
    9. The philosophy of Jesus Christ is basically a sound one.

Type D: Derived Beliefs

    10. People can be divided into two distinct groups: the
        weak and the strong.
    11. Birth control is morally wrong.
    12. The Ten Commandments are of divine origin.

Type E: Inconsequential Beliefs

    13. I think summertime is a much more enjoyable time of
        year than wintertime.
    14. I would never walk through a revolving door if
        I had a choice.
    15. The side from which I get out of bed in the morning
        really does influence how I feel.

FIGURE 2.1   *Examples of Beliefs* (Rokeach 1969)

undesirable. Values are the kinds of beliefs that Rokeach describes as central or primitive in the belief system. Values are derived from culture and will vary accordingly, although some values seem to be shared by all humans. Values are social products that have been transmitted and preserved in successive generations through one or more of society's institutions. E.

If the students value breathing, then they will not walk on the grass.
(Associated Press Wirephoto, Iowa City, Iowa, Summer 1977)

Steele and W. C. Redding have analyzed American values and have concluded that Americans value the puritan and pioneer morality, individualism, achievement, change and progress, equality, optimism, and pragmatism (1962). On the other hand, a more recent survey done by an insurance company found that the prime American values are power, money, and sex (National Public Radio News. KERA-FM 1978).

It is difficult to get agreement on values because they are highly personal and some may even be unconscious. Values also tend to be general and abstract and are applicable to a variety of situations. "I value justice, honesty, and the work ethic; therefore, I have a positive preference for a political candidate who exhibits these qualities." This kind of specific application relates a value to an attitude and possible voting behavior. Rokeach says that we have only a few dozen values, but they may serve as anchors for numerous attitudes.

Rokeach also maintains that values are organized into hierarchies or systems that become guides to action. Different people will rank their values in different orders, but they will also rank their values differently, depending on various situations. Rokeach compares values to our children, whom we love dearly. A parent may say that he/she loves all the children in a family equally. Yet if one child is ill or in need of attention or handicapped in some way, then the parent may be forced to show a preference for one child over the others. When we defend our values or try to share them or teach them to others, we may do so with passion, regarding these values as absolutes. This is especially true if a value is endangered in some way. We may take freedom for granted until it is threatened; then it becomes uppermost in the hierarchy. Rokeach says, "When one value is actually activated along with others in a given situation, the behavioral outcome will be a result of the relative importance of all the competing values that the situation has activated" (1973, p. 6). While values are enduring, they are also changing in character.

Carl Rogers says that, as the result of experience, a mature person's values change. His years as a therapist have allowed him to observe that when people mature and grow in self-esteem, they move away from façades and "shoulds and oughts" to a preference for being and accepting real feelings about the self. When this happens, there is a reordering of values. Deep relationships with others are positively valued along with a high regard for an openness to one's inner and outer experiences. Rogers maintains that when people grow into such self-awareness, they tend to value most those objects, experiences, and goals that make for their own survival, growth, and development, and for the survival and development of others (1964, p. l66). He concludes his analysis on a hopeful note: "In any culture, given a climate of respect and freedom in which he is valued as a person, the mature individual would tend to choose and prefer these same value directions" (p. 167).

Rokeach suggests the same developments in value change, for he has found that when values are challenged, people react as if their self-esteem had been challenged too. B. Spillman, in reference to Rokeach's message, says that "individuals change their values knowingly not because the value change has been internalized, but as a defensive strategy to prevent them from appearing stupid or immoral" (1979, p. 68).

Over the past several years, we have asked our students to try to reach some consensus of value agreement in order to arrive at lists of value-anchors for persuasive messages. The values that seem to be the most consistent in these consensus-producing activities are freedom, peace, friendship, self-fulfillment, education, wisdom, equality, communication, sensitivity, and open-mindedness. The values the students never seem to be able to agree on are religion, democracy, ambition, success, power, beauty, and wealth.

Values are measuring sticks by which we assess our behavior and obtain our goals. They are concepts of right and wrong, good and bad, true and false. When values are not shared, the potential for communication breakdowns is great. One of the reasons why so many "peace" treaties have been broken has been that assumptions about values were false. The American government's treaties with Native Americans of the Great Plains broke down because the government valued majority rule, but the Native Americans valued tribal rule; the government valued ownership of land, but the Native Americans did not believe in private property. As persuaders and persuadees, we should remember that it is dangerous to assume that we share the same values. If we can be sure that a value is shared, then it constitutes a very important anchor for persuasion.

GROUP NORMS

Group norms are both beliefs and values that are derived from membership in groups or from positive references to non-membership groups. Citizens of the United States believe in the freedom of speech and value free enterprise. These are culturally derived beliefs and attitudes. On the other hand, a person may not belong to an esteemed group, but because he/she respects that group, he/she may adopt its beliefs and values.

If television commercials reflect group norms accurately, the American people as a group believe in success. Even if they are not members of those groups, they admire youth, the nuclear family, and athletes.

Bem says that the major influence on people is *people* (1970, p. 75). We tend to accept judgments made by people who are like us and whose approval we seek, and by groups to which we belong. Throughout our lives we have been rewarded for conforming to group norms. Since elementary school, we were rewarded for doing what everyone was told to do and punished if we departed from the norm. The child who sits quietly with hands folded on the desk listening to the teacher is considered acceptable, but the child who gets up in the middle of a lesson to go check on the fish in the aquarium by the window is chastised for disobedience. Later on, in junior and senior high school, there is tremendous group pressure to conform to one's peers. Peer pressure influences how young people dress, talk, and behave. They want to be like the group in order to be accepted by it.

People are also subject to what sociologists call "tunnel vision." Anxiety leads to an inability to make rational judgments under conditions of panic. Thus people will impulsively follow the crowd. This is why people were trampled to death at the rock concert in Cincinnati in 1980, when a huge crowd who had come to see The Who rushed into a space too small to hold everyone. This is also why people are unnecessarily killed in theater fires as they follow the crowd to a single exit even though there are alternative exits available.

Much research on conformity in group behavior has been con-

Pearl Cadwell— Personnel Administrator

Jim Taniyama— Personnel Administrator

Dr. Thomas Mills— Engineering Department Manager

Jackie Garnett—Engineering Section Head

Carrie Wong—Business Analyst

Aida Villalobos—Project Control Administrator

Rudy Ontivares—Programmer Analyst

Bobbi Kyman—Lawyer

THESE ARE THE PEOPLE OF TRW. Productive people doing jobs they like. Looking forward each day to new challenges, new solutions, satisfying careers. There are over 90,000 of us worldwide. Before a company is anything else, it is people. TRW Inc., 23555 Euclid Avenue, Cleveland, Ohio 44117.

A COMPANY CALLED
TRW

ducted. It has been found that people will go along with the group even when the group makes a decision contrary to privately held beliefs and values (see Karlins and Abelson 1970, pp. 41–67).

In one study of the effect of group influence, a recorded speech was presented that contained statements contrary to previously tested norms of the audience. Applause for some of these statements was also presented on the recording. Some audiences in the study were told that the original listeners were different from themselves. Other groups were told that the audience on the recording was similar to themselves. The "similar" audiences tended to exercise a more favorable influence on the listeners than the "dissimilar" audiences (Kelley and Woodruff 1956).

Lawyers who select jurors often use group norms to weed out undesirable jurors. Percy Foreman, the famous Houston lawyer, said in a television interview that he prefers women and members of oppressed minorities as jurors because they will be more sympathetic to the underdog. He also says he avoids people from "exacting" professions like architects and mathematicians because they demand precise proof. This sounds like stereotyping on the part of attorneys. Nonetheless, it is a common practice. Clarence Darrow had his own formula for jury selection: "Never take a German; they are bullheaded. Rarely take a Swede; they are stubborn. Always take an Irishman or a Jew; they are the easiest to move to emotional sympathy. Old men are generally more charitable and kindly disposed than young men; they have seen more of the world and understand it" (Allen 1975).

Group norms can also negatively affect people. If people are openly hostile to a group, its norms can be used to persuade an audience in a negative direction. "You would not want to endorse a candidate who has the support of the Ku Klux Klan!"

Rowland Evans and Robert Novak reported a political speech by Abner Mikva, who was running for the United States House of Representatives in Illinois and spoke at Evanston Township High School in October 1978. He pulled from his pocket a letter from the National Rifle Association that attacked him as "the foremost anti-gun spokesman in the House" but called his opponent, Republican John Porter, "immensely preferable." Evans and Novak said, referring to a negative group norm, "In Chicago's North Shore suburban district, a candidate with the NRA as a friend needs no enemies" (1978).

A persuader can effectively use group norms in two ways. (1) Appeal to membership groups, the ones to which the members of the audience belong, for standards and beliefs that those groups share. Emphasize the current opinions of groups (age, educational level, occupation, political affiliation, geographical location, clubs, interest groups, ethnic groups, etc.),

This ad appeals to a variety of ethnic groups and shows them employed in jobs they enjoy.

and remind them that these are probably their standards as well. Terry Jordan, a geographer at North Texas State University who has done years of research on ethnic groups and voting patterns in Texas, tells about the community of New Braunfels, which is made up of Germans who keep the traditions and language of Germany very much alive in their pretty town. The people of New Braunfels had only voted Democratic once in a presidential election, and that was for Franklin D. Roosevelt's fourth term. They also were openly adverse toward Lyndon B. Johnson. When Johnson ran for president in 1964, he invited the chancellor of Germany, Konrad Adenauer, to visit him at his Texas ranch. He took the German chancellor with him to a political rally in New Braunfels, where Adenauer praised Johnson to his "fellow Germans." For the second time in history, the people of New Braunfels voted for a Democrat for president in 1964!

During the 1980 presidential campaign, both Jimmy Carter and Ronald Reagan courted the blue-collar workers for their votes. In uncharacteristic fashion for a Republican candidate, Reagan spoke in mines, factories, and mills in Pennsylvania, New Jersey, and Michigan in an attempt to capitalize on economic discontent and to persuade workers to vote for the Republican ticket. His press secretary described his group norm appeals to the workers as the "blue woo" (*Newsweek*, October 13, 1980, p. 39).

(2) Appeal to nonmembership groups that are admired or disliked by the audience. Emphasize the standards and actions of such groups, admonish the audience to follow the groups they admire ("We should follow the path set by our community leaders") and warn them not to believe or do anything similar to groups they dislike ("The bigots and racists of this country want our schools to be closed to Mexican alien children. Do you want to be a party to bigotry?").

SUMMARY

A persuader can use anchors to create belief from that which is already believed by the persuadees. Beliefs are statements that tend to be inferential and to draw relationships between the object of the belief and some other object, value, concept, or attribute. All beliefs are not equally important, but vary in terms of centrality and periphery. Primitive beliefs are more resistant to change, but have greater impact on deriving peripheral beliefs from them.

Values are particular kinds of beliefs that are abstract "measuring sticks" about how a person ought or ought not to behave. Rokeach makes

The National Bureau of Standards ad appeals to a membership group of Chicano readers of Nuestro magazine, a periodical written in English and Spanish for Mexican-Americans.

five assumptions about values: (1) the total number of values that a person possesses is relatively small; (2) all people possess similar values but to different degrees; (3) values are organized into hierarchies that may vary according to different situations; (4) the antecedents of human values can be traced to culture, society and its institutions, and personality; and (5) the consequences of human values will be manifested in behavior and behavior change. Rogers believes that the mature person achieves a sense of values based on self-awareness and experience. Differing values are often the cause of communication breakdowns.

Group norms are specific beliefs and values derived from principles agreed upon by people who wish to operate together. Membership group norms represent standards held by people who belong to certain groups. Nonmembership group norms represent standards held by groups to which people may not belong. The groups are capable of influencing nonmembers because these persons admire or dislike those particular groups.

Attitudes, the subject of the next chapter, are less numerous than beliefs and much more numerous than values and are derived from beliefs, values, and group norms. Whatever consistency attitudes have can be related to the consistency of beliefs and values. However, they are much more likely to change than the beliefs, values, and group norms from whence they came.

KEY WORDS

Anchors	Inconsequential beliefs
Beliefs	Values
Primitive beliefs	Group norms
Authority beliefs	Membership groups
Peripheral beliefs	Nonmembership groups

EXERCISES

1. Select one of your peripheral, derived beliefs, and trace it back to (a) an authoritative belief and (b) a primitive belief with 100-percent societal consensus and/or a primitive belief with 0-percent societal consensus.
2. Once you have located your primitive belief in exercise 1, try to remember when and how you acquired that belief. Did one of your parents teach it to

you? Try hard to remember the earliest time in your childhood that you were exposed to the belief.

3. Select another peripheral belief, and locate the source (another belief, belief in an authority, and/or experience) from which the belief is derived. Discover if it is a differentiated belief—that is, derived from more than one source. Write it out in syllogistic form.

4. List thirteen things that you use around your house, apartment, or dormitory. Cross out three that you can live without. Circle three that you cannot live without. What values can you discover from this? (For example, you may not be able to live without your hair dryer, and, therefore, you value attractiveness; or you may not be able to live without your alarm clock, and, therefore, you value punctuality.)

5. If you were president, what would you most want to accomplish? What value does this represent?

6. Review a major decision in your life, and see if you can determine the value(s) that helped you decide. Was the decision a good one? Do you still believe strongly in that value?

7. Make a list of ten of your values, and rank them from 1 to 10 in order of strength. Compare your list with those of your classmates, your best friend, a sweetheart, a brother and/or sister, and your parents.

8. Write your own obituary, and tell what you want most to be remembered for. Be sure to include a statement like "He/she believed in . . .," "He/she valued . . .," "He/she belonged to _____ groups."

9. Take the cards out of your wallet, and make a list of the groups to which you belong.

10. Select one membership group, and write out its norms.

11. Select a group that you do not belong to, but admire. Which of its norms influence you?

READINGS

Bem, Daryl J. *Beliefs, Attitudes, and Human Affairs.* Belmont, Calif.: Brooks/Cole, 1970.

Fishbein, Martin, and **Ajzen, Icek.** *Beliefs, Attitudes, Intentions, and Behavior.* Reading, Mass.: Addison-Wesley, 1975.

Karlins, Marvin, and **Abelson, Herbert I.** *Persuasion: How Opinions and Attitudes Are Changed.* 2d ed. New York: Springer, 1970.

Rogers, Carl R. "Toward a Modern Approach to Values: The Valuing Process in the Mature Person." *Journal of Abnormal and Social Psychology* 68 (1964):160–67.

Rokeach, Milton. *The Open and Closed Mind.* New York: Basic Books, 1960.

———. *Beliefs, Attitudes, and Values.* San Francisco: Jossey-Bass, 1968.

———. *The Nature of Human Values.* New York: Free Press, 1973.

———. *Understanding Human Values.* New York: Free Press, 1979.

ATTITUDES AND ATTITUDE CHANGE

OBJECTIVES

Upon completion of this chapter you should be able to:

1. Define attitudes and understand the characteristics of attitudes.
2. See how attitudes can be measured.
3. Be aware of the functional nature of attitudes.
4. Understand the concept of psychological balance.
5. Be aware of the interrelationship among the beliefs and attitudes of the source, the message elements, and the persuadee.
6. Appreciate the nature of attitude change.

Persuasion emphasizes influence over others' attitudes. The persuader attempts to influence the response of the persuadee in a way that will elicit an "I agree with that" response. In the model of persuasion presented in Chapter 1, the persuadee is depicted as an autonomous individual with a special blend of his/her own attitudes and other psychological sets. The persuadee's psychological sets and the persuader's communicative abilities influence the persuadee's decoding of the message through the persuadee's perceptual filters. The psychological sets will also influence the expectations that the persuadee will have in the interactive-dependency exchange with the persuader.

The persuader must be sensitive to the numerous attitudes in the various persuadees who may make up an audience. When individuals come together as an audience, they do not lose their uniqueness. The heterogeneity of audiences and the difference in the attitudes held by them is of major concern to persuaders. In order for the persuader's message to be received and survive the persuadee's filtering process, the persuader must have some knowledge of the persuadee's attitudes and their propensity for change.

A persuader who wishes to persuade someone basically wants to create or change an attitude concerning an object, person, or idea. The persuader may want the persuadee to "like" or "dislike" someone or to be "for" or "against" an issue or idea. To "like" or "dislike," to be "for" or "against," is to hold an attitude. As we saw in the previous chapter, it is almost impossible to change people's values and primitive beliefs. Attitudes, however, can be changed. That is why one of the most important aspects of learning how to persuade and why we are persuaded is learning as much as possible about attitudes.

DEFINITION OF AN ATTITUDE

Theories of attitude and attitude change attempt to define the concept of attitude, to explain how attitudes operate within a person's psychological make-up, and to predict how attitudes can be changed. People frequently give indications of attitudes without consciously knowing that they are making attitude statements. For example, if you were asked, "What is your attitude toward spinach?" you might respond, "I don't like it!" On the other hand, if you were asked, "What is your attitude toward ice cream?" you might respond, "I like it!"

In each case, you have expressed an attitude, which is a statement of positive or negative preference. An attitude is a statement of readiness to respond to an idea, an object, or a course of action. *An attitude may thus be defined as a learned and relatively enduring predisposition to respond favorably or unfavorably to an idea, object, or behavior.* It is expressed as a specific evaluative statement such as "I agree" or "I feel strongly about that."

Beliefs were defined in the previous chapter as inferences that people make about the world, cognitions about the existence of things, events, ideas, and persons, and the perceived probability of relationships between them and characteristics of them. Attitudes are products of beliefs that cluster together to form preferences for or against an object or an idea. Attitudes are, therefore, derived from our views about the world.

Beliefs and attitudes are formed from direct observation or information received from external sources. Martin Fishbein and Icek Ajzen refer to this as the *information processing* approach, which "views man as an essentially rational organism, who uses the information at his disposal to make judgments, form evaluations, and arrive at decisions" (1975, p. 14).

For example, if a student has gathered favorable information about school and has developed salient beliefs such as "School is fun," "School is a good place to make friends," or "The information learned in school is important," his/her attitude might be "I like school." The information processing stage produced enough "facts" to justify salient beliefs and attitudes about education.

One might infer that the attitude "I like school" reveals that the person will pursue an education. Such a conclusion regarding the person's behavior, however, cannot be drawn because attitudes are not necessarily predictions of behavior. Attitudes can only be used to give others indications of how people feel about a given behavior.

Fishbein and Ajzen's model (1975, p. 15) further explains the relationships between beliefs, attitudes, and intentions with respect to the object and behavior (Figure 3.1). We have added examples about school to make the model clearer.

CHARACTERISTICS OF ATTITUDES

With the definition of attitude and the concept of information processing in mind, let us look at the characteristics of attitudes. Attitudes have six essential characteristics: (1) they are learned; (2) they are determined by salient beliefs; (3) they tend to be lasting; (4) they indicate a relationship between a person and his/her perception of the attitude object; (5) they are characterized by direction and intensity; and (6) they can be measured.

Attitudes Are Not Innate, but Learned

M. Sherif and C. Sherif (1967, p. 112) tell us that attitudes are acquired through the learning experiences that occur in an individual's life. They are not inherited genetically, but can be acquired through direct or indirect

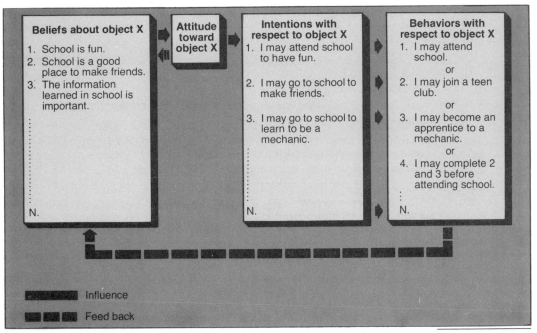

Beliefs and attitudes have a reciprocal effect on each other and, in turn, directly influence people's intentions toward the belief and attitude object. There are, however, many options for resultant behavior. There is no consistent correlation between attitudes and behavior. The consistency exists only between the attitude and the intentions toward the attitude object. The behavioral act would depend on the person's attitude concerning the behavior. This concept will be discussed in detail in Chapter IV.

FIGURE 3.1

experience and from significant figures in one's social environment. A child learns that playing in the street is dangerous because "Mother says so" or by the example of a beloved pet being run over by a car. The latter occurrence reinforces the mother's admonition, thus further hardening the attitude "Playing in the street is dangerous."

Individuals also receive indirect messages from parents, peers, and the mass media without any direct experience to verify these messages. Racial prejudice can be a firmly entrenched attitude without a direct experience, either favorable or unfavorable.

Attitudes perceived from important social groups such as family, church, and peers are usually general. The generalized attitude "I don't like school" may be drawn from unpleasant experiences that generated specific attitudes such as "I disliked Ms. Smith's class."

Racial attitudes tend to include entire racial groups (all blacks, all

Native Americans, or all Asians). If a male golfer has the attitude "I don't like female golfers," it includes all females who play golf, from the sixty-five-year-old lady who holds up the foursomes on Sunday afternoons with her fifty-foot drives, to Nancy Lopez Melton, one of the highest money winners on the women's professional golf tour.

Attitudes are also derived from what Fishbein calls *concept formation*. He defines concept formation as "the conditioning or learning of a common response to sets of particular stimuli" (Fishbein and Ajzen 1975, p. 27). A person develops an attitude at the same time he/she develops a new concept. For example, as a child learns what "desserts" and "vegetables" are, attitudes are formed through repeated tasting experiences of the varieties of desserts and vegetables. Subsequently, many attitudes may be formed from learning a single concept such as what "vegetable" or "dessert" is to "I like ice cream" or "I don't like Jell-o."

Salient Beliefs Are Determinants of Attitudes

Fishbein and Ajzen (1975) tell us that as a person forms beliefs about an object or an idea, he/she automatically and simultaneously acquires an attitude toward that object. Whereas each belief is an association of an attribute with an object, our attitudes are essentially attribute evaluations.

Suppose I buy a novel about which I know nothing. As I start to read the book, I discover that it embodies a feminist ideology. Since I have already positively evaluated feminism, I will begin to develop a positive attitude toward the book. I may now also *believe* that this book was written by a feminist. Thus, because I am favorably predisposed toward feminism, my previously neutral attitude toward a book (object) that contains a feminist ideology (attribute) has shifted to become a positive attitude toward the book, and, furthermore, I have acquired an inferential belief that the book was probably written by a feminist.

Associations cause us to acquire attitudes toward new objects. We will develop positive and negative attitudes toward new objects when we learn how those objects embody attributes toward which we already have attitudes. We have been doing this since infancy, when we learned to acquire a positive attitude toward milk because it embodied the important attribute of reducing our hunger.

The acquisition of an attitude will be related to the *salience* of an individual's belief, which may serve as a determinant of the attitude formation. Salience refers to the perceived importance of a belief for an individual. Fishbein and Ajzen feel that a person's attitude toward an object may be based on approximately five to nine beliefs that are salient at a given point in time (1975, p. 218).

The feminist ideology of the book just mentioned is a salient belief for me. Other salient beliefs embodied in the book had to do with other attributes of it: the main character was (1) female, (2) a college professor, (3) a mother, (4) engaged in research, (5) on sabbatical, (6) in England, and (7) romantically involved with an attractive man. Because being a professional woman, a mother, doing research, spending time in England, and having a relationship with a man are important to me, they helped determine my positive attitude toward the novel.

It is also possible to discuss salient beliefs in relation to a general population. These are called *modal salient beliefs*. Marketing research attempts to ascertain modal salient beliefs within a population by sampling a representative number within the population. The most frequently elicited beliefs are then considered as determinants of attitudes toward a product.

Sometimes having different salient beliefs can produce a conflict in attitudes. The negative attitude may change because one salient belief may be considered more important than another.

For example, in relation to the fuel shortage and energy crisis in America, the majority of Americans possess a salient belief with regard to physical comfort. We are accustomed to having the freedom to set thermostats in our homes to the temperature of our choice. We are accustomed to driving our automobiles without consideration of either gas mileage or the cost or availability of gasoline.

Yet, many of us also have a negative attitude concerning nuclear power that is probably derived from the salient belief that "atomic radiation from nuclear power sources has harmful effects." An attitude derived from this belief might be "Nuclear power is undesirable because it endangers physical health and the environment." The possibility of a meltdown at the nuclear power plant at Three Mile Island in Harrisburg, Pennsylvania, in 1979 produced a fear of health hazards to anyone in the area of a nuclear facility. The film *The China Syndrome* dramatized some of those fears. Each of these experiences confirmed the negative attitude toward nuclear power and the attitude that was related to it.

Then the development of nuclear power was offered as a solution to the energy crisis through statements such as "Nuclear energy may be our best hope to alleviate the energy crisis." Now, what was once a negative attitude ("Nuclear power is undesirable") might be changed to "Nuclear power is desirable" because of its tie to the strong salient belief we have in the need for physical comfort. The change to this belief would also result in a change in the other attitudes concerning health and the environment. New attitudes might include "Nuclear power is not a threat to the environment because of the maximum safeguards that surround its production and development, and it is not physically dangerous because the tests relating cancer and nuclear production are inconclusive." Obviously, this change would lead to some inconsistency, which would have to be alleviated or reduced. This change could occur because of its tie to a belief more salient (comfort) than the belief that atomic radiation has harmful effects.

Attitudes Tend to Be Lasting in Nature

Attitudes are not fleeting feelings, but tend to last once formed. Even though they are not static and do have a propensity for change, they are not subject to change on a moment-to-moment basis or as a result of each relevant stimulus (Sherif and Sherif 1969, p. 334).

Learning theorists believe that attitudes are made to endure through repeated reinforcing experiences or verbal information from those significant in our environment. Attitudes can change, but the change must occur in the same manner the attitude was formed in the first place—through constant reinforcing experiences over a period of time. It is not difficult to understand how the attitudes derived from the family unit tend to be so enduring because of our constant exposure to reinforcement during our formative years.

R. Zajonc's theory of exposure learning lends insight into the enduring nature of attitudes. His thesis is that if a person is exposed to something on a continuous and increasing basis, he or she will come to favor that thing more and more. He states, "Mere repeated exposure of the individual to a stimulus is a sufficient condition for the enhancement of his attitude toward it" (1968, p. 1).

Zajonc's compilation of research in this area reveals that (1) the frequently used words in our vocabulary are liked better than the infrequently used words; (2) subjects exposed frequently to nonsense words later responded favorably toward those words; (3) more frequently used alphabet letters are more pleasing to most people than less frequently used ones; (4) subjects respond more frequently to the Chinese letters that they have seen more of than to those letters they have not often seen; and (5) photographs are rated increasingly positively after being seen several times (Littlejohn 1978, p. 173).

We may conclude that an attitude's exposure to reinforcement is relative to its enduring nature. Certainly, those attitudes that we perceive as important to our place in the social environment are enduring in nature. This further emphasizes the relationship between the subject and the object or idea.

Attitudes Are Indicative of a Relationship between the Person and His/Her Perception of the Object or Idea

The Sherifs tell us, "Attitudes are not formed in thin air, nor are they self-generated" (1969, p. 334). They are the product of a person's relationship to a particular object or idea in the environment. For example, the "moral majority" see Senator Lloyd Bentsen (D-Texas) and Senator Charles Percy (R-Illinois) as liberals who need to be voted out of office, while Democrats view these men as politically conservative. Attitudes, then, are judgments made about objects and ideas in the environment based on the norms that prevail in groups important to us, such as family and cultural institutions.

Attitudes also have motivational-affective properties. Once an attitude has been formed toward an object or idea, the individual is no longer neutral toward that object or idea (Sherif and Sherif, 1969, p. 335). He or she now has definite feelings about it. One attitude may be more important to a person than another attitude. Both direction and intensity are also characteristics of attitudes.

Attitudes Vary in Degree along a Continuum, Characterized by Direction and Intensity

The concept of direction and intensity was developed by Sherif and Sherif in their social judgment theory. People respond to ideas and objects through their perceptions of the world or a particular social situation. Such perceptions or reference points are used as yardsticks to measure new information. The six year old who says "I like being a big boy" is making a statement about "bigness" in relation to his perception of the size of his brothers, sisters, or other children in the neighborhood. Social perception has as its basis a reference point that is internal and derived from our past experiences. The response to communication is influenced by such reference points.

Social judgment theory not only develops the concept of the direction of an attitude (like-dislike), but it also examines the intensity of that attitude revealed through the level of ego-involvement. If attitude direction was considered alone, the assumption could be made regarding two people whose reference points fall at the same place on a linear scale concerning a given object or idea that they would also have the same attitude. This assumption, however, could be incorrect because each person's ego-involvement has not been taken into account. *Ego-involvement* is the degree of involvement of a person and how the person's life is affected by the issue.

The intensity of ego-involvement is a central concept in social judgment theory along with three placements of attitude direction: (1) the latitude of acceptance, (2) the latitude of rejection, and (3) the latitude of noncommitment. The latitude of acceptance position includes a person's position plus all other acceptable positions to that person on a linear scale. All positions that are rejected constitute the latitude of rejection. The remaining positions that are neither accepted nor rejected fall into the latitude of noncommitment (Sherif and Sherif 1967).

For example, you may live in an apartment off campus and possess the same negative attitude toward existing curfew hours in all campus housing as your friend who lives in the dorm. Certainly, though, your friend, whose life is directly affected by the curfew restrictions, is going to be more ego-involved than you. In essence, you would have the same directional attitude toward the issue as your friend; but since the issue does not affect your life style, you would not feel as intensely ego-involved as your friend does.

If a person's perception of a message falls within the latitude of acceptance, he/she tends to perceive the message closer to his/her position than it actually is, which results in *assimilation* effects. If the message lies in the latitude of rejection, it will be perceived much further from a person's position than it actually is, which produces *contrast* effects. The intensity of ego-involvement produces a wide latitude of rejection.

Figure 3.2 (see page 43) presents an interpretation of how receivers distort a communicator's position. These distortions are shown in relation to low, moderate, and high ego-involvement. It can be seen from this model by Kiesler, Collins, and Miller (1969, p. 247) that

(1) within the latitude of acceptance, 'true' discrepancy is underestimated as an increasing function of discrepancy, (2) within the latitude of rejection, true discrepancy is interpreted as a decreasing function of distance, (3) both of these effects are exaggerated by the highly involved respondent and minimized by the uninvolved respondent, (4) for all involvement levels, the shift in direction of distortion presumably occurs within the latitude of noncommitment but close to the latitude of rejection, and (5) for all levels of involvement the latitude of acceptance is approximately equal in size. (Kiesler, Collins, and Miller 1969, p. 247)

Back to the example of you and your friend, both of whom oppose curfews in campus housing. Suppose both of you attend a meeting where the student-body president advocates as a compromise measure eliminating the curfew on weekends and retaining it during the week. Even though you and your friend are "opposed to curfews," because of your different levels of ego-involvement you would respond in entirely different ways.

Your position might be described in the part of the model labeled "Low Involvement." You would have a wide latitude of acceptance, a wide latitude of noncommitment, and a narrow latitude of rejection. Notice that your perception of the message (theoretically predicted judgment) is close to the unbiased correct judgment. Your response to the student-body president's message might be "That's reasonable and sounds much like what we were requesting."

Your friend's position might be described in the part of the model labeled "High Involvement." He/she shows a wide latitude of rejection,

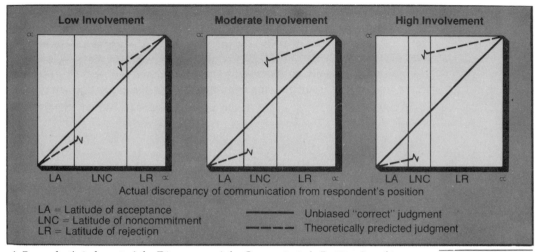

A Respondent's judgment of the Discrepency of the Communicator's Position from his own.

FIGURE 3.2

little or no latitude of acceptance, and no latitude of noncommitment. Your friend's ego involvement causes rejection of the student-body president's position or any position differing from his/her own. His/her response is "This proposal is the opposite of what we were requesting and is untenable."

Social judgment theory is useful to the persuader because it makes possible predictions of persuadee response. How the persuader's proposition is subjectively categorized by the recipient is crucial to the success of the persuader's efforts.

Attitudes Can Be Measured

Various measurement techniques have been designed to reveal the components of attitudes. Most measurement techniques are based on single-response measures. They are drawn from subjects' responses to attitude statements. The choices of responses can be ones such as "approve-disapprove" with linear points in between. They can also be a four- or more point scale where each point is labeled, such as "extremely beautiful," "quite beautiful," "slightly beautiful," and "not beautiful."

In order to better understand how attitudes are measured, six types of measurement will be discussed: (1) Bogardus's Measure of Social Distance; (2) Thurstone's Equal-Appearing Interval Scale; (3) Likert's Method of Summated Ratings; (4) Osgood's Semantic Differential Technique; (5) the

Own Categories Procedure; and (6) the Galileo System, a multidimensional scaling technique. It is important to note that the concept of attitude differs somewhat with each measuring technique that follows. The reaction measured is not always "attitude" as defined in this chapter because what is measured may depend on the type of measurement instrument used. We have designated in the discussion of each measurement technique whether or not the concept of attitude is significantly different from the way we have defined it.

Bogardus's Measure of Social Distance   This measuring technique grew out of E. Bogardus's interest in the intimacy and the prejudice or distance that members of one group felt for an outgroup. An outgroup is any group that a person perceives as significantly different in race, gender, profession, religion, class, or nation. Bogardus's (1925) technique consists of asking the subject to identify one or more of the following statements the subject thought to be appropriate to the specific outgroup in question:

"I would willingly admit members of the outgroup"

1. To close kinship by marriage
2. To my club as personal chums
3. To my street as neighbors
4. To employment in my occupation
5. To citizenship in my country
6. As visitors only to my country
7. Would exclude from my country

A social distance measure is then obtained by counting the statements the subject would exclude. A score of 6 is obtained when the subject only agrees with statement 7. A score of 0 would be obtained by accepting items 1 through 5 and rejecting 6 and 7. A high score indicates a great degree of social distance between the subject and the outgroup in question and thus a negative attitude. A low score indicates a positive attitude. This measure is limited because it can only apply to problems concerning attitudes toward outgroups and their members. It does not measure favorable or unfavorable reactions to groups; the reactions must be inferred from social distance.

Thurstone's Equal-Appearing Interval Scale   The Thurstone scales (Thurstone 1931) are probably the most elaborately constructed of the attitude-measurement techniques that are widely used. An instrument or form that contains a number of statements ranging from the most favorable stand to the most unfavorable stand is presented to a group of subjects. The statements are presented in mixed order to avoid a direction set. A sample is:

- There is no conceivable justification for war.
- War is a futile struggle resulting in self-destruction.
- War is an unnecessary waste of human life.
- The benefits of war are not worth its misery and suffering.
- We want no more war if it can be avoided without dishonor.
- It is hard to decide whether wars do more harm than good.
- There are some arguments in favor of war.
- Under some conditions, war is necessary to maintain justice.
- War is a satisfactory way to solve international difficulties.
- War stimulates men to their noblest efforts.
- The highest duty of man is to fight for the power and glory of his nation.

Prior to testing, a group of statement items are given to a panel of judges, who, through an involved procedure, choose eleven statements (like the above example) and weight these statements in equal distance from each other.

One disadvantage of the Thurstone method has been related to how much influence the judges' attitudes have on the weighting of these items. Partly in response to the complexity of scaling as well as the possible bias of the judges, Likert developed a simpler scaling procedure.

Likert's Method of Summated Ratings   The Likert method (Likert 1932) is one where the subject commits himself or herself on a linear scale concerning a belief or intention statement. The Likert scale has been one of the most widely used attitude-measurement techniques. This scale consists of categories indicating attitude strength with a "strongly approve" answer graduating down to a "strongly disapprove" response on a 5 point scale. An example of belief statements in the original Likert test (1932) is stated below.

"No Negro should be deprived of the franchise except for reasons which would also disenfranchise a white man."

Strongly Approve (1)	Approve (2)	Undecided (3)	Disapprove (4)	Strongly Disapprove (5)

So far, all the attitude testing discussed has been unidimensional with regard to the evaluative property of attitudes in that the tests are capable of revealing only motivational-affective properties. They tend to oversimplify attitudes that are not simple. Other dimensions of attitudes, however, can be brought out in the discussion of Osgood's Semantic Differential Technique.

Osgood's Semantic Differential Technique   Osgood's Semantic Differential Technique (Osgood and Tannenbaum 1955) basically asks the subject to make semantic choices. Its theoretical base is twofold. It is based on connotative meanings rather than denotative meanings. If you said, "Lake Tahoe is a vacation resort in Nevada," it would be a denotative statement because it states a fact. If you said, "Lake Tahoe is a wonderful place where my husband and I spent our honeymoon," your statement would be connotative because it indicates what meaning the object (Lake Tahoe) has to you personally. Semantic differential is a technique whereby those connotative meanings can be tapped for research purposes. Feelings and images can be gleaned from the subject's responses. These responses may be unrelated to favorable and unfavorable responses to an object. Thus, the measurement instrument does not measure an attitude as defined in this chapter; only the evaluation portion of Osgood's scale fits that definition.

Osgood noticed throughout his studies that three basic characteristics of subject responses emerged. He and his associates referred to these characteristics as evaluation, potency, and activity. The *evaluative* characteristic was the same thing that other studies referred to as motivational-affective qualities or, simply, attitude. The *potency* characteristic was discovered by using binary terms such as "big-little," "strong-weak." The characteristic of *activity* was discovered when words in the testing form included "fast-slow," "hot-cold." An example of each characteristic could be as follows:

President Reagan

Good	(evaluative)	Bad
Strong	(potency)	Weak
Active	(activity)	Inactive

The results of the Semantic Differential Technique, then, provide much more than the evaluative dimension, for they include potency and activity as well.

The Own Categories Procedure   In the Own Categories Procedure (Sherif and Sherif 1969, p. 351) the subject is given a packet of individual statements on cards and is asked to put the statements into stacks that are associated enough to belong together in terms of favorability toward an object or idea. The subject is not restricted to a specific number of categories, as in the Thurstone method.

The number of stacks is indicative of ego-involvement. The fewer the categories, the higher the ego-involvement of the subject. During the second part of the procedure, the subject is asked to indicate (1) which stack is closest to his own position, (2) which one is furthest from his own position, (3) which stacks are acceptable, and (4) which stacks are unacceptable to him. The number of statements in both of the acceptable stacks indicate the subject's latitude of acceptance, and the number of statements in both of the "unacceptable" stacks indicate the person's latitude of rejection.

Multidimensional Scaling Technique Multidimensional Scaling (Gilham and Woelfel 1977) consists of a set of techniques that takes advantage of the aggregate character of cultural variables to provide reliable, precise, ratio-scaled and multidimensional measurements of cultural processes.

This theory of measurement presents hypotheses that are sufficiently accurate to measure both stable patterns and small changes in cultural configurations. The assumption is made that the process of identifying an object occurs when individuals learn to differentiate among the stimuli that are the mechanisms of the perception of one object from those stimuli that are the mechanisms of the perception of another object.

For example, chess pieces such as the bishops are perceived as different because one is white and the other is black. The single attribute of color indicates to the individual that the two objects are dissimilar. Two individuals are more complex because they possess more attributes, such as sex, race, weight, height, and age. A collection of all of these dissimilarities can be taken as a measure of the difference between these two people through a series of ordinal ratings of the distance between the attributes. A multidimensional program such as Galileo can then be used.

In a study done by J. Gilham and J. Woelfel, twenty-nine students and faculty members of a large sociology department were asked to estimate pairwise dissimilarities among nineteen professors in the department by the method of ratio judgments of separation. Following a brief paragraph of instructions in the use of the technique, respondents were given the standard "If Professor Jones is ten Galileos from Professor Smith, how far apart are Professor X and Professor Y in the areas of political position and style of research?"

A Galileo is defined by the authors as an arbitrary measure of *distance* between concepts by whatever criteria the subjects individually may choose to use. The dimensions may not overtly reflect favorability. Thus, the concept of attitude is not the same as defined in this chapter.

Some examples of results after the test was administered three times were that Professor E had an average distance of twenty-two Galileos from Professor J, the largest in the study. One of these persons was known to be quite liberal and the other to be quite conservative. The average distance, on the other hand, between Professor P and Professor R was only nine Galileos. Both of these persons were rural sociologists of moderate political stance, and their research was considered moderately quantitative.

All of the results remained stable throughout the three testings. It can be said that when dissimilarities based on a person's perceptions are measured, they tend to remain stable over a period of time.

FUNCTION OF ATTITUDES

Now that attitudes have been described by discussing their characteristics, we will see how attitudes *function* for the individual and why their functioning is important.

It is also useful to understand that attitudes are not only important to an individual, but they are also necessary. They function "as mediators between our internal demands and the reality of our external environment" (Cronkhite 1969, p. 67). In Daniel Katz's functional theory of attitudes (1960) shown in the chart on page 49, he describes the attitude as filling this need through four distinct functions: (1) adjustment, (2) ego defense, (3) value expression, and (4) knowledge.

Adjustment

The adjustment function of an attitude is theoretically based in behavioristic learning theory. Adjustment serves to increase possibilities for rewards and to decrease possibilities for punishment. From infancy one acquires favorable attitudes to those objects, ideas, or events that are associated with pleasure and/or rewards. One of the reasons why obesity is a national health problem in the United States is because eating has traditionally been associated with pleasant times. Obviously, we have a positive attitude toward eating Thanksgiving and Christmas dinners, and it is also common to celebrate a raise, an engagement, or passing a test with a meal. Meetings are often combined with breakfast, lunch, dinner, or at least coffee and doughnuts. Eating is added to the agenda so the event will be "fun." Also, eating can be used negatively. For instance, there was always pressure to "clean your plate" or be considered wasteful or to "take a second helping so the hostess will not be offended."

DETERMINANTS OF ATTITUDE FORMATION, AROUSAL, AND CHANGE
IN RELATION TO TYPE OF FUNCTION
TABLE 1.2

FUNCTION	ORIGIN AND DYNAMICS	AROUSAL CONDITIONS	CHANGE CONDITIONS
Adjustment	Utility of attitudinal object in need satisfaction. Maximizing external rewards and minimizing punishments	1. Activation of needs 2. Salience of cues associated with need satisfaction	1. Need deprivation 2. Creation of new needs and new levels of aspiration 3. Shifting rewards and punishments 4. Emphasis on new and better paths for need satisfaction
Ego defense	Protecting against internal conflicts and external dangers	1. Posing of threats 2. Appeals to hatred and repressed impulses 3. Rise in frustrations 4. Use of authoritarian suggestion	1. Removal of threats 2. Catharsis 3. Development of self-insight
Value expression	Maintaining self identity; enhancing favorable self-image; self-expression and self-determination	1. Salience of cues associated with values 2. Appeals to individual to reassert self-image 3. Ambiguities which threaten self-concept	1. Some degree of dissatisfaction with self 2. Greater appropriateness of new attitude for the self 3. Control of all environmental supports to undermine old values
Knowledge	Need for understanding, for meaningful cognitive organization, for consistency and clarity	1. Reinstatement of cues associated with old problem or of old problem itself	1. Ambiguity caused by new information or change in environment 2. More meaningful information about problems

Ego Defense

Ego defense protects the individual's ego from the unacceptable forces from within, the threatening forces from without, and the anxieties that accompany both.

Ego-defensive attitudes of prejudice are usually a characteristic of persons with extreme feelings of inferiority because certain ethnic, religious, or other groups pose a personal and economic threat to their lives. The recent revival of the Ku Klux Klan is an example of certain white people's defensiveness toward black people's progress in America. The Klan opposes equal opportunity because, they say, it takes jobs and educational opportunity away from white American males in order to give them to minorities and women. The Klan perceives equal opportunity to be robbing them of advantages that are rightfully theirs because of white male supremacy. Equal opportunity threatens their self-esteem, which they feel can be retained only through superiority of race and gender.

Value Expressions

While ego-defensive attitudes are adopted to conceal one's real identity, there are those attitudes that function as a means of expressing central values and are referred to as the *value-expressive* function. Value-expressive attitudes give clarity to one's self-image and also serve to create that image as close to the one desired as possible.

The physical artifacts that are a part of our personal environment are value-expressive. Our clothes, our cars, and our homes are part of an image of ourselves we wish to project to important others. Our choices of membership in certain groups stem from a desire to articulate to those around us that the values adhered to by these groups are ours as well.

Street gangs are an example of the enactment of the value-expressive function. The members dress alike, use the same language, and project a feeling of superiority to themselves and to others. A person joins a gang because he/she wants people to think he/she is superior, tough, and brave. These characteristics are important to him/her as part of the self-image.

Knowledge

All people desire order in and understanding of their universe. When the exterior world seems vague and/or chaotic, it can be frightening. The knowledge function of an attitude provides one with the necessary information to give meaning to the external environment. We all desire a world where our habits, capacities, comforts, and hopes fit in harmoniously. Our perception of this world may be an incomplete or inaccurate one, but we seek enough knowledge to make it orderly and comfortable for ourselves. The term *knowledge* is not used in the same manner as the educator or social reformer would use it to mean a state of awareness or understanding gained through reading and study.

In the 1980 presidential campaign, a major issue that probably contributed to Jimmy Carter's defeat was inflation. Although America may have had inflation regardless of who was president, the Republicans pounded away at Carter for being responsible for the economy. Following Ronald Reagan's victory, many news analysts suggested that the voters' "knowledge" of inflation was determined by their own individual economic problems (unemployment, high cost of living) rather than a knowledge of how a president could control inflation.

BALANCE THEORIES

Balance theories are based on the premise that a conflict between beliefs or attitudes causes psychological discomfort. It is human nature to dislike this noxious state and to seek psychological comfort or, to use the words of the learning theorists, *homeostasis* or *balance* or, to use the word of the consistency theorists, *congruity* or, to use the word of the dissonance theorists, *consonance*. There are many studies of balance theories, but the more prevalently used are (1) Heider's Balance Theory, (2) Osgood and Tannenbaum's Congruity Principle, and (3) Festinger's Theory of Cognitive Dissonance.

Heider's Balance Theory

Fritz Heider (1946) was interested in the ways in which people view their relationships with other people and with objects in their environment. He believed that everyone desires balance or a state of harmony (membership, ownership, proximity). Heider interpreted the relationships through the prism of the person's own perception of the relationships between elements—that is, how the person perceives the relationship of the basic elements to one another. If a person perceives no relationship among the basic elements, then imbalance will be tolerated.

The basic elements that are usually involved are the focal person (P), another person (O), and an object or idea or event (X). The focal person (P) may like (L) or dislike (Ł) O or X or both. If the triad includes three people, the third person is indicated as (Q).

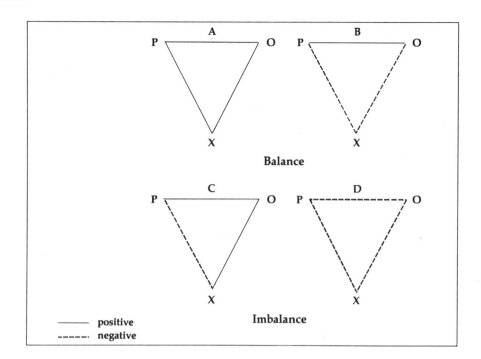

The basic principle of Heider's theory can be stated thus: *Balance exists if all three relations are positive in all respects, or if two of the relations are negative and one is positive. Situations that consist of one negative relation and two positive relations or three negative relations are imbalanced.*

What about some of the truisms that individuals have heard all their lives such as "Opposites attract"? Heider maintained that the mutual attraction could be accomplished by arriving at a common goal; thus, the two may become similar through commonalities that exist other than their opposite personalities (Insko 1967, p. 162). What happens when a man and his best friend love the same woman? This is a case of three positive relations. If Heider's triad is applied to this situation, it would appear that balance exists (Insko 1967, p. 163). For example, John (P) loves (L) Mary (O); John (P) loves (L) Max (Q); Max (Q) loves (L) Mary (O).

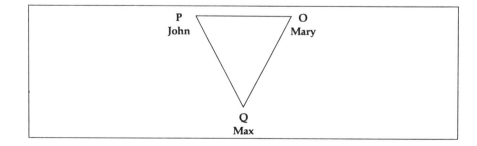

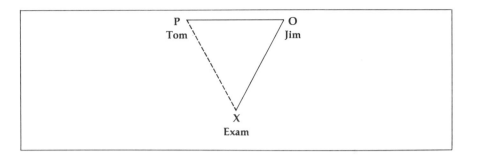

Heider explains this example's obvious imbalance in this manner: John (P) does not want Mary (O) to fall in love with Max (Q) because if Mary loves Max, in this case, it implies that Mary does not love John, which conflicts with John's loving Mary. This example cannot be balanced because of the obvious potential for imbalance between John and Mary.

Imbalance, then, occurs as a result of existing tensions, urges, or forces that motivate a person to move in the direction of balance. For example, Tom (P) likes Jim (O), who has cheated on an exam (X). Tom disapproves, and imbalance occurs.

Tom has several alternatives which could restore balance. He could decide that Jim was forced to cheat because of extenuating circumstances, or he could decide that it was all right since "everybody does it," or he could decide that he no longer cares for Jim because Jim cheated.

In summary, in algebraic terms Heider's triad is balanced if the product of the signs is positive and imbalanced if the product of the signs is negative. The model is not clear, however, about how imbalance is restored. I. D. Steiner and E. D. Rogers (1964) conducted a study that revealed how subjects resolved imbalance when they found their evaluations contradicted by someone whom they respected. The ways in which the subjects resolved imbalance were (1) to conform to the respected person's judgment; (2) to reject the respected person for being less competent than they had thought; (3) to not be able to recall the extent of the conflict; and (4) to devaluate the importance of the topic under discussion. Essentially, some people tend to conform, others reject, others forget, and others deemphasize. Rarely do people use all four of the means of reducing imbalance, but there is a strong tendency to use one of them. H. C. Triandis (1971) suggests that "when persons are rewarded in childhood for conforming, or rejecting, or for making any of the other responses, they develop a tendency to use that particular method for the resolution of imbalance" (p. 70).

In addition, Triandis (1971) offers other ways of handling cognitive imbalance. A person can shut down thinking about the imbalanced situation or think about all of the ways in which he/she is right. Another possibility is to point out respected people who resemble him/her who also engage in the contradiction, or he/she may choose to transcend the inconsistency by justifying the inconsistency with a good reason for it (p. 71).

The point is that inconsistencies themselves are not usually tolerated by an individual. Thus, individuals develop coping mechanisms to reduce or resolve the imbalance. Sometimes they maintain their present attitude toward the object of disagreement, and other times they will change their attitude toward the other person.

Osgood and Tannenbaum's Congruity Principle

Just as Heider's theory deals with relationships between units, C. E. Osgood and P. H. Tannenbaum's (1955) congruity principle is based on the premise that two units are linked together by an assertion. Heider's units were viewed through a person's (P) perception of the relationship between himself and O and X. In the congruity theory, P encounters an assertion about O and X that causes both positions to change in order to restore balance due to the nature of the assertion. The assertion itself is qualitative, whereas the units are quantitative in nature (Fishbein and Ajzen 1975, pp. 36–37).

There are two types of assertions, both of which act as "coupling actions" (Fishbein and Ajzen 1975, p. 36). They may be associative or dissociative (favors–are, opposes–are not). The authors use the semantic differential as a means to measure the shifts in O and X as a result of the associative or dissociative assertion (Insko 1967, p. 112).

Associative assertions are represented by statements such as "Bill likes Susan, Susan likes Bill, or Bill goes with Susan." These units (person, objects, or ideas) are then associated by an assertion such as "Bill (P) cares more for Susan's roommate (O) than he does for Susan (X)."

Another example from the pre-Watergate revelations demonstrates this point. In spite of rumors of Richard Nixon's involvement in a cover-up, Billy Graham, the evangelist, made a public statement proclaiming Nixon to be an honest man (associative assertion). To a person (P) who respected Graham (O) and distrusted Nixon (X), that person's attitude toward both persons would alter toward congruity. Suppose Billy Graham ranked +1 on the semantic differential scale and Richard Nixon ranked −2. As a result of the associative assertion, the person's attitude would move both positions to a −1 to establish congruity. Figure 3.3 shows results that researchers could derive from the use of Osgood and Tannenbaum's formula (Insko 1967, p. 115).

Dissociative assertions further separate or dissociate (O) and (X) such as Bill (P) dislikes Susan's roommate (O) more than he (P) dislikes Susan (X).

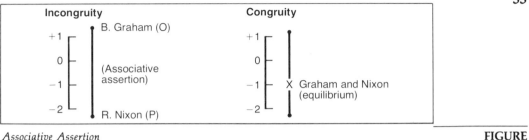

Associative Assertion

FIGURE
3.3

One must keep in mind that the crux of the congruity principle is that when two units are associated by an assertion, whether it be associative or dissociative, a shift occurs. In the case of dissociative assertions, equilibrium is established by maintaining a continuing comfortable distance between the two units.

To use the Nixon-Graham example again, suppose that Graham (O) had made an uncomplimentary assertion concerning Nixon's (X) honesty. This dissociative assertion and its possible results would be as shown in Figure 3.4 (Insko 1967, p. 117).

The congruity principle has useful predictive qualities related to both the direction and extent of attitude change. It extends the Heider model by its precise measuring technique and its attempt to predict outcome. It also is important in persuasion because it helps us to understand the relationship of the persuader to both message and source elements and their impact upon each other as well as how that relationship affects balance and changed perception.

Dissociative Assertion

FIGURE
3.4

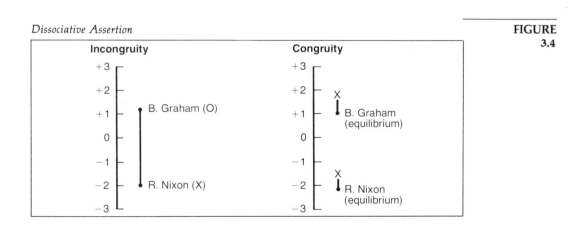

Festinger's Theory of Cognitive Dissonance

Leon Festinger (1957) based his theory on the relationship between two cognitive elements. These elements include attitudes, values, behaviors, perceptions, and knowledge. The relationships between the two cognitive elements could be consonant, dissonant, or irrelevant. *Consonance* is Festinger's term for psychological comfort; *dissonance* is his term for psychological discomfort or tension; and *irrelevance* is when two cognitions have no relation to each other.

Inconsistency between two cognitive elements creates dissonance. The amount or degree of dissonance created depends on the importance of the two cognitive elements to the individual. A decision about whether to wear shorts or jeans to a picnic creates little conflict, but making important life decisions can be quite discomforting. During the senior year in college, there is often a conflict between the decision to get a job immediately in order to make an attractive salary or to pursue a graduate degree, which would mean living on a tight budget for several more years. Such decision making is painful. Once the decision is reached, however, a sense of relief is obtained if the psychological elements are in balance.

Festinger distinguishes between *conflict* and his term *dissonance* in the following manner:

> The person is in a conflict situation before making the decision. After having made the decision, he is no longer in conflict; he has made his choice; he has, so to speak, resolved the conflict; he is no longer being pushed in two or more directions simultaneously. He is now committed to the chosen course of action. It is only here that dissonance exists, and the pressure to reduce this dissonance exists, and the pressure to reduce this dissonance is not pushing the person in two directions simultaneously. (1957, p. 39)

In 1957, four psychologists conducted a study concerning automobile-advertising readership after the recent purchase of a new automobile. It was based on Festinger's concept that since the purchase, all "good" features of the makes of automobiles the individual considered but did not buy and the "bad" features of the make of automobile purchased are now dissonant information (Ehrlich 1957).

Ehrlich and his associates tested 125 male residents of Minneapolis who owned one of eight popular automobile makes. Sixty-five of the respondents were new-car owners selected at random from a list of new auto registrations. The other 60 respondents owned cars purchased at least three years prior to the study.

It was found that new-car owners read advertisements relating to their cars more often than to those relating to the models they rejected. These selective tendencies were much less significant among old-car owners.

But what are the initial causes of dissonance? According to Festinger, there are five situations in which dissonance usually occurs: (1) decision making, (2) forced compliance, (3) involuntary exposure, (4) voluntary exposure, and (5) disagreement with important others.

Decision Making   In decision making, the degrees of postdecisional dissonance will be a result of the importance of the decision, the relative attractiveness between the choice made and the alternatives, and the degree of similarity or difference between the two cognitions.

Decisions vary in degree of importance. Buying an automobile is more important than buying a cold drink. If, however, the choice that is creating the conflict is whether to buy a Toyota Celica Supra or a Datsun 280Z, the dissonance would be less because of the similarities of the two models than if you were choosing between a Mercedes and a Volkswagen Rabbit. There is quite a bit of difference between the latter two models and, therefore, more dissonance.

Forced Compliance   The second dissonance-producing situation is where one is forced to do or say something contrary to his/her beliefs, values, or desires. Some type of promise of reward or reinforcement or threat of punishment usually puts one in a position of complying. It may seem strange, but the least amount of force used creates the most dissonance-producing situation.

For an example of a forced-compliance situation, how many times have you found yourself helping "the nice lady next door" with chores that really go beyond your concept of neighborliness? Why do you feel bad while returning home after performing the third or fourth chore in one day for your "nice" neighbor? Probably your answer is "Well, she asks me in such a nice way that . . ." Whatever forced you to comply has put you in a siutation where you are behaving in a way that is in opposition to your attitude.

Involuntary Exposure   Individuals are constantly exposed to information either involuntarily or voluntarily. In involuntary exposure, there does not have to be a decision-making experience for dissonance to occur. Something as insignificant as a bumper sticker on the car in front of you can create dissonance. A bumper sticker that is prevalent in the South says, "Honk if you love Jesus." A person might feel strange honking to indicate his/her Christianity; but in not honking, does he/she declare himself/herself an athiest? Or perhaps while casually listening to the news (an involuntary exposure to information) you hear the commentator say that tuition is going to be raised at the university you are attending, or you hear your fiancée's employer announce that there will be a considerable cutback in employees during the next two months. Since the new information concerns one's education and wedding plans, the exposure, although involuntary, is immediately dissonance-arousing.

Voluntary Exposure   This situation is unique because it comes as a result of postdecision dissonance. It involves an information-seeking excursion that will assure one that the decision he/she made was the correct one.

If, in the example above concerning the choice between the Mercedes and the Rabbit, the Rabbit was chosen, the individual would only read the fine print of the ads in magazines concerning his/her choice, he/she would strike up conversations with other Rabbit owners, and he/she would make sure he/she did not miss the ads on television that tell him/her "how elegant the Rabbit is."

Disagreement with Important Others   The fifth dissonance-inducing situation is when a person is placed in the position where he/she disagrees with significant or important people in his/her social environment. The degree of dissonance depends on the number of people disagreed with, their importance, and the importance of the issue to the person taking the stance.

An example would be of a wife and mother who divorces her husband and grants him permanent custody of their children. The knowledge that she will be criticized by her family, other relatives, close friends, and society creates dissonance in her.

When dissonance exists, how does one reduce it? According to Festinger, there are five ways individuals may reduce dissonance: (1) change one of the cognitive elements—that is, change attitude; (2) add new elements to one side of the tension or the other; (3) come to see the elements as less important than they used to be; (4) seek consonant information; or (5) distort the information involved.

Using some of our former dissonance-producing examples, we can see how dissonance in their cases could be reduced by one or more of the above. In the case of the "nice lady next door," we could decide that we do not like her anymore (changing one of the cognitive elements). For reducing dissonance in the choice of buying a car, seeking only favorable information is certainly adding new elements to one side and seeking only consonant information. In the example of the senior making a decision of getting a job or going to graduate school, he/she may decide to stay in graduate school because money is not important, which would be seeing one element as less important than other elements. In the example of the woman who chooses a life style that means granting custody of her children to her husband, she may reduce dissonance by weighing one cognition with more information than the other by saying, "They are better off without me" or "He's a better mother than I can ever be," or she may choose to ignore the void she may be leaving in the lives of her children (distortion) by saying, "I can give them more by seeing them once a month than I am able to by unhappily living with them."

The basic difference in the three balance theories may be summed up by pointing out that Heider's theory deals with a person's perception of his or her relationship to others, Osgood's theory is based on how a person views two units that are connected by an assertion, and Festinger says dissonance exists between two cognitive units, and dissonance occurs after the conflict has been resolved.

THE NATURE OF ATTITUDE CHANGE

Although cognitive imbalance may lead to attitude change, people ask questions such as: "Even if an attitude appears to have changed according to pencil-and-paper measurements, will the attitude change last?" "Is it a temporary change rather than a deep-seated change?" Such questions bring us to the subject of the nature of attitude change. H. D. Kelman (1958) discusses attitude change through three processes: (1) identification, (2) internalization, and (3) compliance. Compliance, the engaging in behavior that may result in changed attitudes, is discussed in Chapter IV.

Changes in attitudes occur at different levels. Kelman refers to the agent for change as the processes of social influence. He considers attitudes as a function of motives with antecedent social influences. His theory is based on the concept that in order to know how to change an attitude, one must first know the type of attitude that he/she is trying to change.

Identification and internalization are processes of influence by which different types of attitude change can be identified.

Identification

Identification occurs when someone else's attitudes are adopted because an association with those attitudes results in a "satisfying self-defining relationship" with another person. This relationship is encompassed in one's self-image. Our closest friends, our roommates, our confidants all fall into this category.

When attitudes change as a result of identification, it is an actual change, not just a behavior change. The attitude change is an avenue to a satisfying relationship.

An example might be a student from a conservative family who develops a strong admiration for his or her sociology professor. Through discussions in class, the student becomes aware of the professor's strong commitment to the rights of the oppressed and minorities. When, in an informal setting in the student center, the professor asks the student to be his/her guest at an ACLU meeting, the student's acceptance of the invitation and perhaps subsequent adoption of the attitudes embraced by this group might be motivated by a need for a more lasting and meaningful relationship with the professor.

Also, identification embraces the concept that no one wants to be different. People want to believe that there are others who think as they do, hold the same beliefs and values, and are like themselves. This is known as an assumption of similitude. How often has one said or heard someone else say, "I am so glad to hear you say that. I feel exactly the same way, but have said nothing because I thought everyone else was thinking just the opposite." A feeling of relief occurs when a confederate has been discovered.

Take note of all the commercials that use the technique of assumption of similitude to persuade us to buy certain products. They show the grateful housewife whose neighbor has just told her about the new orange juice, detergent, cooking oil, or roach killer that "everyone" is using.

If one were to play devil's advocate at this point, he or she might say, "But what about the commercials that seem to be appealing to a person's desire to be different?" The devil's advocate might use the example of the advertisement for Cachet perfume, which says, "The perfume no two women can share." Surely this approach is using a technique appealing to the desire to be different rather than similar. Yet the assumption-of-similitude premise is working in this example as well. Maybe no two women want to share a pleasant fragrance, but all women want to exude a pleasant fragrance. Herein lies the similarity.

It is the function of the persuader to tell the persuadee that the persuadee is not different and that what the persuadee believes is shared by others. The persuader can also imply that if the persuadee has an alternative viewpoint from the persuader's, the persuadee is basically alone or in the minority. If the persuadee accepts the persuader's stance, however, the persuadee will be joining others of similar values, beliefs, and goals.

The concept of identification, then, tells us that we change attitudes based on motivations that come from the desire for special relationships with significant others and the desire to share with others our attitudes, beliefs, and goals.

Internalization

Internalization, according to Kelman, occurs when an attitude is adopted because it coincides or is congruent with one's value system. The reward involved in the attitude change produces internal psychological comfort rather than external compensations, as is the case in identification. Dissonance theory and social judgment theory deal with attitude change based on the internalization process.

Dissonance Theory When a persuadee has been convinced that he/she is not in the mainstream on a given issue, he/she will often experience dissonance. If the persuader knows the general attitudes and beliefs of the persuadee, the persuader may decide to take a position that would be in conflict with one of the persuadee's attitudes or beliefs even though that position may be the opposite of what the persuader originally believed. This would, then, create imbalance in the persuadee. It would then be the task of the persuader to provide his or her own point of view in such a manner that it would convince the persuadee that to accept the advocated position would make the persuadee feel comfortable again or restore balance.

There are times when the most the persuader can do is to cause a shift in an attitude. Osgood and Tannenbaum's theory can also be of assistance here. The persuader must keep both units in mind when making his or her assertions. Being aware that a shift occurs in the position of both units, the persuader's efforts, through the shifting of both positions, could possibly get these positions closer, if not make them congruent.

The Resolution of Dissonance   A persuader also must be aware of the fact that if he or she is asking the persuadee to make a choice, not only does he or she have the responsibility of resolving the conflict between choices in the mind of the persuadee, but he or she must provide the persuadee with dissonance-reducing material as well.

Place yourself in the role of the persuadee. You are Catholic, and your best friend has asked you to attend a proabortion rally with her. She may resolve your conflict, according to Festinger's definition, by telling you that you have nothing better to do that afternoon or that there are supposed to be some excellent speakers or that a lot of your friends will be there.

You may give an affirmative answer that resolves the conflict of whether to go or not. If your friend is astute, she will be aware of the dissonance in you, such as "I shouldn't go because I am against abortion for religious reasons" or "My attendance could lead others to believe I'm for it."

To relieve your dissonance, your friend might point out that an issue much greater and equally as important as abortion is going to be discussed—the freedom of choice. She might also point out that discovering what the opposition is saying on the subject might help you to become better prepared to defend your own stance on the issue.

Dissonance theorists also tell us that when there is high discrepancy between the persuader's communication and the persuadee's stand on the issue, these two variables are two dissonant cognitions and can only be alleviated by an attitude change. Philip Zimbardo (1960) indicated that the amount of dissonance that is created in this situation depends not only on the degree of discrepancy, but on the importance of the two elements of the situation as well.

However, the key to whether or not attitude change will occur as a result of discrepancy depends on whether or not alternative methods to reduce dissonance are available. For example, during the day of the attempted assassination of President Reagan, people were interviewed by the media for their reactions to the event, and some said that they did not feel unhappy about Reagan's getting shot. Suppose that one of these people was a prominent Democrat from your community with whom you had worked in the past. Since his view about the shooting of Reagan may be highly discrepant with your attitude, which is one opposed to the shooting of *anyone*, you may have to explore the alternative of derogating the prominent Democrat, or you may have to decide that he is an ineffective spokesperson for the Democratic Party. If, however, these alternatives are not viable ones for you, your attitude toward the situation may change.

The balance and consistency theories give persuaders valuable insights into the persuasive process. They provide valuable options and a variety of approaches to use in persuaders' efforts to persuade.

The conclusion can be drawn from the study of attitudes and balance theories that communication may result in change and that persuasion is the process by which attitude change may occur.

Social Judgment Theory   Social judgment theory (Littlejohn 1978, p. 191) makes predictions concerning attitude change such as (1) attitude change can occur when the message falls within the latitude of acceptance; (2) attitude change is significantly reduced or even impossible whenever a message falls within the latitude of rejection (indeed, this can produce a boomerang effect, which reinforces the original attitude); (3) attitude change will be greater in relation to the discrepancy from the original attitude when the message is within the latitude of acceptance and noncommitment (when the message reaches the latitude of rejection, change will not occur); (4) attitude change will be less in relation to a person's ego-involvement in the issue—that is, the greater the ego-involvement, the larger the latitude of rejection, and the smaller the latitude of noncommitment, the less the attitude change.

As is mentioned in the third prediction, above, discrepancy plays a role in social judgment theory as it does in dissonance theory. R. Rhine and L. Severance (1970) conducted a study in which subjects were told that the experimenters wished to determine their attitudes on the issues of (1) increased tuition at the University of California, which was a high ego-involvement issue, and (2) the amount of new park acreage that should be developed in Allentown, Pennsylvania, which was a low ego-involvement issue.

Among their results, the authors discovered that a significant ego-involvement change resulted in those subjects with low ego-involvement in the issue after these subjects heard a highly discrepant message. It is easy to understand, perhaps, why the highly ego-involved do not change since they have considered all aspects of the issue before making a highly ego-involved commitment. The authors suggest that when an individual is required to consider a topic that he/she has never thought about and is also required to make some kind of commitment, his/her perception of the importance of the topic will tend to shift.

This study also revealed that perhaps in certain situations the latitude of rejection may be a better predictor of a person's attitude than the traditional approach of looking at the latitude of acceptance. Some attitudes appear to reflect what an individual is against instead of what he/she is for.

There are many instances where people are very well informed on the side of the issue they oppose but are vague about the finer points of their own position. Many Americans who support President Reagan's budget and its cutbacks know "everything" about the proclaimed balanced budget and lower taxes, but they are not necessarily informed about the probable increase in state and local taxes which may result. The Rhine and Severance study presented another significant finding—that social judgment theory is a much better predictor of attitude change than dissonance theory.

Perceived Consequences As a Factor in Attitude Change

A person's perceptions of the consequences of an attitude change is a good predictor of whether or not the change will occur. An important study concerning the effect of perception of consequences on attitude change was conducted by D. A. Infante (1975) in a series of five studies. Each study rated the subjects on their perceptions of the consequences on topics such as guaranteed minimum annual income, compulsory national service, and tuition increases.

The first two studies showed that there was a relation between one's perception of desirable consequences of an issue and one's attitude toward that issue. It also indicated that perception of desirable consequences was more of an indicator than perception of undesirable consequences.

The results of the third and fourth studies suggested that arguments about likely undesirable consequences are more persuasive than arguments regarding unlikely favorable consequences when the persuader wishes to induce unfavorable attitudes toward an issue. If the persuadee already has favorable attitudes toward the proposal as well as an awareness of the possibility of favorable consequences, it is most effective for the persuader to include arguments concerning likely undesirable consequences and unlikely desirable consequences.

The results of the fifth study indicated that when persons perceive undesirable consequences as more likely than desirable ones, the perceptions of the undesirable consequences are the better predictors of unfavorable attitudes.

These studies by Infante appear to support a "likelihood" hypotheses—that is, whatever we perceive as the "most likely" consequence will be the best predictor of attitude change. The persuader who uses arguments claiming consequences that are "likely," whether desirable or undesirable, will be more successful in effecting attitude change.

These studies also revealed that the importance of the consequences to self and others is also a key variable. For example, we have a colleague who is politically conservative and who campaigned for the first Republican governor in Texas. In his campaign, the candidate advocated negative proposals for the state's educational system, mainly a cut in funds. Between the period of the campaign and after Governor Clements's inauguration, our friend's son became a state employee and married a schoolteacher. Suddenly, the consequences of the governor's stand on state salaries became important as far as our friend was concerned. He now holds a negative attitude toward the governor for whom he actively campaigned during the last election.

Since an attitude is a feeling that an individual has toward an object, person, or idea, one needs to take into consideration how the attributes one assigns to the object affect attitude change.

ATTRIBUTION THEORY

The most prominent theory of the process of attribution is H. Kelley's (1973). His theory consists of two aspects. (1) In some incidents the individual has information that he/she has gained from more than one observation and from which he/she draws perceptual conclusions concerning which effects are attributed to which causes. (2) In some situations the attribute is made from a single observation that discounts any prior observations (Littlejohn 1978, pp. 233–34). Kelley refers to the first aspect as covariance and the second as discounting. There will be further discussion of attribution theory in Chapter IV. Attributes are also a part of the next theory to be discussed—the Fishbein-Ajzen theory (1975).

In the previous discussions of attitudes, theorists agreed that attitudes are derived from salient beliefs. The major problem in changing attitudes appears to be twofold. Fishbein and Ajzen explain it is this manner:

Any belief that assoicates the attitude object with some other object, concept, or property and that is part of the person's salient belief hierarchy constitutes a primary belief. It is important to note that the object of the primary beliefs is exactly the same as the object of the attitude which is to be changed. (pp. 396–7)

An example might be a salient belief in American "democracy," around which the individual would develop primary beliefs concerning freedom, equality, and voice in government. If the persuader, however, tried to tie in an argument concerning politics in England (a democracy), it would be inappropriate. Just because these are primary beliefs about democracy, it does not necessarily mean that tying any democratic government to this belief would be successful. Democracy in England is very different than American democracy because it has a socialist economy. The argument would need to be tied to more salient beliefs concerning England's particular concept of democracy or to England itself.

Target beliefs must be linked to the individual's salient belief system in order for attitude change to occur. Appropriate target beliefs are only a portion of the primary belief influencing attitude. Two other factors that make up the salient belief system are influence attempts and evaluation of those attributes associated with the primary beliefs. These factors can also influence the degree of attitude change (Fishbein and Ajzen 1975, p. 397).

A significant study concerning the impact of influence attempts and attribute evaluation was done by R. J. Lutz (1973, in Fishbein and Ajzen 1975, p. 398). Through a free elicitation procedure, a list of modal salient or primary beliefs was obtained. Four experimental groups were used to attempt to change or alter one of these beliefs. One group was told that a detergent could be used in all temperatures. The second group was told that the detergent could not be used in all temperatures. The third group was told that the detergent was costly. The fourth group was told that the detergent was not costly. Lutz found that attitude change could be predicted on the basis of change in the target belief.

The influence attempt also had significant effect on some of the primary external beliefs. Attitude change turned out to be related to both the direction of belief change and of attribute evaluation. When a person's belief that the detergent was all-temperature was increased or when a person's belief that the detergent was expensive was decreased, he/she developed an increasingly favorable attitude and vice versa (Fishbein and Ajzen 1977, p. 398).

SUMMARY

The concept of attitude plays a central role in persuasion. Attitude has been defined as a learned and relatively enduring predisposition to respond favorably or unfavorably to an idea, an object, or a person.

It is important to remember that attitudes are derived from beliefs, values, group associations, and other attitudes. Although attitudes are not as difficult to change as salient beliefs or values, they are not transient either. Attitudes tend to be lasting by nature, but they are susceptible to change. It is this feature that makes attitudes and the knowledge about them crucial to the persuader. When attitudes are changed, the change can be measured both in direction and intensity.

Finally, it is essential to the understanding of attitudes to remember the relationship between the person holding an attitude and his/her perception of the attitude object.

The study of attitudes is related to other psychological processes. The conceptualization of attitudes includes the affective component of attitude, which is evaluative in nature, the cognitive component, which includes beliefs about or factual knowledge of attitude objects, and the behavioral component, which is the overt action taken toward the attitude object. This dimension of attitudes, behavior, and behavior change is the subject of the next chapter.

To understand attitudes and attitude change, we must understand the complexity of human nature. Human beings cannot tolerate psychological inconsistency. When inconsistency exists, we will try to eliminate it or reduce it. Balance theories account for the conflict of attitudes and behavior, the resultant psychological discomfort, and the resolution or reduction of the conflict, which sometimes can result in attitude change. Heider's Balance Theory shows us how our attitude toward a source and an idea can be balanced or imbalanced. Osgood and Tannenbaum's Congruity Principle extends the Heider model with a more precise measuring technique and an attempt to predict outcome when two units are associative or dissociative. The shifts that occur establish psychological equilibrium, bringing predictable congruity out of incongruity. Festinger's Cognitive Dissonance Theory is an important conceptualization of what happens in a postdecision state. Cognitive dissonance assumes that an individual will not, perceptually at least, tolerate more than a minimal amount of psychological inconsistency in his/her perceived environment. When dissonance is provoked due to an imbalance in a cognitive element about the self and the attitude object, there is a need to reduce dissonance. There are numerous ways to achieve dissonance reduction, one of which is attitude change. Yet, what is essentially being sought is psychological equilibrium, and this is purchased at the price of some kind of change, either in behavior toward, or perception of, the dissonant elements. Free choice is always dissonant-producing. Therefore, people who make choices need to understand what happens to them in choice-making situations.

The ways in which a persuader attempts to alter attitudes must include an understanding of balance theories and practical applications of them, the assumption of similitude, and social judgment theory. It is important to try to know the persuadee's latitude of acceptance and/or rejection as well as his/her level of noncommitment in order to affect shifts of opinion and to predict what direction the shifts might take.

Finally, attribution theory gives the persuader knowledge about what attributes to attach to an attitude object in order to create favorable responses to persuasion. Fishbein and Ajzen target the necessity of understanding the salient beliefs of a persuadee's hierarchy. This concept, as well as many others discussed in the chapter, provides essential understanding of the complex nature of attitude and attitude change. When a persuader and persuadee interact, whether they are the same person, an interpersonal dyad, a small group, a persuader and an audience, or the mass communication network of multiple persuaders and audiences, the knowledge of attitudes will greatly assist the persuasion process, the choices that are made within it, and, perhaps, the successes or failures that result from it.

KEY WORDS

Attitude
Information-processing approach
Concept formation
Identification
Potency
Activity
Internalization
Direction and intensity of
  attitudes
Assimilation and contrast

Ego-involvement
Balance
Congruity
Dissonance
Consonance
Associative assertion
Dissociative assertion
Assumption of similitude
Attribution theory

EXERCISES

1. State one of your salient beliefs, and make a list of attitudes that relate to that belief. For example, you probably believe in protecting your health. What new attitudes result from such a belief?
2. List four attitudes that you feel are firmly entrenched in your make-up. (a) Try to trace them back to salient beliefs and other attitudes. (b) Relate them to other attitudes that you are sure you hold.
3. Name four attitudes that you hold without any actual experience or factual knowledge to base them on. From what do you think they are derived?
4. Select a controversial group such as the American Nazi party or the John Birch Society as a subject, and test five of your friends according to Bogardus's Measure of Social Distance.
5. Briefly tell of an instance in which two people with the same reference point on the Sherif Linear Scale react in completely different ways as a result of different levels of ego-involvement. You might want to use a campus problem similar to the one about curfews in campus housing.

6. Have you ever involuntarily received information that created imbalance, incongruity, or dissonance? How did you resolve or reduce your psychological discomfort?

7. Can you think of an instance in which you have an attitude that is inconsistent with your behavior? For example, do you smoke knowing that cigarettes are dangerous to your health? Do you spend more time socializing and drinking in college than you do studying when you know that in order to get good grades you should study more? How do you explain that to yourself? How do you reduce your own dissonance?

8. Write or develop a portion of a persuasive speech in which you point out to an audience conflict between their behavior and salient beliefs or strong attitudes that you are pretty sure they hold. Attempt to create dissonance in your audience, and then offer audience members an acceptable way to relieve the dissonance with the proposition of your speech, which is an attitude or behavior change. Later on, try to incorporate this technique into a longer speech.

9. Use one of the attitude measurement scales discussed in the chapter when one of your class members gives a speech. Maintaining anonymity, tabulate the results, and tell the class what shifts in attitude, if any, took place. Discuss the reasons why. Also, you might want to administer the test a few days or a week later to see if the attitude shift endured over a period of time.

10. To what extent do you think your attitudes are culturally bound? How much alike are the attitudes that you and your peers hold compared to those that your parents hold? Listen to a presidential address, and compare the president's attitudes with yours. Try not to be influenced by the office of president in the comparison.

11. Go to an action-type film (a Western, a detective film, or some type of horror–science-fiction film), and notice if you experience any psychological imbalance during the chase scene or other scenes in which a character with whom you identify is threatened. Note how you reduce your imbalance during or after the film.

12. Look back on a relationship that has been severed (a friendship, a love affair, a marriage), and examine the psychological imbalances that you experienced as a result of differences in attitudes related to the strong feelings you held for the other person.

READINGS

Fishbein, Martin, and Ajzen, Icek. *Beliefs, Attitudes, Intention, and Behavior: An Introduction to Theory and Research.* Reading, Mass.: Addison-Wesley, 1975.

Insko, Chester. *Theories of Attitude Change.* New York: Appleton-Century-Crofts, 1967.

Kiesler, Charles; Collins, Barry E.; and Miller, Norman. *Attitude Change: A Critical Analysis of Theoretical Approaches.* New York: Wiley, 1969.

Littlejohn, Stephen W. *Theories of Human Communication.* Columbus, Ohio: Charles E. Merrill, 1978.

4

ATTITUDES, BEHAVIOR, AND BEHAVIOR CHANGE

Upon completion of this chapter you should be able to:

1. Know the difference between attitude toward an object and attitude toward a situation.
2. Define self-perception theory.
3. Know the determinants of behavior.
4. Know the components of behavioral intentions.
5. Understand the conditions that facilitate behavioral change.
6. Understand the concept of modeling as a means of behavioral change.

n the previous chapters, we discussed beliefs and attitudes and how they relate to the persuasive process. This chapter is about what is often the ultimate goal of any persuader—behavior change. The variables that influence behavior, the determinants of behavior and behavioral intentions, and the components of behavioral intentions are discussed in this chapter. The goal is to know what elicits changes in behavior and which situations hold the highest probability of change.

Some people would like to believe that attitudes are precursors of action. Unfortunately, it is not that simple. Many of the studies that have attempted to link attitude to behavior change have been unsuccessful. In fact, there has been a profound disenchantment with the utility of attitudes for understanding human activity. If, however, we measure the attitude toward the object or the situation in which the behavior would occur, then behavior can often be predicted (Steinfatt and Infante 1976).

ATTITUDE TOWARD OBJECT

M. Rokeach and P. Kliejunas (1972) conducted a study in which 108 students who were enrolled in two intermediate psychology courses were examined to determine the relationship between class-cutting behavior and the attitude toward cutting class. The experimenters selected attitude toward instructor as "attitude toward object" and the general activity of the class as "attitude toward the situation." They hypothesized that how often each student cut class should be a function of each of these attitudes, their interaction, and their perceived importance. The results showed that by considering these two attitudes separately as well as their cognitive interaction, behavior could be predicted. This study served to explain why, in some of the early studies, there was such high discrepancy between attitude and behavior. The early studies had tested attitudes toward the object, whereas Rokeach and Kliejunas tested attitudes toward the situation as well as toward the object.

ATTITUDE TOWARD BEHAVIOR

Three studies by J. G. Jaccard, W. King, and R. Pomozal (1977) were conducted to find out if a person's attitude toward a specific behavioral criterion was the best attitude predictor of behavior. In one of the studies, students were given questionnaires concerning blood donations. This distribution of forms occurred one week prior to a student blood drive on campus. Two attitude measures were acquired: (1) the attitude toward "donating blood at the upcoming drive" and (2) the attitude toward "blood donation" in general. Each attitude was determined by semantic differential ratings such as "good-bad," "pleasant-unpleasant," and "nice-awful." The sum of these responses constituted the attitude measure.

During the week following the blood drive, all subjects were contacted by phone and asked if they had donated blood. These answers were checked against the official blood-donor records. There was a much more significant correspondence between the attitude toward "donating blood at the upcoming drive" and subsequent behavior than there was between the general attitude toward "blood donation" and behavior.

A woman may indicate proabortion attitudes on an attitude test, but a clearer indication of her attitudes would be a measure of her intentions to have an abortion should she become pregnant. M. Fishbein and I. Ajzen (1975) report that a person's attitude toward the object is also related to the set of intentions that he/she has toward the performance of a wide choice of behaviors available to him or her. Included in these attitudes are those that involve one's attitude toward performing the suggested behavior. Fishbein and Ajzen refer to this concept as the expectancy-value theory.

EXPECTANCY-VALUE MODEL

One of the best-known expectancy-value models is the subjective expected utility model (SEA) (Edwards 1954). This theory suggests that when faced with behavioral choices, people tend to choose the alternative that has the highest expected utility or the alternative that seems likely to result in a favorable outcome.

Not only are attitudes about intentions toward a behavioral object clues to behavior, but also if the performance of a given behavior is contrary to an existing attitude, the old attitude will change to coincide with the new behavior. Self-perception theory and other self-attribution theories have been useful in explaining the behavior-attitude relationship.

SELF-PERCEPTION THEORY

Daryl Bem's self-perception theory (1970) states that an individual, in identifying his/her internal states, partially relies on the same external cues that others use when they infer the individual's internal states. Bem uses the example of the question "Why do you eat brown bread?" with its response "Because I like it." A clearer example of what really happens is exemplified in the question "Why do you like brown bread?" The answer "Because I eat it" is indicative of a behavior-attitude sequence.

To better understand how we judge our internal feelings by our behavior or other external clues, we need to remember our early days, when we learned the names of objects from the adults in our lives who told us what they were. Yet, how did we learn to identify our internal states? Our parents, unable to "see inside" us, taught us the names of internal states by evaluating our behavior. If we cried and pulled at our ear, we were told that "we had an earache." If we rubbed our eyes and were cranky, we were told that we were "sleepy." In other words, in our formative years we learned to identify our internal states from the adults who judged and named our internal states by observing our external behaviors.

As adults, we also draw conclusions about our inner feelings from observing our external actions. We say, "I must not be feeling well or I wouldn't be so rude to my boss" or "I must be enjoying this persuasion book because I'm reading it so carefully."

SELF-ATTRIBUTION THEORIES

Other self-attribution theories reinforce Bem's ideas. R. E. Nisbett and S. Valins (in Jones, *et al* 1972) noted that if we perceive the cause of our behavior as an internal reaction to the stimulus toward which the behavior was directed, then changed attitudes may result from the observation of our own behavior. A changed attitude will not result, however, if we perceive that the behavior was caused by other circumstances that were separate from the stimulus.

S. Valins (1966) conducted a demonstration that supports this premise. Male subjects who were shown slides of scantily clothed women were told that the experimenter was measuring the subjects' physical reactions to the pictures. The men could hear a heartbeat each time they were shown a slide, and each man was told that it was his heartbeat. The experimenters manipulated the supposed heartbeat by increasing or decreasing the rate when the subjects were shown certain slides. When the men were asked to rate the slides at the conclusion of the experiment, they chose those pictures that they had looked at when they believed that their heartbeat had increased or decreased. They believed that they were evaluating the slides on the basis of their own internal states, whereas they had actually evaluated them on the basis of external information. When rechecked after several weeks, the subjects still preferred the same pictures.

From this and other studies, we know that individuals tend to stand by their previous statements. If you were a witness to a hit-and-run accident, you would be asked to make a statement. Suppose this statement was made under noncoercive circumstances, and you stated that the driver was blonde, dressed in a suede jacket, and approximately thirty years old. Later, at the trial, when other witnesses gave conflicting stories, you would be inclined to stay with your original story because you would think "If I said it, it must be true."

ATTRIBUTION OF ATTITUDE TO BEHAVIOR

When we observe our own behavior, we can have one of many reactions. Harry C. Triandis gives this example: "I acted that way so it must mean that I wanted to act that way or I wouldn't have" or "I acted that way more than once, so I must like to act that way" (1977, p. 5). When we attribute new attitudes to behaviors, those attitudes tend to remain changed. If, however, we attribute the behavior to an unusual situation such as "I was sick that day" or "I was pressured by my boss," then there may be only a temporary attitude change and not necessarily a permanent one.

Bem's theory suggests that new attitudes may result from various kinds of behaviors; Nisbett and Valins differentiate between ordinary situations and unusual circumstances, only the former causing permanent attitude change (Triandis 1977).

Since a change in behavior can cause a change in attitude, it is from behavior observation that a persuadee may draw conclusions about what he or she feels or believes. Can a persuader then predict the behavior of a persuadee? For the persuader, the emphasis in this chapter will be on changing behavior, thereby producing changes in attitudes. If we are aware of the determinants of behavior and the components of behavioral intentions, types of behavior, and the influence of the weight of all these variables on behavior and behavior's propensity for change, we should become not only effective persuaders, but also understanding of our own behaviors and their resultant effects.

GOALS AND INTENTIONS

Behavioral acts are related to goals and intentions. A *goal* is a desired outcome of a series of specific acts, and behavioral intention is "a cognitive antecedent to a behavioral act" (Triandis 1977, p. 5). If you were asked "Why are you going to school?" or "Why do you jog three miles a day?" your answers would be considered goals. If your apartment caught fire, your rush to the phone would be motivated by a behavioral intention to "call for help" (Triandis 1977).

"Goals specify the requirements for positive self-evaluation" (Bandura 1977, p. 161). Once an individual has formed a concept of self-satisfaction that is dependent on attaining a goal, he/she tends to pursue that goal until certain end states are achieved. Most goal achievements do not necessarily bring permanent satisfaction, but rather elicit further positive self-evaluation related to achieving higher goals.

The degree to which goals create incentives for behavior can be determined by the specificity of a goal. Albert Bandura states that "explicitly defined goals regulate performance by designation of the type and the amount of effort required and they foster self-satisfaction by furnishing clear signs of personal accomplishment" (1977, p. 161). Naturally, more effort is put forth when satisfaction is dependent upon difficult goals than with simple ones.

Behavioral intentions are special forms of beliefs "in which the object is always the person himself and the attribute is always the behavior" (Fishbein and Ajzen 1975, p. 12). The strength of an intention can be measured by procedures that place the subject along a subjective-probability dimension involving a relation between himself or herself and a specific behavioral act (Fishbein and Ajzen 1975).

DETERMINANTS OF BEHAVIOR

The above definitions help us to understand the determinants of behavior and their relative importance in given situations. Such knowledge gives us clues about the probabilities of heightening behavior change. Triandis (1977) has explored a concept that specifies the parameters to be considered in attempting to predict social behavior. The determinants of the probability of the behavior that Triandis develops are (1) habit (2) the behavioral intention to perform the act, and (3) behavioral potential.

HABIT

A behavior, according to Triandis (1977, p. 9), is a habit when it has been performed repeatedly for a long period of time. Most scholars accept the premise that patterns in past behaviors or habits are fair predictors of future behaviors. Consider our classic answer to the question "Why do you do that that way?": "Because I've always done it that way!" In other words, after we have engaged in a given behavior many times, we develop a script for that situation. Each time we encounter a similar situation, it "does not require a great deal of consciousness to carry out the same behavior" (Roloff, in Roloff and Miller 1980, p. 50).

When an act is recurrent by nature, it comes under the influence of habit (Triandis 1977, p. 10). A casual observer can see the influence of habit on behavior in daily life. The person who "just can't get moving until he/she has had that first cup of coffee" is a victim of habit. Roommates fare well if one is in the habit of bathing in the morning and the other is in the habit of bathing at bedtime. In many of the police shows on television, the wrongdoer is discovered because the clues he/she leaves behind at the scene of each crime are similar to each other. Police officials make such statements as "That's his M.O. all right!"

Even if the persuader convinces the persuadee to behave in a recommended fashion, if the persuadee already has habits to the contrary, the changed behavior is unlikely to occur. The intensity of the habit is also a significant variable. Is voting the Democratic ticket for the past five or ten years as intense a habit as smoking? The difference in the two examples lies in the strength of the two habits. The overwhelming victory of Ronald Reagan in the 1980 presidential election never would have occurred if a significant number of habitual Democrats had not revised their voting habits.

BEHAVIORAL INTENTIONS TO PERFORM THE ACT

Behavioral intentions can be understood by studying their components, which are: (1) social factors; (2) affect or feeling about the behavior; and (3) the perceived value of the consequences of the suggested behavior (Triandis, 1977).

Social Factors

According to Triandis, the social factors that determine behavioral intentions are norms, roles, contractual arrangements, self-monitoring, and self-concept. We have also included values.

Norms As discussed in Chapter II, norms are beliefs and values derived from membership in groups or from positive references to groups to which we do not belong. Norms are often cultural rules that specify appropriate and correct behaviors in specific situations. How to greet dignitaries, how to behave as a house guest, and table manners all fall into this category. Norms often regulate automatic behavioral responses such as shaking hands or saying "Thank you."

When following the norms of a valued or esteemed group, people do not have to stop and think about their behavior. They can conform to the norms of behavior of the group, which requires less effort than making decisions about how to behave. Of course, some norms are stronger than others. Thus, the influence of these norms on behavior is dependent on their importance to an individual. A strong norm for Americans is cleanliness, and the subsequent behavior is frequent bathing. The soap and bath-oil manufacturers assume that Americans bathe regularly and try to persuade Americans to use their products when they do.

Gang behavior is another example of norms that strongly influence behavior. Gangs often value power and physical strength. Thus, physical aggression is acted out to fulfill these norms. Some gangs enforce the norms with strong punishment if acts of physical aggression are not used to respond to affronts (Wolfgang and Ferraciti 1967).

Values   Values, also discussed in Chapter II, influence behavior as well. When values are consistent and strong, behavior change is not likely to occur. In fact, Rokeach tells us that a behavior will remain consistent as long as the values are intact (1973). He suggests that persuaders pay more attention to the change in value that underlies a behavior because a change in a value, which is not easy, may lead to behavior change.

Roles   Roles are clusters of norms that apply to specific individuals in given positions. Roles influence behavior according to the position a person presumes to have. As a son or daughter, your behavior is somewhat regulated by the norms of your parents. Your behavior may be drastically different when you are cast in the role of employee, fraternity brother or sorority sister, lover, or sports fan. Also, there are behaviors that are considered appropriate in one situation, but not in another. Your father assumes multiple role behaviors as husband, father, son, boss, and employee. The role we feel we are in at the time a behavior is suggested will influence whether or not we will perform the behavior.

Contractual Arrangements   In our culture, we are very committed to contractual arrangements. Appointments with doctors and to have lunch as well as attendance of classes and meetings are seen as behavioral contracts or commitments. We behave according to the intensity of a contractual arrangement. An early-morning appointment causes behaviors such as hurried dressing and rushing to the car to fight the traffic so that we can arrive on time. People who are late elicit a negative response. It has become common for people to be irritated when a doctor makes a patient wait for a long time.

Self-monitoring Self-monitoring (Snyder 1974 in Triandis 1977, p. 14) is one's self-observation and self-control guided by clues for what is socially appropriate. According to M. Snyder, individuals monitor emotional behavior in five different ways: (1) by accurately communicating their true emotions by means of expressive presentation; (2) by communicating an emotional state that is not a true representation of their feelings; (3) by concealing an inappropriate emotional state and appearing to experience a more appropriate one; (4) by pretending to be emotionally unresponsive when actually they feel inappropriate emotions; and (5) by appearing to experience an emotional state when actually they feel nothing. Translated into appropriate behavior, choices for a given situation would look like this: "I am emotional, and I'm going to show it"; "I am emotional, but I shall pretend I'm not"; "I am envious, but I shall pretend that I am magnanimous"; "I shall act cool even though I'm angry"; "I am not emotional, but I shall pretend I am." These decisions to behave are examples of self-monitoring. We all vary in the amount of self-monitoring in which we engage. Triandis states that persons who score high in self-monitoring "are good at learning what is socially appropriate in new situations, have good control over their emotional expressions, and can effectively create the impressions they want" (1977, p. 14). Theater actors scored higher while hospital-ward patients scored lower than university students in experiments measuring self-monitoring.

Self-concept Self-concept is a theory that we construct about ourselves (Epstein 1973). It is derived from our perceptions about the world, the self, and the interactions among the self, others, and the world. We devise self-theories that enable us to maintain a pleasure-pain balance and organize our experiences in ways by means of which we can effectively cope with life (Triandis, 1977).

Self-concept may thus be defined as self-attributed traits or behaviors (Triandis 1977, p. 14). We all perceive certain behaviors to be more consistent with the "image in our heads" than other behaviors. For example,

Nice 'n Easy ad. This ad depicts how a woman's self-concept is based upon her self-attributed characteristics.

a woman who thinks she is glamorous will buy more glamorous clothes than a woman who considers herself practical or plain. A study (Kraut 1973) was conducted in which the experimenter discovered that subjects who were labeled charitable by the experimenters gave more to charity than those who were labeled uncharitable. We tend to perform behaviors that are consistent with our self-images. If we perceive ouselves to be lazy and stupid, then we will procrastinate and make failing grades. This phenomenon is referred to as the self-fulfilling prophecy.

Behavior change can occur as a result of a change in self-concept. When a behavior is suggested and the persuadee answers "I can see myself doing that," change in behavior is likely to occur. The person who perceives himself or herself to be athletic will be more inclined to join the company's softball team than a person who perceives himself or herself to be athletically inept.

When a man contemplates asking a woman for a date, he sees himself as being successful in receiving an affirmative answer or he would never have the courage to perform this behavior. Since behavior is influenced by our self-concept, a behavior change can result from an alteration in the self-concept.

One of the major elements that cause social factors to be so important is compliance. Compliance is a form of social influence that causes a person to do what is expected of him/her by another person, not because of agreement and willingness, but because of his/her fear of punishment or expectation of a reward (Kelman 1958). We have all engaged in compliant behavior in order to achieve goals. If a professor requires a lengthy term paper but gives us insufficient notice, we go ahead and write the paper to the best of our abilities, not because we think the professor has asked for reasonable behavior, but because we wish to pass the course. The degree to which we feel pressure from significant others to comply proves to be a strong variable in bringing about a specific behavior (Fishbein 1967, Dulaney in Horton and Dixon, 1968, and Acock and De Fleur 1972).

Affect or Feeling about the Behavior

The suggestion to behave produces in an individual a pleasant or unpleasant feeling about the behavior. A suggestion that you need to see the dentist probably gives you an unpleasant feeling. The thought of the behavior acts as a conditioned stimulus, and the pleasant or unpleasant feeling acts as an unconditioned stimulus.

Affect refers to our feelings about a given behavior. If a friend invited you for a dinner that was going to include fried rattlesnake, your feelings about eating rattlesnakes would have a strong bearing on your behavior. (We didn't make it up. There are people in Texas who actually eat rattlesnake meat.) We all have feelings concerning given behaviors, and it is to the persuader's advantage to know those feelings. Feelings are unique within an individual. The suggestion to learn hang-gliding may conjure up pleasant feelings in one person while causing another person to pale at the thought.

Because of pleasant or unpleasant experiences related to a given behavior, we begin over a period of time to respond without realizing what feeling state in the past caused the response. If, in childhood, you were forced to eat watery, boiled squash, you may now refuse a very elegant squash casserole without realizing that you are responding to an old stimulus. When this behavior occurs, the response has moved from being a behavioral intention to a habit. If your immediate response is negative, your intention will be to not perform the behavior.

Perceived Value of the Consequences

Behavioral intention is also linked to the consequence attached to the behavior as well as to the perception of the consequence's value. Will the suggested behavior cause something favorable to happen to us? Will it cause us to lose something of value? Gambling is attractive to some people because of their perception of the consequence of making a lot of fast money. Others, however, perceive gambling to be a case of the odds being against them. In the example of hang-gliding, there could be a situation where the person's belief that "it could be fun" (affect) was stronger than the consequence factor "it is dangerous" or "I could be injured."

There is a difference in perceived consequences when they are considered as immediate or long-range. A student may activate study behavior to achieve the immediate goal of a passing grade, whereas a smoker may not change behavior if there are no immediate ill effects from smoking. The long-range consequences have less impact on the behavior than the immediate consquences.

When asked why we performed a given behavior, our answer will usually reflect the social, affect, or consequence component of behavioral intentions. The statement "I played football in high school because boys were not accepted if they didn't" reflects the social component as well as the consequence component. The statement "In spite of my allergy to shellfish, I ate shrimp for dinner last evening because I love it" would be an example of the affect component taking precedence over the consequence component.

Triandis (1977) reports on a study that involved self-reports as explanations of the subjects' behavior (Collins, Martin, Ashmore, and Ross

(*Wichita Falls Record News* February 22, 1980, p. 6A)

1973). Three of the four findings that emerged were similar to the three components that Triandis discussed. The social component was reflected in the subjects' agreement with statements such as "In order to get along and be liked, I tend to be what people expect me to be rather than anything else" or "I guess I put on a show to impress people" or "I know I'm not the person I pretend to be." A second factor reflected the affective component by subjects' agreeing with statements such as "I can only argue for ideas to which I am strongly committed." The consequence component was reflected through items such as "All one's behavior should be directed toward a certain number of definite goals" (Triandis 1977, p. 18).

BEHAVIORAL POTENTIAL

If the behavioral potential is low, behavioral intentions can be deterred. Behavioral potential is the presence or absence of facilitating conditions that would allow the performance of the act. When conditions exist that disallow the performance of the behavior, then habit and intentions have little influence. If a person is a habitual smoker but finds himself or herself in the nonsmoking section of an airplane, then he or she will not smoke because conditions do not allow this behavior.

A study that examined the subjects' attitudes toward the attendance of football games and the intentions of attending specific games on specific dates was conducted by P. A. Holman (1956). He discovered that overall attitude results were different from the results relating to intentions. Specific attendance on certain dates was negated for reasons such as "I have to work that day" or "It's my mother's birthday."

An example that effectively demonstrates the difference between the components of behavioral intentions and behavioral potential was cited by R. Bostrom:

After hearing a persuasive message, urging me to vote for a particular candidate for water commissioner, I may feel more kindly toward the candidate (affective component), see in him many good qualities (belief component), decide that I am going to vote for him (behavioral intention), and the sum of these might be described as my "predisposition" to get out and vote. Unfortunately, before I actually vote there are a number of other factors that influence me. I may not be registered, so that voting would be impossible. I may have a job that keeps me a significant distance from the polling booth; the election may take place during the week that I have already scheduled for my vacation, and so on. Even if all those obstacles were not present, I may not know where the polls are located. The sum of all these factors that are necessary to elicit the behavior may be called the behavioral *potential*, and it should be clear that is is quite different from behavioral *intention*. (Bostrom in Roloff and Miller 1980, pp. 177–78)

Behavioral potential must be considered as a strong determinant of a person's follow-through behavior.

BEHAVIOR AND BEHAVIORAL DIFFERENCES

According to Triandis (1977), behaviors can be divided into three categories, and the same laws do not govern each category. The behavior we observe in ourselves and others is considered *overt behavior*, which is both verbal and nonverbal. When a person is in love with another person, the first person may say "I love you" (verbal) and follow this statement with an embrace (nonverbal). *Attributive behavior* is derived from conclusions one draws about the internal states of others from their behavior, such as "She appreciated my report, so she must be intelligent." Our emotional reactions to people and events are referred to as *affective behaviors*. All behaviors fall into one of these categories.

Just how much might the components of intentions and whether or not a behavior is already a habit give us clues about the probability of a behavior occurring? Researchers have discovered that most social behaviors are determined by intentions to behave. When these behaviors happen frequently over a period of time, they become habit. The influence of the components of intentions may vary when the situation and the behavior are taken into consideration.

Triandis gives an example of how the influence of the components can vary in a given situation:

For example, suppose a politician attends a picnic sponsored by a particular ethnic group. The norms in such a case call for the politician to voice highly complimentary attributions about the ethnic group. These attributions may or may not be believed but the point is that they are appropriate in that setting, and they may get the politician some votes. Thus, the social and the consequence components will combine to determine the attribution that the politician will make. It is even possible that the politician dislikes making such attributions because he really dislikes the particular ethnic group. However, unless the weight of the affective component is much greater than the combined weights of the social and consequences components, the positive attributions are likely to be made. (1977, p. 25)

The social, affective, and consequence components have different effects according to the type of situation, type of behavior, and the type of individual. Certain situations demand certain behaviors. Norms, roles, and contractual obligations are strong behavioral influences. In church, for example, we behave according to community and religious norms and roles. More intimate behaviors occur at parties in comparison to more formal behaviors in the classroom.

When a behavior is new and not yet learned, a behavioral intention is used to explain or predict behavior. Habit and intention are related in the sense that intentions, when relatively constant over time, will cause some behaviors to occur over and over. Habit results from the frequency of times a behavior has occurred. Also, habit controls behavior when that behavior is triggered by emotion (Triandis 1977).

LEARNING NEW BEHAVIORS THROUGH MODELING

Most behavior is learned through the observance of other people as models. From the observation of others, we form concepts of how new behaviors are performed. Later, this information can serve as a guide for new behaviors of our own. According to Bandura's social learning theory (1977), modeling influences produce new behaviors because they give us new information about how to behave. Through observation we acquire symbolic representations of modeled activities, which serve as road maps for our own behavior.

"Mom, would you think me effeminate if I told you
I want to grow up to be an executive like you?"

Role-modeling. (*New Woman* February 1980, p. 14)

Observational modeling, according to Bandura, is governed by four processes: (1) attentional processes, (2) retention processes, (3) motor-reproduction processes, and (4) motivational processes (see Figure 4.1).

Attentional processes

In order for observed behavior to influence our own behavior, it has to gain our attention. What we attend to and how we relate to it determines, in part, whether and in what ways we will be influenced by it. The factors of attention are discussed in Chapter VIII, but it is important to note here that our attentional processes are related to perception, motivation, needs, and goals (see Figure 4.1 on the next page).

Also, behavior of individuals with whom we associate on a regular basis provides strong models for behavior and behavior change. Attractive

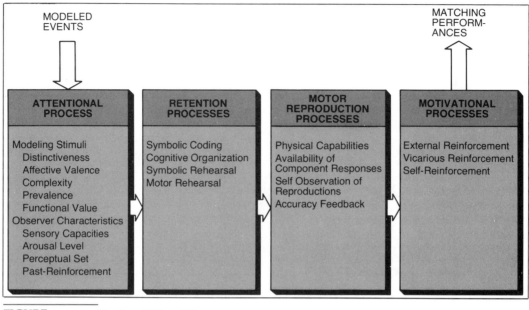

**FIGURE
4.1**   (Bandura 1977, p. 23)

models who possess engaging qualities gain our attention more than those with unattractive qualities. For example, certain models presented on the media who are attractive may cause us to imitate their hair styles, dress, speech, and mannerisms.

From time to time a movie or television star will have widespread impact on the public. In the early 1930s, it was customary for men to always wear undershirts, yet in 1934, when Clark Gable ripped open his shirt in the film *It Happened One Night* to reveal a bare chest, undershirt sales plummeted all over the United States!

Retention Processes

If a new behavior gains our attention, then there will be something about that behavior that will cause us to remember it when the model itself is no longer in sight. According to Bandura (1977), the behavior must be stored in memory in some symbolic form. Through symbols, transitory behavioral modeling experiences can become permanent in the memory system. The processes of imagery and verbal coding provide us with the means to retain concepts of modeled behaviors. Studies by Bandura and his associates (1969, 1971, 1973) showed that subjects who expressed modeled behaviors in words, concise labels, or vivid imagery remembered those behavioral patterns better than those subjects who observed or were distracted during the observation period.

Eldridge Cleaver's account of his initial contact with the Black Panther party provides a good example of an observed behavior stored in symbolic form. Cleaver was looking for and was ready to pay attention to new kinds of behavior for blacks in the late 1960s, when he attended a meeting of activists planning a commemoration of the death of Malcolm X. Cleaver described his reaction:

"Suddenly the room fell silent. . . . From the tension showing on the faces of the people before me, I thought the cops were invading the meeting, but there was a deep female gleam leaping out of one of the women's eyes that no cop who ever lived could elicit . . . the total admiration of a black woman for a black man. I spun around . . . and saw the most beautiful sight I had ever seen: four black men wearing black berets, powder blue shirts, black leather jackets, black trousers, shiny black shoes—and each with a gun!"

"Where was my mind at? Blown! . . . Who are these cats? . . . They were so cool and it seemed to me not unconscious of the electrifying effect they were having on everybody in the room." (Bowers and Ochs 1971, p. 13)

Cleaver was susceptible to the attractiveness of the Black Panthers because he was looking for an attractive behavior. Obviously, he stored the vivid image in his mind as symbols of males dressed in black, carrying guns, evoking female admiration.

Motor Reproduction Processes

When symbolic representation is converted into appropriate action, motor reproduction processes are activated. For new behaviors to occur, there must be an involvement of cognitive organization of responses, their intitiation, their monitoring, and their refinement on the basis of feedback. If all these components can be coordinated effectively, then a new behavior may occur (Bandura 1977, p. 27).

We can all remember when we first learned to drive an automobile. We studied the manual, which gave us the step-by-step procedures (cognitive organization). We then took our place behind the wheel, where we endeavored to turn our cognitive learning into reality (initiation). We made sure that we did not put our foot on the accelerator when we meant to put our foot on the brake (monitoring). When the automobile jerked and weaved, it provided us with the signal that we needed to "regroup" and refine our skills (feedback). Unsatisfactory behavior can occur when one of the four steps is deleted.

Motivational Processes

Bandura's social learning theory (1977) separates acquisition of modeling experience and the actual performance of the modeled behavior. The key difference is motivation, and the primary motivation appears to be the observation of positive consequences consistently associated with the behavior. The weight and importance of perceived consequences and the value of those consequences have already been discussed. Thus, we know that repeated observation of pleasant consequences occurring as a result of a behavior would provide a strong motivation to change one's behavior to the one that is observed.

Social learning theory cannot be discussed without also examining the role of reinforcement. Reinforcement acts as an important antecedent influence rather than as the traditional consequent influence. The anticipation of positive reinforcement, according to Bandura, can effectively influence what is observed and the degree of attention paid to the observation of a given behavior (1977, p. 37). In other words, learning new behaviors through observation can be more successful if those observing the behavior are told ahead of time that they will benefit from performing the behavior.

Persuaders should remember that if they can provide models whose behavior consistently demonstrates desired responses, can encourage others to reproduce the behavior, can monitor others' failures if these failures do occur, and can provide encouragement when the persuadees succeed, the persuaders may produce the desired behavior change. This is something every parent knows or hopes.

When failure occurs, it can be because the persuadee was not observing the behavior, was engaged in mistaken symbolization, was not retaining key aspects or the importance of the behavior, was unable to perform the behavior, or the persuader was not providing the persuadee with sufficient motivation to engage in the changed behavior.

SUMMARY

Behavior change is often the ultimate goal of the persuader. Attitudes, by themselves, are not always precursors of action, especially attitudes toward objects. Studies have shown, however, that one's attitude toward a given behavior is a predictor of behavior.

Expectancy-value theory tells us that a person, when faced with behavioral choices, will select the behavior that would appear to bring about the most favorable outcome. If the behavior performed is contrary to an existing attitude, that attitude will change in order to remove feelings of inconsistency.

Self-perception theories lend insight into the behavior-attitude relationship. A person relies on external clues to interpret his/her own internal states. These are the same clues that other people use to determine the person's internal states. A changed attitude does not result, however, if the behavior is attributed to some other cause.

Behavioral acts are related to goals and intentions. A goal is a desired outcome of a series of specific acts. A behavioral intention is an antecedent to a behavioral act. Goals specify the requirements for positive self-evaluation, which, once established, causes the goal to be pursued until certain end states are achieved. Goals must be specific in order to be incentives to behavior. There is also more motivation to pursue difficult goals than simple ones.

Behavioral intentions, on the other hand, are special forms of beliefs in which the object is always the person and the attribute is the behavior.

The determinants of the probability of a behavior occuring are (1) habit, (2) the behavioral intention to perform the act, and (3) behavioral potential.

Behavioral intentions of a person have certain components, which are (1) social factors such as norms, values, roles, self-monitoring, self-concept, and compliance; (2) affect or feeling about the behavior; and (3) the perceived value of the consequences of the behavior.

Behavioral intentions can be deterred if the potential to perform the behavior is low. Behavioral potential is defined as the presence or absence of facilitating conditions that allow the performance of the act. It is a strong determinant of a person's follow-through behavior and must be a consideration of the persuader.

There are three types of behavior: (1) overt; (2) affective; and (3) attributive.

The persuader can influence new behaviors through observation learning, referred to as modeling. Through observation, symbolic representations of modeled activities are acquired that serve as guides to a person's behavior. This observation is governed by four processes: (1) attention processes, (2) retention processes, (3) motor-reproduction processes, and (4) motivational processes.

What a person attends to and how he/she responds to it

determines how and if influence occurs. For modeling to occur, the person must remember that which has gained his/her attention. There must exist in the memory a symbolic representation of the behavior. These symbolic representations are then put into action through the stages of their initiation, their monitoring, and their refinement on the basis of feedback.

A persuader can gain much by observing the behavior of a persuadee and analyzing what influenced or acted as determinants of those behaviors. The persuader must consider what the possibilities or capacities are of the persuadee to perform the persuader's recommended behavioral act. Knowing whom the persuadee admires may, perhaps, provide a model that the persuader can use as an example.

The more we know about why a person performs a behavior, when a behavior is likely to occur, and how these patterns tie in with the person's attitudes and beliefs, the greater the possibility of success as a persuader and the greater the understanding of a persuadee.

KEY WORDS

Behavior-attitude relationship
Expectancy-value model
Self-perception theory
Goals
Behavioral intentions
Motivational processes
Habit
Behavioral potential
Roles
Self-concept
Self-monitoring

Affective component of behavior
Perceived value of consequences of behavior
Overt behavior
Affective behavior
Attributive behavior
Social component of behavior
Observational modeling
Attentional processes
Retention processes
Motor reproduction processes

EXERCISES

1. Make a list of foods you like and foods you dislike. Can you link them to the "Try it (behavior)—you'll like it (attitude)" premise?
2. Observe people in public places. What characteristics do you attribute to them based on their behavior?

3. Provoke a behavior in someone else—offer a stranger a flower or sit with a stranger in a restaurant. Write a paper on what social, affective, or consequence components could have influenced the resultant behavior.

4. Reflect on a behavior that you have performed that conflicted with one of your attitudes. Did your attitude change at all as a result?

5. Give an example of a behavior that you performed because you were persuaded that there would be favorable consequences.

6. Give an example of a person after whom you and your peers modeled your own behavior.

READINGS

Bandura, Albert. *Social Learning Theory*. Englewood Cliffs, N.J.: Prentice-Hall, 1977.

Fishbein, Martin, and **Ajzen, Icek**. *Beliefs, Attitudes, Intentions, and Behaviors*. Menlo Park, Calif.: Addison-Wesley, 1975.

Jones, E. E.; Kanouse, D. E.; Kelley, H. H.; Nisbett, R. E.; Valens, S; and **Weinger, B.**, eds. *Attribution: Perceiving the Causes of Behavior*. Morristown, N.J.: General Learning Corporation, 1972.

Triandis, Harry C. *Interpersonal Behavior*. Monterey, Calif.: Brooks/Cole, 1977

 # ENVIRONMENTAL PERSUASION

OBJECTIVES

Upon completion of this chapter you should be able to:

1. Understand how the individual is affected by his/her environment.
2. Know the difference in the "perceived" and the "real" environment.
3. Observe how the environment reflects our culture and its ideology.
4. Understand how persuasive forces in the environment operate below the level of awareness.
5. Be aware of approach-avoidance behaviors in yourself and others.
6. Have a more acute awareness of the symbols in the environment.
7. Analyze your own movement, encounter, and rest behaviors in your environments.
8. Know why you are uncomfortable in foreign environments.

n the previous chapter, behavior and the factors that determine and influence behavior were discussed. It is also important to consider the environment in which behavior occurs and to examine the relationship between the environment and behavior. People usually think of their lives as being separate from the environment because they move in and out of different environments during the course of daily life. Yet, behavior is the product of the complex functioning of variables related to the individual on the one hand and variables related to the environment on the other. Various kinds of researchers, who are identified by labels such as "environmental psychologists," "behavioral ecologists," "environmental engineers," and "behavioral geographers," are attempting conceptually and empirically to study the link between the environment and behavior. The study of environment and behavior, a new field, is the study of change—not change that is imposed by an external force, but change that grows out of a process in which people play a central role. As Robert Sommer has said, "All people are builders, creators, molders, and shapers of the environment. We are the environment" (1969, p. 7). Since the study of environment includes change, behavior, and human influence, it can be considered within our definition of persuasion. Thus, we choose to call this chapter "Environmental Persuasion." In it, we define environment, discuss its functions, look at the behavior-environment relationship, and explore the physical, cultural, and symbolic variables inherent within the environment.

Knowledge of the environment broadens the persuader's options and adds new insights into persuadee behavior. An environment has different effects on people. The attitudes that one has toward a particular environment and the experiences one has had with such environments help determine whether or not that environment is perceived as familiar, comfortable, strange, or threatening. Not only does the environment contribute to the outcome of communication within that environment, but the environment is itself a communicator capable of influencing the people within it.

The environment consists of a combination of physical and psychological components that continually influence one another in a dynamic and interactive way. People in the environment are considered components in the total process. David Seamon defines environmental experience as "the sum total of a person's first-hand involvements with the geographical world in which he or she typically lives" (1979, p. 16). Albert Mehrabian claims that people react emotionally to their surroundings. He says that emotional reactions can be accounted for in terms of how aroused, pleasurable, and dominant people are made to feel (1976).

Consider a situation in which you have decided to read this chapter for a class assignment. When you enter your dorm room or apartment and approach your desk, you discover that it is cluttered with study materials from the test you took this morning. Your bed is still unmade. Your response may be that so much clutter will inhibit your work. So you tidy up. Just when you have created a comfortable environment, the jackhammer and tractors used in work on an adjoining building are set into motion, and you are distracted. Your discomfort with your surroundings motivates you to go to the library to study. You find the library warm, spacious, neat, comfortable, and quiet. Thus, you complete the assignment.

When you attend class the following day, you feel confident. Instead of taking one of the back-row seats, where you usually sit, especially when you feel unprepared, you take a front center seat. You enjoy exchanging greetings and chatting with fellow classmates. When the professor arrives, however, you focus your attention on him or her. Your behavior, as well as that of your classmates, changes from active to more passive as the class begins.

Through these examples, we have shown how a familiar environment influences one's behavior. Yet, there are some individuals who would react differently in the above examples. Many people are not bothered by clutter and thus would not feel uncomfortable studying in a room with a cluttered desk and an unmade bed. Others could mask outside noises by turning on the stereo very loud. To many students, libraries are too quiet, too sterile, and too uncomfortable. We do not all respond to the same environment in a similar manner, but our response to an environment is dependent on how we perceive it.

THE RELATIONSHIP BETWEEN BEHAVIOR AND THE ENVIRONMENT

In order to understand the relationship between people's behavior and the environment, we must again emphasize that people and their environment are interactive by nature. In previous chapters, we have discussed beliefs, attitudes, values, group norms, and self-concepts, all of which make up a psychological framework from which people draw their perceptions of and reactions to their physical environment. The behavior-environment relationship will be discussed according to six underlying assumptions concerning this relationship.

(1) The "perceived" environment is not necessarily the "real" environment. *Perception* here is defined as the process by which one attributes characteristics to his/her environmental situation through a prism of values,

attitudes, beliefs, needs, and past experiences. These, of course, are the perceptual filters from the model of persuasion in Chapter I.

Environment perception is, as W. H. Ittelson, H. M. Proshansky, L. G. Rivlin, and G. H. Winkel maintain, "the source of our phenomenal experience of our world" (1974, p. 123). What we know about the external world, we apprehend through our senses. The phenomena we perceive have the characteristics we attribute to them because we interpret them, assign meaning to them, and give some sense of structure to them. The human brain is designed to order and interpret the stimuli that are fed into it.

Most of us would regard the jungle, with its screeching sounds, muggy humidity, and strange creatures, as a dangerous and threatening environment. Yet to Tarzan, it is a warm and friendly place where he has many friends. Imagine Tarzan in an American disco. Here he would feel fear and discomfort because it is a strange and unfamiliar environment, whereas most of us would be at ease in such a place.

When we perceive the environment in a specific situation, we take in valuable information on which to base our behavior. We may observe how much space we have, what demands it places on us, and what consequences can result from given behaviors under consideration. At a disco, a person may feel free to ask someone at another table to dance. Yet the same person dining at an expensive restaurant would not cross the social barriers to ask a stranger to dance. The cultural and social implications of the environment supersede the physical elements in this case.

(2) Physical environment reflects the principles of a social and cultural system. Cultural systems are composed of values and social norms. The physical artifacts of a culture reflect its values, and the behavior of its citizens reflects its norms.

Architecture can be viewed as a symbol of a nation's ideology, but it can also be viewed as a persuasive force that perpetuates that ideology. Architecture, therefore, can be viewed as an influence on our values, beliefs, attitudes, and behavior.

When touring Europe, one views the architectural structures in order to better understand the societies that created these structures. It is impossible for an American citizen to take a tour of Washington, D.C., and view the memorials to the great leaders in our history without being persuaded that our nation is also impressive and is as big, massive, and indestructible as the monuments that represent its past.

In the much loved movie of the 1940s, *Mr. Smith Goes to Washington*, there is a montage sequence in which Smith takes his tour of the capital. A low camera angle causes the spectator to look up at the Lincoln Memorial, the Jefferson Memorial, and the Capitol while a high camera angle looks downward on Jeff Smith to make him appear small and in awe. The audience identifies with Smith because they are reminded of their own awe-inspiring experiences and feelings of patriotism when they visited Washington for the first time.

One of the most outstanding examples of architecture as a persuasive force was in Nazi Germany. Hitler had Albert Speer design buldings that would be a visual dimension of Nazi ideology. Hitler wanted his buildings to act as permanent statements of the beliefs of the Third Reich and as symbols of Hitler as a great unifier and leader (Stuart 1973). As a result of the monuments that were erected during his regime, he was referred to as the "masterbuilder."

The massive size of Speer's buildings symbolized force, superiority, and power. The Lutzpold arena is an example of how a structure magnified Hitler and his rhetoric. The huge slab platforms were designed to symbolize the "new" Germany; and when Hitler spoke there, his stature and his message were viewed as massive, as strong, and as indestructible as the arena itself (Stuart 1973).

Architectural symbols represent a nation's ideology, but the ideology dictates the use of time and space in the environment. Cultural norms tell us how to use space, such as how far apart we sit or stand from others and how long we stay that way. It is acceptable to lie prone on the beach for hours, but the same position at the office or in the classroom is culturally unacceptable. Cultural norms provide us with "house rules" for our behavior in any given context.

The use of distance in an interaction between two people in a particular situation is controlled by cultural expectations. When we violate another person's space, it is a cultural and societal violation. Sommer states that "sitting next to someone on a piano bench is within the expected distance but also within the bounds of personal space and may cause discomfort to the player" (1972, p. 27). Sommer refers to personal space as "portable territory" that a person carries with him/her wherever he/she goes.

Another cultural rule that operates at a subconscious level is that furniture arrangements in public spaces must remain in place. Even though the arrangement makes communication difficult, we tend to be reluctant to move furniture in hotel lobbies, waiting rooms, and restaurants. People who rearrange tables in a restaurant without consulting the hostess are frowned upon. At a party, we may carry on a conversation across a distance without ever presuming to rearrange the host's furniture.

Our culture also tells us how to structure our time, and this has a major influence on how we act in our environment. Hall (1976, p. 14) refers to two cultural uses of time: monochronic and polychronic. American culture is monochronic because we are dominated by schedules and prefer to do one thing at a time. There are, however, instances when we choose not to be monochronic, such as on the weekend, when we might say, "I'm just going to relax tomorrow and do what I want to do when I want to do it."

One of the massive platforms designed for Hitler by Albert Speer to symbolize power, to suggest distance from the masses, and to represent a new and modern age. (Photo from the German film *Triumph of the Will*)

Toward the end of the weekend, thoughts begin to occur such as "Well, back to the routine tomorrow!" The pressures of our culture require making and maintaining time schedules. People in our society who do not conform to time expectations are considered disorganized, inconsiderate, and/or ir-responsible.

Polychronic time systems, on the other hand, are characterized by events that happen simultaneously. The emphasis is on involvement with people and completion of the business at hand rather than adherence to previous schedules.

The Vietnam war emphasized the different time perspectives of America and Vietnam. The Vietnamese viewed the conflict in terms of dec-ades, while the Americans felt that the war seemed endless and wanted to "get it over with" (Sommer 1972, p. 72).

(3) We have a basic need to feel psychological as well as physical comfort in our environment. Our homes provide rooms or spaces for eating, resting, socializing, and sanitation. We may be uncomfortable when the bedroom is being painted and we have to sleep on the sofa. When a person's favorite chair has been sent out for repairs, his/her comfort in the den is affected.

Even the layouts of our cities give us psychological comfort (Hall 1966, p. 97). Most of the cities in America are laid out in a similar fashion. Americans traveling in foreign countries get very frustrated in European cities. The French plan of the radiating star or the Roman grid layout is unfamiliar and thus discomforting to the American visitor.

When the plans were made to rebuild the House of Commons in England after World War II, Sir Winston Churchill fought against new plans, which departed from the traditional intimate space pattern that caused opponents to face one another across a narrow aisle. He felt that if the environment of the House of Commons was changed, then British government would change also. He believed that people shape buildings and that buildings, in turn, shape people (Hall 1966, p. 97).

Suppose your parents sell the family home to move into a small condominium. During your first visit you discover that there is no longer "your room" nor a large kitchen table for family gatherings. Your reaction to all these new variables would be one of psychological discomfort.

People have immediate and long-range goals. When the environment is incongruent with our goals, then psychological discomfort occurs. For example, suppose a person has two markets where he/she shops for groceries. The first one has many bargains and gives green stamps, but has narrow aisles and long lines at the check-out counter. The other market has few bargains, does not give green stamps, but is well lit, has wide aisles, and has fast-moving check-out procedures. The person may discover that he/she shops more frequently at the latter market because it is more comfortable and convenient. The environment enables him/her to reach an immediate goal, which is to get the grocery shopping done as quickly and as painlessly as possible.

(4) We are often unaware of the persuasive effects that the environment has upon us. Because of automatic behavior as well as cultural norms, much of our response to environmental forces is subconscious or, at least, nonconscious in nature. We may not stop to think about it. Our responses are either those of approach or avoidance.

Approach and avoidance behavior means more than just rushing toward or turning away from a given situation, for we also indulge in approach or avoidance behavior within an environment from which we cannot escape. Suppose you take someone who has been seriously injured to the emergency room of the local hospital. Your concern over the life-and-death status of the person causes you to be lost in your thoughts rather than involved with your surroundings. The only part of the environment that gains your attention is an approaching nurse or doctor, who may have information concerning the welfare of the injured person. The signs stating "Donate Blood" or "Thank You for Not Smoking" are unnoticed. This behavior is one of avoidance. If, on the other hand, after the person is out of danger you take him/her to the doctor's office for a routine checkup, you would probably notice the furniture, the magazines, and the receptionist. This environment is no longer a threatening one to you. Thus, the behavior is one of approach. Each of you has your own list of avoidance behaviors in which you engage during dull classes, such as dozing, daydreaming, wearing sun glasses, or fantasizing. Approach behaviors may be straightening your posture, leaning forward at your desk, taking careful notes, and maintaining eye contact with the instructor.

We use approach-avoidance behavior in relation to other people. Here, our weapon is a subconscious use of space. If someone keeps his/her distance or turns his/her body away from us, we regard this as avoidance behavior. If we enter a room at a party and we wish to have fun, we tend to move about, go up to strangers, and stand close to those with whom we are talking. This is approach behavior.

The use of space is a cultural phenomenon. Americans keep greater distance between one another than the French or Latin Americans. Americans can tolerate closer distance on each side of them than they can directly in front of them (Sommer 1969, p. 26).

Environmental psychologists believe they can predict how one will behave in a given environment. A particular room can provoke people to be subdued, stiff, and anxious to leave or can cause them to be outgoing, friendly, and eager to stay (Mehrabian 1976, p. 4). The persuader, in order to be effective, must consider where his/her persuasive efforts will take place. What aspects will operate on the persuadee below the level of awareness? If, for example, you are calling a meeting of a committee, it is worthwhile not to meet "just anywhere," but to choose surroundings that the committee members will find pleasant and conducive to staying the necessary length of time without feeling trapped. In 1980, the Danforth Foundation sponsored a two-day seminar at North Texas State University on effective teaching. The planners made a horrible mistake by holding it in a wide and shallow banquet room at a local motel. The room had mustard-yellow walls, dark-brown drapes, and harsh, square, dirty ceiling lights. The two hundred teachers who attended sat at long, narrow tables with sixteen chairs on each side. It was impossible to move, let alone interact. Although the guest speaker was warm, witty, clever, and wise, his intimate and soft-spoken style was lost in the harsh, impersonal surroundings.

We are manipulated without awareness by the business establishments we frequent. Restaurants, for example, differ in style, and their environments reflect this. Fast-food restaurants consist of small tables, uncomfortable chairs, and bright lighting. This environment does not encourage leisurely dining, which, of course, would defeat the purpose of the fast-food concept. An industrial engineer who designs the bar stools that are placed at the lunch counters of small restaurants said in an interview in Dallas, on February 26, 1980, "I have several customers in the downtown section of large cities. They make ninety-five percent of their money between eleven and two-thirty in the afternoon. During the lunch rush, their problem is to turn over those seats often enough so they may serve a set number of lunches every day. With people waiting in line for those seats—and they do wait—you're doing nothing but losing money whenever someone lingers over his BLT or stops and leans back to smoke a cigarette. So, for these customers, I design a stool that is initially very comfortable, but within about fifteen minutes, it becomes uncomfortable due to the angle that the spine is resting at. This means that the luncheon customer won't dawdle."

A more expensive restaurant will have comfortable seats, pleasant table settings, and subdued lighting to encourage leisurely and luxurious dining. The same industrial engineer quoted above said, "For a plush tavern, I design chairs that are tremendously comfortable, that encourage the patron to linger over drinks and bring his friends back for leisurely meals. The tavern owner makes a higher percentage of profit on the drinks than on the food. Therefore, he wants you to sit around and chew the fat over a couple of drinks."

Hotel lobbies and airports are designed for short waiting periods. It is hoped that those waiting will become uncomfortable enough to wander to the bar, restaurant, or shops, where the chances are good that they will spend some money.

Psychological balance can be affected by the environment. In the recently completed Loews Anatole Hotel in Dallas, there are many examples of dissonance-producing and dissonance-removing environments. Dan Pryor, a former graduate student at the North Texas State University, made these observations:

As one enters the lobby of the hotel, he/she quickly becomes aware of the formality and lack of warmth found there. Knapp (1978) suggests that cool, formal environments cause a person to be less relaxed, more superficial, and linger for shorter periods of time. The kinds of materials used in the lobby construction contribute to the environmental atmosphere. A neutral, polished marble is used for the walls and floors, and accents are done in polished brass. If the color scheme of the environment lacks diversity of color, the individual becomes bored and unstimulated causing the person to be attracted to more diverse areas with more color and warmth (Deabler, 1957). The only seating area is found in the center of the lobby. The couches are arranged in a large circle, all facing toward the center. None of the couches [is] placed at right angles to each other, thus making interaction more difficult. Research indicates that the greater amount of interaction among persons occur when they are seated at right angles from one another (Mehrabian, 1976). The carpeted area is not unpleasant, but it is not

The registration desk at the Loews Anatole Hotel in Dallas is dominated by neutral, polished marble, and brass accents. It is a cool and formal environment which causes people to stay for a short time.

The seating area in the lobby of the Loews Anatole Hotel in Dallas is not conducive to interaction. Here, a man waiting has no opportunity to talk with another who may also be waiting because they are too far away from each other for interaction.

Here are two different eating-drinking areas in the Loews Anatole Hotel in Dallas. The one with the round tables and wicker chairs is a fast-food, cafeteria lunchtime restaurant. The chairs are comfortable enough for a short lunch but do not encourage lingering over a meal. The environment suggests that diners eat comfortably but not linger. The area with the plush upholstered chairs and cube-shaped tables is a bar. This environment encourages a long and relaxed conversation not only because of the comfort of the chairs but also because of their arrangement and the accessability of the table. (These pictures were not posed. The men in the second picture appear to be more at ease than those in the first.) (Photographs courtesy of Dan Pryor)

conducive to long-term conversation. According to Knapp (1978), this type of environment is often found in hotel lobbies.

There are two restaurants in this hotel the environments of which dictate entirely different concepts of dining behavior. In the less expensive restaurant, the color scheme is basically red. Red is known to stimulate the senses, but causes one to tire of surroundings after a short period of time. As a result, one does not want to linger for an extended period of time. In the other restaurant, which is considerably more expensive, the color scheme is blue and green. Most people find these colors relaxing and soothing and will linger longer than in the restaurant where the major color is red. In both of the restaurants, one finds numerous plants and architectural barriers that allow persons a sense of privacy.

Different bar environments also affect behavior. James Schaefer conducted a study of bar behavior and discovered that bar atmospheres affect drinking behavior (in K. Mills 1980, p.3). Country music, dim lighting, and action pictures of calf-roping and cowboys encouraged bar patrons to consume more alchohol.

Seating arrangement also affects people. A round table usually impresses upon us that all group members are of equal status. Even if this is not always true, the table's roundness tends to deemphasize the differences. King Arthur used the round table as a symbol of equality between himself and his knights.

A table of rectangular shape creates sharp contrasts among members of the group. A study by F. L. Strodtbeck and L. H. Hook showed that jury foremen were chosen from persons who were male, who had "prestigious" occupations, and who were seated at one of the end positions of a rectangular table (1961).

Another interesting study was conducted by H. J. Leavett (1951). Four different seating arrangements were provided for the subjects, who were assigned a group task. In order for the task to be completed, all group members were dependent on the information in the possession of the other members of the group. The group arrangements were as follows:

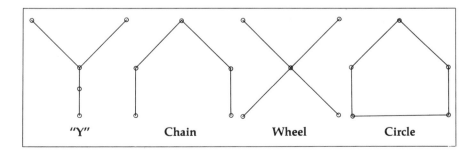

"Y"   Chain   Wheel   Circle

The results of this study showed that the "wheel" was the most efficient, and the "circle" was the least efficient. The "wheel," however, provided the least amount of satisfaction for its members, while the "circle" provided the most satisfaction for its members. The other configurations limited independence, recognition, and individual participation and achievement, all of which are strong cultural predispositions in our society that operate at a subconscious level.

(5) The environment takes on the value and function of a social symbol when it is representative of social meaning (Appleyard 1979). High-rise buildings might be seen as symbols of corporate power, while a "people's park" could be perceived as a symbol of youthful rebellion against society. An airport may be shaped like a bird with the visual symbolism being openly metaphorical. Social symbolism links the physical environment to the sociopolitical structure.

Low-income housing is often "hidden" from the rest of the city. The poor, like the prisons, dumps, and industry, are kept at the back of the city. The suburbs, which are also away from the mainstream of a town or city, are not "hidden," but "secluded" to invoke a sense of privacy. Fences and walls symbolize territorial rights forbidding entry.

Height and length are also symbolic components. The rivalry between New York and Chicago for the highest buildings is well known. The lengthy façades of Versailles and the Winter Palace at Leningrad were status symbols. In fact, in America, the distance one has to commute from the suburbs to work has become a sort of status symbol. Many people with families who work in cities go home to the suburbs even if it means a two-hour train ride.

Buildings, like people, have attributes that are perceived as positive by society. People in San Francisco, for example, in these days of dieting, prefer slender buildings to bulky ones (Appleyard 1979). Research in perception of buildings indicates that there is a strong connection between various architectural characteristics and character itself. Pictures of two San Francisco hotels were shown to a group of students. One was garish, plastic, and brightly colored. The other was drab, restrained, and concrete. The students predicted that orgies took place in the former, while more dignified behavior occurred in the latter. Appleyard, who cites this study, says that he has not yet checked out the accuracy of the students' predictions (1979, p. 150).

Analysis of two large shopping centers in Dallas by students in Professor O'Donnell's persuasion class has revealed that not only are the prestigious and expensive shops clustered together in subdued, lighted areas with many plants and natural wood façades compared to the cheaper shops in harshly lighted areas with concrete façades and plastic plants, but that the mall floors actually begin to slope downward in the approaches to the less expensive shops and go up in the approaches to the more expensive ones.

Our private homes with our material possessions can also be seen as symbolic of our income, interests, tastes, and life style. Appleyard says, "Possessions—both the hardware of purchasable objects and the software of beliefs and ideas—become precious in exact ratio to their expressiveness, their capacity to define the relationship of the self to the environment" (1979, p. 146).

(6) People become most aware of the characteristics of an environment when change is introduced or when a different or unfamiliar setting is encountered. We tend to perceive familiar environments as neutral environments. It is when the aspect of unfamiliarity enters into the picture that the environment becomes a part of our level of awareness.

Familiar objects in the environment go unnoticed until they are removed. During the tornado of April 10, 1979, in Wichita Falls, Texas, Professor Kable's fence, along with the neighbors' fences, was blown away. As a result, people gathered in backyards and chatted and exchanged greetings, a form of behavior that had not occurred before. The patios, kitchens, and breakfast rooms were no longer private, but were in open view to the many automobiles going through the alleyways and to the neighbors. Evidently, there was more discomfort than enjoyment in the new situation, because the neighbors rebuilt their fences before they repaired any other damages.

An individual's sense of identity is inextricably tied to those familiar objects and places in his/her environment. We have all experienced those feelings that occur toward the end of a vacation. In spite of the fun and excitement, we begin to yearn for our own bed, a visit with friends, a taste of our own cooking, or a reunion with our pet.

Psychologists and psychiatrists have their appointment books full (with cases of depression or disorientation) after an area has endured a flood or a tornado. The loss of objects and familiar surroundings contributes to a blurring or a loss of self-identity.

Explanations of Patricia Hearst's criminal behavior after being abducted by the Symbionese Liberation Army have included the observation that, as a result of abrupt removal and isolation from her own environment, she believed that she was dependent on her captors for survival and safety. Her only alternative seemed to be to adapt her behavior to that of her captors in order to survive and to have some identity.

Ittelson and his associates contend that we respond to unfamiliar environments in six different ways: affect, orientation, categorization, systemization, manipulation, and encoding (1974, p. 96).

One of the first responses to new surroundings is that of affect or emotion. If we are driving late at night and our automobile stalls on a secluded road, our first response might be fear. When you entered college as a freshman and your parents took you to the dorm to check in, you probably felt a range of *emotions*, such as excitement, anxiety, fear, or loneliness. When you arrived in your room, you began to unpack. A familiar coverlet was placed on the bed, personal items were placed on the desk, and toilet articles were arranged in the bathroom. These actions can be referred to as the process of *orientation*. The familiar objects placed in the new environment provided comfort and a sense of order and familiarity. After that, you probably began to ask questions, such as where the nearest drugstore, post office, and record shop were. The process of orientation is also at work here, motivated by a desire to know one's location in relation to important environmental entities. We feel better when a mental map of our environment begins to emerge.

After we pick up information about our surroundings, we begin the process of *categorization*. This process is the sizing up and making decisions about positive and negative factors that exist in our environment. The new student may decide to avoid the student next door because the student next door is a compulsive talker. The new student may opt to walk three blocks farther to a drugstore with more reasonable prices than to the one located nearest the campus. He/she may decide that the best time to go to the student center is in the afternoon rather than in the morning. Pieces of information are chosen over other pieces to form a behavior map that will constitute desirability and familiarity. This process is referred to as *systemization*.

After registration, the student may discover that an anatomy and physiology class at eight in the morning is too grim to bear. So he/she goes through late registration to substitute another course in an effort to change factors in the environment to make it more pleasant. This process is referred to as *manipulation*. This is not always possible, however. For example, the anatomy and physiology class at 10:00 A.M. may be closed, which would leave the student powerless to manipulate his/her environment.

Finally, we *encode* or give names to environmental objects either because we wish to specify something or because the name represents a common meaning to those who need the information that the name contains. We may refer to the "big boulder" near the union building, or we may call the remedial English class "dumbbell English." The coding has to be understood by others in order to systemize and manipulate.

Seamon characterizes our behavior within the environment as movement, rest, and encounter. Movement includes the role of the body, habit, and routine in the day-to-day environmental dealings; rest is the human attachment to a place; encounter includes the ways in which people observe and notice the world in which they live (1979, p. 16). When we move through an environment, we encounter various stimuli that arouse our senses, and we eventually seek rest as a form of relief from the stimuli. This is why there are resting plazas with soothing fountains and places to sit in our shopping malls. The plazas give us relief from the stimuli of the shops, the merchandise, and the sales techniques.

A merchandise area inside the Dallas World Trade Mart. A prospective buyer moves into it in order to encounter the stimuli of the wholesale goods on display.

The plaza on the first floor of the Dallas World Trade Mart has a placid reflecting pool where the buyers can gather for some tranquility. It is an oasis of sorts.

Also on the first floor is a round seating area where the buyers can rest after their encounter with the wholesale goods on the upper floors.

The vertical elevators at the Dallas World Trade Mart carry the buyers up and away from the restful oasis-like plaza to the display areas which are filled with merchandise. Only buyers wearing official tags are permitted to ascend to the merchandise floors. (Photographs courtesy of Suzanne Aplin)

SUMMARY

There is a persuasive connection between the environment and behavior. Environmental persuasion refers to changes that may take place in an individual as the result of environmental influences.

People are affected differently by the same environment because the environmental impact is related to an individual's previous experiences. What an environment communicates and how communication within an environment takes place are dependent on how aroused, pleasurable, and dominant people are made to feel. These reactions are the result of people interacting with the environment.

There are six underlying assumptions concerning the relationship between people and their environment: (1) The "perceived" environment is not necessarily the "real" environment. How we perceive the environment is dependent on how people interpret it according to beliefs, values, attitudes, and social norms. (2) Physical environment reflects the principles of a social and cultural system. Architecture, the use of space, and how we structure time, either monochronically or polychronically, are revealing of cultural ideologies and societal expectations. (3) People have a basic need to feel comfortable in their environment. Our homes, our cities, our government buildings, and our stores need to offer us familiarity and convenience. (4) The environment frequently affects us below our level of awareness. When we approach an environment, we have an observing, positive attitude toward it. When we avoid an environment, we may be distracted or feel threatened by it. We are also manipulated by the environment's lighting, color, décor, furniture, and seating arrangement. (5) The environment has social-symbolic value. Buildings, their size, and their characteristics convey symbolic meaning and intent. (6) People become most aware of the characteristics of an environment when change is introduced or when a different or unfamiliar setting is encountered. We respond to change with emotion, orientation, categorization, systemization, manipulation, and encoding.

Our behavior within an environment is characterized by movement, rest, and encounter.

The concept of environmental persuasion offers us a way to understand that we are not totally separate from the environment and its influences, for they can shape and determine our behavior within it.

KEY WORDS

Environmental persuasion   Encounter
Environment   Movement
Environmental perception   Orientation
Monochronic time   Categorization
Polychronic time   Systemization
Approach behavior   Manipulation
Avoidance behavior   Encoding
Rest

EXERCISES

1. Examine the architecture in your community. How does it reflect your community's cultural norms?
2. Ask a realtor to show you a house that is for sale. Draw a profile of the family that lives there on the basis of the décor of the house and the possessions in it.
3. Observe your shopping habits, and analyze why you shop in certain stores.
4. Look around your classroom in which you are taking this course. Is the environment conducive to learning?
5. The next time you go out to dinner, observe the seating arrangements, color, and lighting to see if they influence whether you eat in a hurried or leisurely fashion. If you are on a date, notice how the surroundings influence your behavior.
6. Go to a large, indoor shopping mall, and notice if the expensive shops are clustered together in certain ways. Check their proximity to the cheaper shops. Notice the lighting differences, materials used, and the plants.
7. When you shop at a mall, observe your movement, encounter, and resting behavior.
8. Look at the different parts of a city. How do they symbolize societal ideology? What is hidden?
9. What constitutes a comfortable environment for you? Do you know why it is comfortable? What does it tell you about yourself?
10. Think of a place that makes you feel threatened. Try to analyze why it threatens you.

READINGS

Altman, I. *The Environment and Social Behavior.* Monterey, Calif.: Brooks/Cole, 1975.

Hall, E. T. *Silent Language.* Garden City, N. Y.: Doubleday, 1959.

———. *The Hidden Dimension.* Garden City, N.Y.: Doubleday, 1966.

Ittelson, W. H.; Proshansky, H. M.; Rivlin, L. G., and **Winkel, G. H.**
Environmental Psychology. New York: Holt, Rinehart and Winston, 1976.

Mehrabian, A. *Public Places and Private Spaces.* New York: Basic Books, 1976.

Sommer, Robert. *Personal Space.* Englewood Cliffs, N.J.: Prentice-Hall, 1969.

6

SOURCE CREDIBILITY

OBJECTIVES

Upon completion of this chapter you should be able to:

1. Understand that a persuader's image resides in the mind of the persuadee.
2. Understand that source credibility is a multidimensional construct.
3. Relate a persuader's credibility to the goals that are relevant to the situation and to the goals that are operable and achievable in light of the situation.
4. See how you can attribute certain unobserved characteristics related to a persuader's credibility on the basis of observed characteristics.
5. Understand the importance of identification between the persuader and persuadee.

t is well established in our society that a positive communicator image has a significant relationship to one's persuasive efforts. Source credibility is that part of persuasion that says, "Listen to me because of who I am." Politicians spend huge sums of money to achieve a certain "image" in the minds of their listeners and viewers. While the image may, in part, be determined by the communicator's expertise, status, and reputation, it is also influenced by his/her appearance and general demeanor. President Lyndon B. Johnson was very concerned with his image. When Bill Moyers was Johnson's press secretary, Moyers had a "box" rigged up for the president with specially placed lights to prevent unflattering shadows on Johnson's face, carefully placed microphones to produce even sound, and a Teleprompter so the president would appear to be looking right at the television camera. When Moyers left the White House and George Reedy took over, the first thing that the new press secretary did was "to get rid of the damn box." He advised Johnson to appear before the press equipped only with the rigging of a small, lavaliere microphone. Johnson came across as energetic, less paternal, and much more interesting. The press acclaimed "a new Johnson." Those who knew Johnson from the U. S. Senate said, "Nonsense, that's the real Johnson." Moyers's attempts to create a different image for the president had hidden some of the president's attractive characteristics. On the other hand, Richard Nixon did not project a very positive image to many voters in 1960, when he appeared with John F. Kennedy in the televised debates. The voters remembered Nixon's five-o'clock shadow and his nervousness compared to Kennedy's handsome good looks and air of confidence. When he ran for the presidency in 1968, Nixon hired Johnny Carson's make-up man to prepare him for his television appearances. By the 1980 election, the candidates were sophisticated enough in using make-up and controlling physical quirks so that the public made little comment about their appearance. Visual effects must be considered in today's image impact.

In the world of advertising, image is certainly important. Prestigious personalities are selected to represent certain products. Distinguished actors and actresses who never before made television appearances now sell coffee and life insurance on television along with athletes who hawk deodorant and beer. Sometimes celebrities find their commercial contracts in jeopardy when their images are affected by adverse publicity. Anita Bryant's orange-juice contract was jeopardized due to her outspokenness against the Gay Liberation movement.

In previous chapters we have discussed beliefs, attitudes, behavior, and environment and their influences on the persuasive process. In this chapter, we shall "look unto ourselves" from the standpoint of how we are perceived, how we perceive others, and what influences those perceptions.

When you and your friends gather in the student center after the first day of the semester, the conversation mostly consists of comments on new instructors such as "He/she is going to be easy," "He/she is warm and friendly," "He/she is really going to be difficult to please," "I'm going to change instructors because I could never get an A from him/her."

When you go to your favorite restaurant and ask for a specific waiter's or waitress's table, you may be implying that he/she is competent, friendly, and honest, but you are also saying that he/she will satisfy your needs as a customer in this particular situation.

All of these statements are examples of attributing characteristics to a particular source in a particular situation. What did each source do to create the image in your mind? What personality traits and goals have you contributed to these perceptions? What influence did the situation have on your perceptions? These questions will be answered in the remainder of this chapter.

SOURCE CREDIBILITY DEFINED

Source credibility may be defined as the perception of and attitude toward the source that exists in the mind of the receiver at a given time in a given situation. If we asked you to describe the image of a person, your description would be *your* image of the communicator. If twenty people were asked to describe their images of a famous politician, their descriptions could vary considerably, covering a whole range of positive, neutral, and/or negative adjectives. One of your professors may have a Ph.D. from Harvard University, be an author of many texts and scholarly articles, and be the recipient of numerous honors, yet you may perceive him/her as dull, disorganized, and indifferent to the needs of his/her students. The perception in your mind represents this person's credibility in the classroom situation, not his paper credentials. If, however, you needed a letter of recommendation for graduate school at a prestigious university, your perception of this same professor would be different in this situation, and you would probably seek his/her support.

Source credibility is thus an evaluative construct. Regardless of the stimuli that a sender may emit, those stimuli gain meaning only in terms of the receiver's evaluation of them. Not only does communicator image vary with the receiver's perception of it, it also varies with time. The image of a communicator may change within a given communication. Source credibility can be registered before a communication, during a communication, and after a communication. Furthermore, the way in which a communicator is identified prior to the communication can affect receiver response to the persuader. B. Sternthal, L. Phillips, and R. Dholakia (1978) drew the following conclusions: A high credibility source will induce greater persuasion than a low credibility source when identification precedes the message. A high credibility source is typically more influential than a low credibility source when identification is made before the persuasive appeal. Yet, deferring the identification of a low credibility source until after the message facilitates persuasion (p. 289).

Source credibility is a multidimensional construct. Various dimensions have been attached to the concept of source credibility throughout history. The Greek word *ethos*, which means "character," was used by Aristotle in *Rhetoric* to include a communicator's integrity, character, and good will (Cooper 1960). Research in the recent past has focused upon identifying and measuring the dimensions underlying a communicator's credibility. The first monumental contemporary study of source credibility was conducted by C. I. Hovland, I. L. Janis, and H. H. Kelley (1953), who listed the dimensions of source credibility as expertise, trustworthiness, and intention toward the receivers. These three dimensions are contemporary counterparts of Aristotle's. K. E. Andersen (1961) measured speaker authoritativeness and dynamism as dimensions of source credibility. D. K. Berlo, J. B. Lemert, and R. J. Mertz (1969) investigated the dimensions of safety, qualification, and dynamism.

Between 1971 and 1975, J. C. McCroskey and associates conducted studies in which five dimensions of source credibility were determined through factor analysis: competence, character, sociability, extroversion, and composure. The researchers specifically excluded dynamism because they believed it to be an unstable factor. In a study that they labeled the "ultimate study of source credibility," McCroskey and T. J. Young (1977) sampled over 2,000 college students, asking them to respond to forty-one scales with six special sources to evaluate. This extensive study revealed the same five dimensions as in the previous studies listed above. Most of the recent research in source credibility has concentrated on factoring out the dimensions of source credibility. These studies (Applbaum and Anatol 1972) have demonstrated instabilites in the factor structure of source credibility and have brought the long-presumed generality of factors of credibility perception into serious question. This increasing complexity in the findings concerning the dimensional structure of credibility evaluation has, over the years, contributed to a growing concern regarding the credibility concept. Consequently, new approaches to source credibility have been developed.

J. G. Delia (1976) included the theory of perception in the understanding of source credibility when he stated that one's understanding of another person is never a reflected reality (p. 367). In interpersonal persuasion, people tend to construct their impressions of the actions, qualities, or attitudes of other individuals by interpreting the other person's appearance and behavior (Delia 1976, p. 367). Because the response to communicator credibility is individualized in nature, it contains judgments brought to the situation by the receiver that include both socially similar and individually idiosyncratic dimensions (Delia 1976, p. 369). In fact, a new term, *source valence*, is now being used to designate source credibility plus interpersonal attraction and the degree of homophily (perceived similarity present between source and receiver).

SOURCE CREDIBILITY AS PROCESS

To better understand source credibility in relation to individual responses, it will be discussed as a process. Source credibility can be viewed in situations other than the public speaker-to-audience communication. Source credibility is operative in interpersonal persuasion, small group communication, and organizational communication. The majority of persuasive attempts in modern society take place not behind the podium, but in dyadic or small group situations (Miller and Burgoon 1978, p. 33). There are situations in which our need-satisfaction goals are primary influences upon our perceptions of a source. If a person needs information, his/her perception of the source will be determined by the source's ability or willingness to provide information. Conversely, if a person needs entertainment, a source who provides only information will have poor source credibility.

Different situations and goals and the attributes that are applied to a persuader influence one's perception of the source. Gary Cronkhite and J. R. Liska state it this way: "People choose to participate in the process of persuasion with others who are most likely to satisfy needs and achieve goals which are most salient and important at the moment of choice" (in Roloff and Miller 1980, p. l03).

The role of the source is not static. For example, in a business meeting, where decisions are being made, all members of the group interchange their roles as sources and receivers. It is appropriate, then, to discuss the variables that interact to form one's perceptions of the source.

PROCESS MODEL OF SOURCE CREDIBILITY

Cronkhite and Liska's model of source credibility (Figure 6.1) focuses on the relationship between a source and the receiver's needs. The interactive-dependency of persuader-persuadee is easily illustrated this way. A persuader needs an audience to perceive him/her as credible, but in order to do so, the persuadee must have his/her criteria for credibility satisfied by the persuader. This is still another example of interactive-dependency whereby the persuader's need to be perceived as credible is dependent on the per-

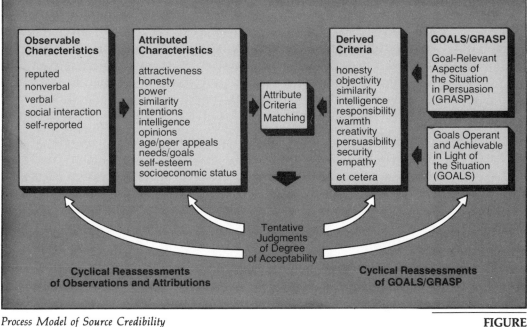

Process Model of Source Credibility

FIGURE
6.1

suadee's perceptions of what is a credible source. A persuader who has impeccable credentials in his/her degrees and honors may not satisfy a persuadee's need for the source to be likable and entertaining. The premise of Cronkhite and Liska's process approach is that an individual attributes certain unobservable characteristics to another person on the basis of observed characteristics. The individual, at that point, evaluates that person by comparing these attributes to his/her own criteria for desirable communicators that have been drawn from his/her own needs and goals and that apply to the specific communication situation (in Roloff and Miller 1980, p. 105).

Observable Characteristics

Most of the observable characteristics have been referred to elsewhere as the extrinsic or external characteristics of source credibility. These characteristics include (1) reputed characteristics, (2) nonverbal characteristics, (3) verbal characteristics, (4) characteristics of social interaction, and (5) self-reported characteristics.

Reputed Characteristics Reputed characteristics are those facts about a potential communicator that we gain from others and not through direct observation. In the previous example of student comments regarding instructors, the students accumulated information during those sessions that influenced their subsequent choices of instuctors. At some universities, books that describe the reputed characteristics of instructors are sold to the students. Press releases that appear in local newspapers concerning forthcoming artists, speakers, or movies influence people's decisions about whether or not to attend the openings or lectures and, further, influence people's perceptions when they do attend. Film distribution is highly dependent on the knowledge that prospective audiences have about the stars. Film critic Arthur Knight presented a very fine film at the Southern Methodist University, U.S.A. film festival in March 1980 entitled *The Ace,* starring Robert Duvall. At the time, the film had no distributor mainly because, according to Knight, Duvall had been a supporting actor in his previous films and was not well known to the public. The distributors were not willing to take a chance on an actor who was not well known even though the film was quite good. It ended up on cable television and trans-Atlantic airplane flights three months later with the title, *The Great Santini.* When word began to spread about the film from those who had seen it on television or in an airplane, the film got a distributor and was shown in movie theaters. The key difference in the reputed characteristics variable and the direct observation variable is that there is a middle source—a third communicator—who plays an active role in the process. That source's perception of the potential communicator is a mediating influence.

An interesting study (Infante 1973) was conducted in which an authoritative and a nonauthoritative middle person was used to discover the influence of forewarnings by a third person. The authoritative source used opinionated language as verbal anticipation of what an authoritative speaker was going to say. Nonauthoritarian forewarnings were accomplished by deleting the opinionated language. The results showed that the opinionated warning had no effect on receivers when applied to the authoritative speaker but did inhibit their responses to the less authoritarian speaker. The nonopinionated warning paved the way to positive perception on the part of the persuadees more than the opinionated warning did.

Nonverbal Characteristics There are two types of nonverbal characteristics that influence the perception of the source: those that are under the control of the communicator and those that are not. Communicators cannot control being short in stature or showing nervousness through rapid blinking of the eyes or excessive perspiration. The 1960 presidential debates between John F. Kennedy and Richard M. Nixon revealed excessive perspiration on Nixon's face. This nonverbal characteristic hurt Nixon's image even though it could not be avoided. Another example occurred during the primaries in 1974 when Edmund Muskie, a strong contender for the Democratic nomination, broke into tears in response to what he considered slanderous comments about his wife. The public's reaction to his emotional display was that "A man who cannot control his emotions should not be president."

The characteristics that are under the control of the communicator and that are usually the first to gain our attention are dress and grooming. Being dressed garishly "like a used-car salesman" can create distrust in a receiver. A woman clad in tight, revealing attire may be perceived as being "sexy and dumb." The meaning of "10" was altered to signify a standard of physical perfection after Bo Derek appeared in the movie *"10."* Gestures are nonverbal characteristics from which we draw impressions or make attributions. Males can communicate negative impressions to others through what some might perceive as effeminate gestures. Facial expressions convey positive and negative impressions. We form negative opinions concerning people who never smile and perceive them to be malcontents or difficult to approach. Conversely, we tend to view the constant smile as affected and insincere. A stiff body kept at a more-than-discreet distance causes us to consider a person "aloof."

People also draw conclusions about a person's character from his/her eye contact or lack of it. We have all used or heard statements such as "He/she never looks me in the eye, and I never trust anyone who won't look me in the eye" or "When she looked pleadingly at me with those beautiful baby-blue eyes, I just couldn't resist."

Voice quality or regional dialects make impressions on people. Geraldine Page's early movie career was short-lived because of her high-pitched voice even though she was considered to be a good actress. Before she could play Tennessee Williams's gutsy leads in plays like *Sweet Bird of Youth*, she had to lower her voice with the help of a coach. Tapes of former Alabama Governor George Wallace's speeches reveal that he used standard Southern speech dialect when talking with businessmen and politicians, but with laborers and the Ku Klux Klan, he would lapse into a substandard version. By a subtle change in dialect, he tried to become all things to all people.

Verbal Characteristics We have rules in our society that govern our system of symbols. These rules are cultural norms, which everyone is expected to follow. A featured comedian in a night club might use off-color language that would bring laughter from most of the audience, but a minister giving a sermon on Sunday or the president at a press conference who indulges in the use of the same language might not be so well received. When President Harry Truman called press correspondent H. V. Kaltenborn an s.o.b., it made headlines in all the newspapers across the country because Truman had defied a cultural norm.

Rollo May, when speaking as part of a lecture series, referred to black people as "colored." The use of the term called attention to itself because it was so dated and considered a racial slur by many. A speaker who refers to women in the audience as "the girls" may do serious damage to his credibility.

Characteristics of Social Interaction   These characteristics come to the fore when we observe how much, for instance, a person speaks and how much he/she listens. To whom does he/she choose to communicate, to how many, and how often? How well does he/she handle different types of communication situations? Some individuals, for example, do well in lecturing, presenting reports or proposals at meetings, but do not fare well when interrogated or interviewed. We all know people who communicate well on a one-to-one basis, but are less than effective when addressing a large group. From these observances of a person's social interactions, we draw conclusions about his or her credibility.

Self-reported Characteristics   These characteristics have been referred to traditionally as the intrinsic or internal qualities of source credibility or those qualities inherent in the communication from which receivers draw their impressions. Communicators express opinions, reveal facts about their backgrounds and past experiences, and share their beliefs or feelings about issues and other persons. When a persuader tells of his/her humble beginnings, he/she may cause listeners to perceive him/her as hard-working and modest.

Other self-reported characteristics include such information as age, education, and experiences, which are presented in such a way as to deem them as qualified in the particular area of communication concerned. The receiver, however, not only relies on his/her perceptions of the qualifications of the source, but on how the source's qualifications compare with his/her own. There appears to be a significant effect on the credibility of the source when the receiver perceives the source's level of qualification to be more than the receiver's own. (Baseheart and Bostrom 1972, p. 744).

The receiver is also influenced by the position the communicator takes on a given issue. The receiver judges the source's credibility to be considerably lower if they disagree on the desirability of the consequences.

Since perceptions of desirability are anchored in our value systems, we may perceive the source, as a result of his/her disagreement with us, to have different values (Infante 1972, p. 180).

These examples are just a few of the observable characteristics from which we form perceptions concerning characteristics that we attribute to the persuader.

Attributed Characteristics

Receivers frequently attribute unobservable traits to a source on the basis of observable traits or characteristics. The unobservable characteristics thus inferred may be honesty, power, similarity, intelligence, age, self-esteem or socioeconomic status, and attractiveness. Obviously, this list does not exhaust the possibilities.

A person may be thought to be honest because one's best friend says so (reputed characteristic) or because the first time one met the person, he/she was relaxed and used direct eye contact (nonverbal characteristic). A person might infer that a source has power because the newspapers report the government positions the source has held in the past and or companies he/she has successfully built into empires. Individuals may also be observed in their interactions with others. If a person is only charming around someone "who can do him/her some good" or is friendly on one day and cool the next, observers may decide, on the basis of these behaviors, that the individual's motives are self-serving in nature.

People also form perceptions about others from the statements these others make about themselves. If the claims are presented believably and if they are consistent with reports and information gained from other sources, positive characteristics may be attributed to the communicator.

Attractiveness   Attractiveness is one of those qualities that can be inferred from a variety of variables. Studies tell us that attitude similarity (Byrne 1971), need similarity (Izard 1961) and personality similarity (Griffitt 1969) all contribute to our perceptions of the attractiveness of others. Persons with these qualities are perceived to be stable, sincere, and warm. Research also establishes a link between an individual's communicative ability and his/her style as well as how others perceive his/her attractiveness (Norton and Pettigrew 1977, p. 259).

Norton and Pettigrew describe communicator style in the following terms: dominant, open, dramatic, relaxed, contentious, animated, friendly, attentive, impression-leaving, and communicator image (1977, p. 260–61). A report from three studies using these style variables as the basis of testing showed that the dominant/open style was considered most attractive (Norton and Pettigrew 1977). This could perhaps be due to the fact that attractive persons receive strokes, feedback, and ego gratification from others so that they, as a result, develop styles of communication that reflect confidence, which in turn presents a dominant and open style of communication.

Attractiveness of a source can also be manipulated by prior knowledge. A communicator in one study (Eagley and Chaiken 1975, p. 137) either praised or derogated college students prior to presenting a persuasive message to them. By manipulating attractiveness in this manner, a separate group of subjects was exposed to the communicator but not to his message. They were then asked to speculate which positions the source would advocate in his message. When the source praised college students he was considered "attractive," and when he used derogation, he was perceived as "unattractive." In other words, "Attractive people say pleasant things" and "Unattractive people say unattractive things" (p. 137).

Age and Peer Appeals   There was a point in time when scholars and advertisers believed that the "lofty ideal," the authority, or the perfect example was the most effective source of influence. But today the trend is to have children in toy commercials, teen-agers in toothpaste commercials, and the like.

Along with the obvious success of peer appeals, the "satisfied customer" approach has proven successful. The ex-smoker, the reformed convict, and the reformed alcoholic all seem to have more influence than those who just have expert knowledge on the subject.

A study (Cantor, Alfonso, and Zillman 1976) that lends insight into the degree of this type of influence was conducted to promote positive evaluations of the intrauterine device as an effective means of birth control and to encourage the selection of this technique. Eight versions of the interview were designed in which the interviewer varied the characteristics that she attributed to herself. The subjects in the study were all female undergraduates, so the interviewer cast herself as either twenty-one (peer) or thirty-nine (nonpeer). The interviewer also manipulated the "experience" portion of the interview by claiming either to be using the IUD at the present time or to have a good friend who was using one and who relayed good reports. The interviewer portrayed expertise (or lack of it) by representing herself as studying or working in the general area of medicine or as not being a part of the medical field at all.

The results of this study showed that the subjects were more inclined to use the IUD when suggested by a peer. This decision was enhanced in the situations where the peer also stated that she was a "satisfied customer" or a user of the device. The expertise of the interviewer had no significant effect on the subjects' decisions.

When you help start a Scout troop, there's no guarantee one of the Scouts will grow up to hit 755 home runs.

But you never know.

For all the facts on how your organization can support a Scout troop, call Boy Scouts of America. The Ebenezer A.M.E. Zion Church of Toulminville, Alabama did, and look what they've got to show for it.

A famous athlete lends his credibility to the Boy Scouts.

Thus, characteristics are attributed on the basis of observed information. What influences exist in the perceiver or who infers these characteristics? Why do we not all perceive persons exactly the same? Obviously, we do not or one political candidate would receive all the votes, one detergent would run the others out of the market, and the selection of best actor or singer for an award would be easy. The situation in which the persuasive event occurs and the goals of the persuadee provide answers to these questions.

Goals/Grasp

Goal-Relevant Aspects of the Situation in Persuasion   The situation in which the communication occurs becomes important in relation to the degree to which it is relevant to the goals of the receiver. Cronkhite and Liska refer to this as the goal-relevant aspects of the situation in persuasion (GRASP). For example, if a college student calls home from school to talk to different members of his/her family, the statement "How are you?" asked by each member of the family comes from the situational context of each person's relationship to the student. When asked by the mother or father, it probably means "Are you eating right and getting enough rest?" or "How's your money situation?" When asked by a sister or brother, it probably refers to the social life at the college.

One member of an audience for an investment counselor's speech may have no money to invest and may not look as acutely for characteristics of honesty and expertise as another person who does have money to invest. The goal-related aspects of a persuasive situation are keys to how persuadees perceive a persuader. Cronkhite and Liska say, "a situational aspect must be taken into account because it restrains or facilitates goal achievement" (In Roloff and Miller 1980, p. 123).

Goals That Are Operable and Achievable in the Light of the Situation
The goal that is operable and achievable in the light of the persuasive situation (GOALS) is a major influence of one's perception of the source.

In any instance, there are certain goals that are only relevant to aspects of the situation of persuasion. When Professor Kable met Tim Kable, who is a physician, for the first time, it was prior to the day he was to perform surgery on her. She had read the degrees and certificates on the wall in his office and had listened carefully to his answers to questions for certain signs of expertise in his field—that is, she sought signals that would allay her fears. Ten years later, they were introduced at a social function. At this meeting, she noticed how handsome, warm, and delightful he was in a social situation. You could say that her goals in each situation affected her perception of this man to the point that what she saw in him the first time was quite different from what she perceived later. Her personal motivations and goals were different each time, which caused the same person to be perceived differently in different situations.

As stated earlier, the source and receiver, each with his/her various qualities and goals, interact throughout the process of persuasion. Each type of communication has its own unique set of variables for evaluation of source credibility.

Criteria for Evaluating Potential Persuadees

According to Cronkhite and Liska (1980 p. 126), the persuader has general criteria for evaluating potential persuadees: (1) persuaders want persuadees who are willing to make themselves accessible to what the persuader has to offer; (2) persuaders want persuadees who are susceptible to persuasion in general; (3) persuaders want persuadees who are susceptible to persuaders' influence in particular; (4) persuaders want persuadees to have goals that can be satisfied by the persuasion; and (5) persuaders want persuadees who are in the position of being able to carry out the suggested proposal and to influence others after they have been influenced themselves.

Criteria for Evaluating Persuaders

Persuadees use different criteria to evaluate persuaders in different situations. Cronkhite and Liska (in Roloff and Miller 1980) cite fifteen situations in which criteria for judging the source would be different in each case. For our purposes, we shall focus on two of these situations.

(1) The first situation is one in which the persuadee's goal is to be informed. Depending on their level of awareness, persuadees will risk being persuaded in exchange for being given needed information. In this instance, they require the persuader to be *competent*. If they are aware that they run the risk of being persuaded, they want the persuader to be *trustworthy*.

Cronkhite and Liska (in Roloff and Miller 1980) list further requirements of the persuader in this situation: (a) that the persuader be in a position to observe pertinent facts; (b) that he/she be physically, intellectually, and/or emotionally capable of observing those facts accurately; (c) that he/she be sensitive to the facts being discussed because of experience; (d) that he/she be motivated to perceive and report facts accurately because he/she has nothing to gain through deception; (e) that he/she share the persuadees' goals; and (f) that he/she have a reputation for reporting events and facts accurately and be in a position of being held accountable for the facts as reported.

(2) A second persuasive situation is one in which two people are in dialogue, each with the GOALS of persuading the other. A tacit reciprocal agreement is at work here. Each agrees to the risk of exposure to persuasion from the other in exchange for the opportunity to persuade. Neither person

is seeking information, as was the case in the first situation. Instead, the criteria persuaders use to evaluate persuadees are at work here, since both persons expect to be persuaders. Also, since each person runs the risk of being persuaded, he/she will choose a counterpart who is perceived to have less expertise in persuasion (Cronkhite and Liska, in Roloff and Miller 1980, pp. 126–27).

This situation is not to be confused with a debate, for in a debate the two adversaries are not trying to persuade one another, but, in fact, are trying to defeat one another in the presence of a third party (Cronkhite and Liska, in Roloff and Miller 1980, p. 127).

An interactive-dependency approach to persuasion assumes that both agents involved in communication do not seek victory or defeat, but rather they seek to satisfy one another's needs. The persuader image plays a significant role in getting the persuadee to accept not just what the persuader has to say, but also in getting the persuadee to feel confident in the acceptance of it.

IDENTIFICATION

Source credibility may be felt by a persuadee, but he/she may feel that its essence is intangible. The persuadee may not "like" a persuader, but he/she may still be willing to believe what is said. Conversely, there may be attraction to the source, yet there may be an unwillingness to believe. This is why the persuader needs to be extrasensitive to the needs of the persuadees in a given situation. The persuader should work to gain the trust of the persuadees by relating to their goals. Identification, which is discussed in more detail in the "language" section of Chapter VIII, plays an important role. To the extent that we can identify, can share common substances in thought, word, and deed, we may be able to establish mutual trust. One of the successes that Gloria Steinem has in speaking to audiences is that she is able to share the often "unspoken" experiences of women, the feelings of restlessness, dissatisfaction, and oppression. As one of our students expressed it: "Gloria Steinem is talking about *me* and my experiences, and she has never met me." This is a true example of identification or, in the word of Kenneth Burke, "consubstantiality," a coming together as one. We may have common sensations, concepts, images, and ideas that make us consubstantial. These qualities give us the feeling of being united in one common substance.

Identification represents a persuader's response to a condition of expectation in the audience. This interrelationship that exists within a situation extends beyond source credibility to include all that happens during persuasion. A persuader analyzes his/her intellectual, moral, social, and experiential substance and tries to have control over his/her communicative theme and its details, its mode of presentation, order, and logical framework to enforce and not distort the basic propositions and insight into the desired results of the persuasion. The persuadee examines his/her understanding of the situation and his/her prevailing goals and motives as they are related to personal and social beliefs, attitudes, and values as well as a concern for the social outcome of the persuasive situation.

The next three chapters, which describe the message facilitating factors, incorporate the strong and necessary interrelationship between persuader and persuadee.

SUMMARY

Source credibility, the perception and attitude that the receiver has of and toward the source at a given time and situation, is a very important construct in persuasion. Politicians are particularly sensitive to their public "image," which can change over time.

Source credibility is a multidimensional construct and has been the subject of much research for at least twenty years. Although some researchers believe that there are five consistently present dimensions of source credibility (competence, character, sociability, extroversion, and composure), others feel that response to communicator credibility is highly individualized. For this reason, a process view of source credibility has been developed. The process view emphasizes needs and goals achievement—that is, the persuader needs to be perceived as credible, but the persuadee needs to have his/her criteria for credibility satisfied.

A process model for source credibility relates certain unobserved characteristics of credibility to those that can be observed. Observable characteristics are reputed, nonverbal, verbal, social interactive, and self-reported.

People also attribute traits to communicators on the basis of attractiveness and peer appeals. Source credibility, however, is also largely determined by goal-relevant aspects of the situation (GRASP) and goals that are operable and achievable in light of the situation in persuasion (GOALS). Goals determine how the persuader and persuadee perceive one another. If the persuadees can see themselves as gaining information, they will submit themselves to the risk of being persuaded. If persuader and persuadee see the situation as one in which they can persuade one another, they will risk being persuaded in order to persuade.

Finally, the extent to which both parties are able to identify with one another affects their mutual responses. They each have expectations, and they may share common substances. Although this interrelationship goes beyond source credibility, it certainly can enhance it as the parties to persuasion are able to move together toward a common goal.

KEY WORDS

Image
Source credibility
Ethos
Observable characteristics
Unobservable characteristics
Attributed characteristics
Situational characteristics

GOALS—goals that are operable and achievable in the light of the situation
GRASP—goal-relevant aspects of the situation in persuasion
Identification
Consubstantiality

EXERCISES

1. Have you ever made a significant purchase on the basis of a friend's recommendation? Did you regard the friend as an authority? How did you know he/she was a trustworthy source?
2. Listen to a political campaign speech. Do you believe the speaker? What causes you to accept the speaker as a credible source?
3. Are you influenced more by your peers or by authorities? In what situations do you prefer authority sources over peer sources?
4. Have you ever resisted changing an attitude or a behavior because someone you did not like or trust wanted you to? Were you aware that your aversion to the source may have influenced your resistance to persuasion?
5. List the characteristics of a professor whom you would consider a credible source of information for a course that you need to develop your own professional abilities.
6. Suppose that you need to find a doctor to perform major surgery on you. How would you decide which doctor to select?
7. Suppose that you are asked to mediate a dispute between your father and brother over the brother's wish to own and ride a motorcycle. How would you use identification to establish some commonality between the two men in order to reduce or resolve the conflict?
8. You missed an important test in a class last week because you had to drive

your mother to the hospital when she had an attack of appendicitis. How can you get your professor to believe that you are a reliable person who should be given a chance to make up the test?

9. What was the last movie you attended? What motivated you to attend? Was there something about the prior publicity that attracted you such as the star, a well-known director, its receipt of an award?

READINGS

Cronkhite, Gary, and **Liska, Jo R.** "The Judgment of Communicant Acceptability." In *Persuasion: New Directions in Theory and Research,* M. Roloff and G. Miller, ed. pp. 101–39. Beverly Hills, Calif.: Sage, 1980.

Delia, Jesse G. "A Constructivist Analysis of the Concept of Credibility." *Quarterly Journal of Speech* 62 (1976):361–75.

McCroskey, James C., and **Young, Thomas J.** "Ethos and Credibility: The Construct and Its Measurement after Three Decades." Unpub. paper (1977).

Sternthal, Brian; Phillips, Lynn W.; and **Dholakia, Ruby.** "The Persuasive Effect of Source Credibility: A Situational Analysis." *Public Opinion Quarterly* 43 (1978):285–314.

MESSAGE FACILITATING FACTORS

OBJECTIVES

Upon completion of this chapter you should be able to:

1. Understand the facilitating factors that pertain to the message.
2. Be aware of how the discrepancy between the persuader's message and the persuadee's stance can effect the success or failure of message acceptance.
3. Understand the importance of the situation to message content.
4. Collect evidence that is valid and can enhance persuasive effect.
5. Understand how effective use of reasoning can redirect the persuadee's perception of the world.
6. Understand motivation and its role in the persuasive process.
7. Be aware of emotion and its use in persuasion.
8. Use intense language in a persuasive manner.
9. Define message strategies.
10. Choose relevant strategies for a given persuasive situation.

The communication model of persuasion in Chapter I describes the internal variables such as beliefs, values, attitudes, and group norms that influence the persuader and the persuadee. External variables such as behavior and environment have added other dimensions that are used in order to understand the persuasion act. Also, perception, the filter through which one sees, hears, and evaluates events, determines how the environment is interpreted. It is within this information framework that the message—M_1, message sent, and M_2, message received—occurs. What constitutes a persuasive message? Are there any guarantees that M_2 will resemble M_1? How can persuasive efforts be put into a message form toward which an audience is likely to be receptive?

These questions will be answered by discussing the facilitating factors pertaining to the message: the message situation, purpose, content, evidence and reasoning, and message strategies. Motivational theory, which also plays a role in message strategies, will also be discussed along with emotional appeals and language intensity.

THE MESSAGE

In order to be an effective persuader, whether in a dyadic, group, or public situation, it is necessary to understand the importance of message preparation. The persuasive message is defined as "consisting primarily of a series of belief statements, each linking some object to an attribute such as another object, a concept, an event, or a goal" (Fishbein and Ajzen 1975, p. 458). The message includes content, the organization of the content, the language used to relate the content to an audience, and the strategical treatment of the content. The facilitating factors are those elements that make possible the reception and acceptance of the message by the persuadee. Message situation, content, evidence and reasoning, motivation, and persuasive strategies are discussed in this chapter. Organization and language as facilitating factors are discussed in the next chapter.

DISCREPANCY

Before designing the message, a persuader needs to determine how discrepant his/her message purpose is from the position held by the persuadee. That is, how far apart are the positions held by the sender and the receiver prior to the presentation of the persuasive message? Message content and strategies will then be selected with the desired end being a reduction or removal of the discrepancy. Also, prior information possessed by the receiver may be discrepant from that being sent in a message. New information needs to be presented with this in mind.

In Chapter III, the discussion of Sherif's social judgment theory indicated that one's acceptance of a message depends on the discrepancy (distance) between the receiver's position and his/her perception of the source's position. This theory also assumes that a persuader puts pressure on a persuadee to change positions. Thus, the greater the perceived discrepancy between the persuadee's perception of the two positions, the more pressure the message exerts. A further prediction is that "the amount of change in position should increase with discrepancy so long as the advocated position is not perceived to fall within the latitude of rejection" (Fishbein and Ajzen 1975, p. 456). If, however, the advocated position falls within the latitude of rejection, persuadee change will not occur.

Discrepancy can also affect source credibility. For example, when a source advocates a position perceived to be widely discrepant from that of the persuadee, the source may be judged as untrustworthy, unattractive, and inexpert, and his/her arguments will be perceived as invalid (Fishbein and Ajzen 1975, p. 463).

MESSAGE SITUATION

Both persuaders and persuadees come to the persuasion act with expectations. The persuader has beliefs that he/she wishes to be accepted by the persuadee. The persuadee, on the other hand, comes to the situation with a set of predispositions, group norms, attitudes, and values. Thus, there is a state of interactive-dependency between both parties. Each wants the other to fulfill his/her goals, purposes, or expectations.

Difficulties arise when a discrepancy exists between the expectations of the persuader and persuadee. There are often situational elements that contribute toward a discrepant state. For example, if an official from the Department of Health chose as a topic for an address to the American Medical Association the advocacy of a national health insurance program, it goes without saying that this position would be discrepant from the position of the audience. The physicians would come to the situation with predispositions concerning their need for autonomy, antifederal control, and government spending. The official, on the other hand, would have hopes that this prestigious group would be amenable to his plan. If the official could convince them that this program would provide physicians with protection against high malpractice premiums and from abusive and unnecessary lawsuits, the two positions would no longer be at opposite poles. If the persuader, however, were a Nobel prizewinning physician, there might be less discrepancy to begin with because of source credibility.

Situations exist in which the discrepancy may not be overcome, but respect for the speaker may be heightened, and this may become beneficial to him/her on other issues. Frances Farenthold, when she ran for governor of Texas in 1972, came out in favor of abortion. It took courage for this Roman Catholic mother of six to do so, and it gained her the respect of some antiabortion advocates. Although they did not change their attitude toward abortion, they regarded her as a woman of courage who, as governor, would probably stand up for what she believed in on other issues as well.

Message situations also differ due to the audience's ability to receive the message. There are situations in which audience members are limited in knowledge and experience. Many young people who voted in the 1980 presidential election were not aware that Ronald Reagan was a movie actor, and there are vast numbers who have never seen his movies. Their perceptions of him and their attitudes toward him may differ from those who remember him as an actor. A working-class group might have no background in philosophy or anthropology; thus, a speaker's favorite piece of information from these disciplines may be wasted. A reference to Plato may be meaningless if the audience does not know who Plato is. A persuader must be aware of the knowledge and backgrounds of the persuadees.

Experience, or lack of it, is a situational variable that must be considered. Much of the "generation gap" that existed in the 1960s between the establishment and youth over the Vietnam war was the result of different experiences and knowledge between the two groups. Many in the establishment still related war to World War II and the feelings of patriotism and self-sacrifice shared by all Americans during that time. To them, the youth who were refusing to fight for their country, protesting against the war, and openly criticizing the values that were inextricably tied to the World War II era were un-American, unpatriotic, and dangerous to society. It was difficult, on the other hand, for the youth to understand members of the establishment because the youth had not shared their wartime experiences.

Another situational variable is time expectation. If the situation calls for a ten-minute presentation and the persuader speaks for thirty minutes, the audience will become restless, hostile, and possibly unwilling to listen. Most people in the audience for the Gettysburg Address did not hear Abraham Lincoln's speech. They expected a speech several hours in length. They had not even settled down to listen when Lincoln concluded his brief address.

Just as different situations require appropriate behaviors, they also require appropriateness in the type and content of the message presented. After a banquet, no one wants to hear about gory accidents, sickness, or unpleasant and complex ideas. It is best to be light and entertaining in this context. If, for example, the situation is an annual gathering where members of a business firm bring their spouses, the audience members will become uncomfortable if the speaker's approach is all "shop talk." The spouses may be bored, and company employees, knowing that their husbands or wives are bored, may become uncomfortable.

Leon Breedon, former director of North Texas State University's famous Jazz Lab Band, tells of an inappropriate story that one of his students told at the White House:

Lou Marini was nineteen-years-old when we were at the White House and were in the private quarters (living room) on the second floor where the president and his family live. President Johnson came into the room from next door where he was meeting with all fifty governors of the states. He talked with our band for a period of about ten minutes, answered questions, and started to leave the room. As he passed by Lou Marini he turned and said: "Son, didn't you raise your hand a minute ago? Did you have a question?"

Lou shuffled from left to right [foot], looked L.B.J. straight in the eyes and said: "No, Mr. President, I didn't have a question—I just wondered if you'd heard the latest Aggie joke?"*

The Secret Service people almost had a heart attack and started giving Lou the once-over thinking that they had a real nut on their hands. President Johnson said: "No. I guess I haven't heard it!" To which Lou said: "Well, it seems that one Aggie said to the other Aggie: What do you think of LSD? The other Aggie immediately said: Why, he's the greatest president we've ever had!"

For a second no one said anything—looked shocked—until Johnson bent over, slapped his knee and laughed very loudly. At that time everyone in the room started to laugh, including Secret Service men. I've always thought that this was America at its best—a nineteen-year-old kid telling the President of the United States a PRESIDENT JOKE!

The *Washington Post* picked up this story and, in their coverage the next day, stated: "It is most likely that President Johnson went back to the Governors' Conference and immediately told them the joke, except this time it was a Republican instead of an Aggie." (*North Texan* 1980)

Thanks to the good humor of President Johnson, the inappropriateness of the joke was overlooked.

OTHER FACTORS

There are factors other than the situation that affect individuals' abilities to relate to a persuasive message regardless of the context. Janis and Hovland suggested that "individuals vary in their abilities and levels of motivation to process messages" (Janis and Hovland 1959, in Littlejohn 1978, p. 193). They grouped these abilities into four categories: attention, comprehension,

---

(*An "Aggie" is a student at Texas A & M University)

anticipation, and evaluation. Attention is the process of selecting and focusing on particular stimuli. Comprehension involves understanding the various elements of the message. Anticipation is the ability of a person to imagine his/her acceptance of a particular message. Evaluation involves a judgment process for scrutinizing arguments. The authors further group these abilities into two categories: learning factors and acceptance factors. Attention and comprehension are learning processes that occur as a result of the message. Anticipation and evaluation are considered acceptance factors, for they reflect the extent to which the message will be accepted or rejected. Attention, comprehension, and anticipation are also facilitating abilities, whereas evaluation is considered inhibitory to persuasion. Thus, if a persuadee has the abilities to attend, comprehend, and anticipate, these characteristics will facilitate change, while a strong evaluative ability may inhibit change (Littlejohn 1978, p. 194). When predicting persuasibility, levels of motivation should always be considered together with the persuadee's abilities to relate to a message. When motivation to use facilitative abilities is low, persuasibility will be low. When such motivation is high, persuasibility will be correspondingly high. When motivation to evaluate is high, persuasibility is low (Littlejohn 1978, p. 194).

MESSAGE PURPOSE

Before selecting any message strategies, a persuader must determine the specific purpose of the message. This purpose can be thought of or written as a statement that says, "When I am finished with my persuasive strategies, I want my audience to . . ." It doesn't matter whether the persuadee is a parent who, "when finished with my persuasive strategies, wants my teenager to help with the yard work" or a company president who, "when finished with my persuasion, wants my board of directors to believe in a relocation of the company's plants" or a minister who, "when finished with my persuasion, wants my congregation to be good Samaritans." These statements ("I want my audience to do, believe, or feel more strongly that . . .") are the desired responses from the audience that the persuader is seeking. They are the target belief statements.

It is also useful for a persuader to think of a declarative thesis statement or central idea that embodies a target belief. "Yard work is good exercise and is also a form of helping with family responsibilities." "Relocating company plants in the Sunbelt will cut down on expenses and lead to increased profits." "Helping others is practicing Christian brotherhood." These types of statements embody the target belief statement of the persuader, that attitude that he/she hopes the audience will change. Belief statements that support the target belief often embody the receiver's values, beliefs, and attitudes. Supportive statements are often added to enhance acceptance of the target belief.

MESSAGE CONTENT

Evidence

Evidence is usually presented in the form of relevant facts and opinions selected to induce understanding and acceptance of an idea or a target belief statement. Evidence in the form of supportive belief statements is presented with the hope that if the evidence is accepted, the target belief will also be accepted. The acceptance of evidence, however, does not guarantee the acceptance of a target belief. Belief change can occur when (1) presenting evidence produces a change in the persuadee's existing supportive belief; (2) there is a probable relationship between supportive and target beliefs; and (3) "there are no unexpected impact effects on relevant external beliefs" (Fishbein and Ajzen 1975, p. 471).

It would be nice to be able to say that if a persuader uses evidence, he/she will be effective. Different types of messages, however, require different types of evidence, which can have varying effects. For example, a rational presentation may enhance persuader credibility. Use of sensational visual aids may increase anxiety in the persuadee. Yet, evidence usually affects the persuadee somehow. It carries some influence on his/her perception of the persuader's target beliefs (Fishbein and Ajzen 1975, p. 4). There will be more discussion of the impact of evidence later in the chapter.

Fact and Inference

It is important to know the difference between a fact and an inference when selecting and presenting evidence. Irving Lee demonstrated the difference in one of his Talking with People films entitled *Do You Know How to Make a Statement of Fact?* Lee said that a fact is something that can be observed, whereas an inference is what is assumed, usually because it cannot be observed. Facts are from past observations; therefore, statements of fact are made after observation. A statement of inference, which is not dependent on observation, can be made anytime. Because a fact has been observed in the past, the statement about the fact can be unchanging. Since an inference is made without observation, it can be changed anytime, especially whenever new observations contradict the statement of inference.

The statement of fact is as close to certainty as one can get, but the statement of inference has varying degrees of probability. It is a fact that President John F. Kennedy was killed by gunshot wounds in Dallas on November 23, 1963, but it is an inference that the shot was fired by Lee Harvey Oswald.

Evidence is data that are sometimes factual and sometimes inferential. Real examples and statistics are usually factual, and predictive statistics and authority statements are often inferential. Both are perfectly respectable to use in a persuasive message, but the persuader has an obligation to be clear about whether a statement is factual or inferential.

In his film, Lee told a true story about a famous Scotland Yard case in which a valuable quantity of silver was stolen from a British estate the night after the dining room was painted. On the window sill a handprint was found that was, upon investigation, discovered to belong to a famous thief who had been released from prison three days prior to the theft. Scotland Yard announced that this particular thief had stolen the silver. A statement of fact? It would seem so except that the thief in question was found dead along the side of the road and missing a hand. It was his handprint all right, but one of his buddies had accidently killed him in a fistfight and then seized the opportunity by amputating the dead man's hand and leaving its imprint for the detectives to find. Needless to say, Scotland Yard detectives were blushing over their failure to make a pronouncement of inference instead of fact because the theft had not been observed.

The acceptance of the target belief statement is usually dependent on the evidence presented for support. There are various types of data that provide evidence choices for the persuader: (1) example, (2) statistics, and (3) testimony or authority.

Example   A belief statement can be clarified, explained, and substantiated by the use of specific examples or general examples. Both types of examples usually include the who, what, where, when, and why. "Mary Ellen White, aged twenty-five, was robbed and beaten by the Silver Blades Gang on Ninety-eighth Street in New York City on April 2, 1979" is a specific example because it singles out certain individuals and one event. More details, making the example a case study, may be added.

A general example includes a whole class, such as "Residents of the suburbs no longer have a feeling of security because of the vast number of muggings that have been occurring in these areas." Often a specific example is presented first as typical of a general example.

Statistics   The use of statistics enables the persuader to compress a vast amount of information and present it through numerical summaries. The source of the statistics should be acceptable to the persuadee. It is not enough, however, to just use statistics. The persuader must convince the persuadee that out of all the statistics available, the ones presented are the most reliable and originate from unbiased sources. Statistics should also be presented in such a way that they are easy to understand and should be related to the target or supporting belief.

Statistics are more meaningful if they are related to personal experiences. Consider the following comparison:

Dr. Gerald Looney of the University of Arizona said in a speech to the American Academy of Pediatrics in 1972 that the average prekindergarten child spent more than 60% of his waking time before a TV set. This means that by the time a child goes to kindergarten he/she will have devoted more hours to watching TV than a student spends in four years of university classes. (*Saturday Review* 1972, p. 39)

Testimony or Authority   The term *expert testimony* is often used in the courtroom and other places where special experts are asked to testify. Authority sources are prestige sources, but not all prestige sources are authority sources. A famous person may make a statement outside of his/her field of expertise. Such a statement may be discarded, not because of the lack of prestige of the speaker, but because of his/her lack of expertise on that subject.

The persuader should use authorities that are unimpeachable as experts in the subject area for which they are quoted. These authorities should be known experts whose word will carry considerable weight. This article appeared in the *Dallas Morning News* on June 11, 1974:

Solzhenitsyn's Ex-Wife's Memoirs Offered

Soviet representatives have been quietly offering the purported memoirs of Aleksandr I. Solzhenitsyn's first wife to Western publishers in an apparent effort to discredit the exiled author.

A manuscript attributed to Natalya A. Reshetovskaya, who was separated from the novelist in 1970, is circulating at a time when stores in the United States are offering the first copies of an American edition of "The Gulag Archipelago," Solzhenitsyn's widely publicized account of the Soviet labor-camp system from 1918 to 1956. The book is being published in the United States by Harper & Row.

Miss Reshetovskaya, who was still living with Solzhenitsyn when he wrote the book and typed at least part of it, was quoted earlier this year as having described it as "Camp Folklore" rather than as a genuine reflection of history.

What the article does not say is that Solzhenitsyn was involved with another woman at the time, became the father of two of her children, and eventually left his wife to marry the other woman. Ms. Reshetovskaya was hardly an unbiased source. The quotation of the expert should be chosen carefully. It is best that these quotations be concise and to the point. The persuader must be sure that relevant portions of the quotation are not lost among remarks that are not relevant to the issue.

It is also the responsibility of the persuader to relate the importance and significance of the authority statement to the target belief. The persuader can also be an authority. If, in a persuasive encounter, a person is advocating martial arts as an effective means of self-protection and that person has not only earned a black belt in karate, but has successfully protected him/herself, he/she would probably be accepted as an authority on this issue.

Tests of Evidence

Evidence can be strong or weak, impressive or unimpressive, appropriate or inappropriate. Evidence should be directly related to the topic and of primary importance to the target belief. It should also be current. Outdated evidence should not be used to support an issue of current significance. Evidence should also be relevant to the issue and should not unwittingly call attention to irrelevant issues.

There should be enough evidence to clearly demonstrate the validity of the target belief in the mind of the persuadee—that is, if the audience is committed, not as much evidence is necessary, whereas a hostile or uncommitted audience will require more evidence.

Evidence should be unbiased. Using statistics published by the National Labor Relations Board in a prolabor argument would not be reliable or persuasive. When a mother states "My daughter should have been elected beauty queen—she is the prettiest girl in the class," persuadees may sympathize with the mother, but may not necessarily believe her.

Usefulness of Evidence

Evidence is useful to the persuader in many ways. It enhances source credibility if the persuader's credibility is low (McCroskey 1969). Audiences expect a persuader to use evidence (Cathcart 1955) even though they may not always be persuaded by it (Dresser 1963). Evidence enhances the learning process in listeners, thereby strengthening what they already know and feel. Evidence enables them to perceive things in a new way ("I didn't know or realize that"). It gives friendly audiences support for their own beliefs, whereas discrepant evidence gives unfriendly audiences a chance to weigh their opposing evidence against the persuader's evidence. It provides neutral audiences with information that might lead to the conclusion "I never realized this was so important; you've caused me to think about it in a new way."

Evidence can give a sense of "logic" to persuasion and enhances the chance of an audience making a logical choice, for its use appeals to the rational nature of people.

Use of Evidence

Caution must be exercised in the use of evidence. A persuader needs to be careful not to display argumentative prowess, for, after all, the goal is to influence, not to impress or repel an audience with argument.

A successful persuader combines forms of evidence for interest and belief reinforcement. When using an example, it may be presented as a well-told case study with names, places, events, and narrative. This, then, can be reinforced with a general example further supported with statistics to give a sense of a widespread problem. The following example from a student-contest speech about suicide among college students illustrates this very well:

One pretty coed—we'll call her Cheryl—was extremely upset by the death of her father; and she was being pressured by exams. One of her favorite places to go and meditate was a nearby pond—so as usual, she took her blanket and went there. Only this time she brought something else—a razor blade. Cheryl methodically cut each wrist—then curled up in the blanket with her teddy bear in her arms to die. She fell asleep, but woke up later with the blood clotted on her wrists—very much alive. Cheryl was disappointed in her failure and returned to her room to find another way. Fortunately, her horrified roommate found her and quickly took her for psychiatric help. Cheryl is typical only in that she was one of 25 students who attempted to commit suicide at Indiana University last year.

Dr. Dana Farnsworth, a leading expert in the field of student mental health, lists some rather ominous nationwide statistics for colleges. He stresses that of each 10,000 students, 1,000 will have emotional conflicts severe enough to warrant professional help, 300–400 will have feelings of depression deep enough to impair efficiency, 5–10 will attempt suicide, and 1–3 will succeed in taking his own life. If these statistics are true, my university should encounter 15–45 suicide attempts of which 3–6 will be successful. (Hayes, in Linkugal, Allen, and Johannesen 1972, pp. 266–67).

When using statistics, a persuader needs to proportionately relate them to the audience to show how many in an immediate audience could be affected. For example, sectional statistics on the prevalence of venereal disease could be boiled down to "In this class of 27 people, 3 or 4 people could have V.D."

Local examples are effective pieces of evidence such as statistics taken from your local hospital on the number of emergency cases of traffic victims. Authorities in the area who are known and liked by the audience, such as a popular college president, student leader, or athlete, provide effective support.

Evidence provides a basis for logical thinking, but can also stimulate emotional responses as well. *Unsafe at Any Speed*, written by Ralph Nader in 1965, was persuasive and controversial because it was influential in getting the Corvair, a Chevrolet automobile, taken off the market because of its unsafe design. An excerpt from this book provides an example of the use of statistics and an example that creates both a logical and emotional impact simultaneously:

A transportation specialist, Wilfred Owen, wrote in 1946, "There is little question that the public will not tolerate for long an annual traffic toll of forty to fifty thousand fatalities." Time has shown Owen to be wrong. Unlike aviation, marine, or rail transportation, the highway transport system can inflict tremendous casualties and property damage without in the least affecting the viability of the system. Plane crashes, for example, jeopardize the attraction of flying for potential passengers and therefore strike at the heart of the air transport economy. They motivate preventative efforts. The situation is different on the roads.

Highway accidents were estimated to have cost this country in 1964, $8.3 billion in property damage, medical expenses, lost wages, and insurance overhead expenses. Add an equivalent sum to comprise roughly the indirect costs and the total amounts to over two per cent of the gross national product. But these are not the kind of costs which fall on the builders of motor vehicles (excepting a few successful law suits for negligent construction of the vehicle) and thus do not pinch the proper foot. Instead the costs fall to users of vehicles, who are in no position to dictate safer automobile designs.

As described by a California Highway Patrol officer, John Bortolozzo, who witnessed the flip over while motoring in the opposite direction, the Pierini vehicle was traveling about thirty-five miles an hour in a thirty-five MPH zone in the right lane headed towards Goleta. He saw the car move towards the right side of the road near the shoulder and then "all of a sudden the vehicle made a sharp cut to the left and swerved over." Bortolozzo testified at the trial that he rushed over to the wreck and saw an arm with a wedding band and wristwatch lying on the ground. Two other men came over quickly and began to help Mrs. Pierini out of the vehicle while trying to stop the torrent of blood gushing forth from the stub of her arm. She was very calm, observed Bortolozzo, only saying that "something went wrong with my steering." (Nader 1965)

The appeal in the first two paragraphs is logically persuasive, whereas the third paragraph appeals to the emotions in a vivid and graphic way.

Where to Find Evidence

Persuasive communication is interesting if it has a variety of evidence. Many alternatives are available, and all of these alternatives need to be explored by the student of persuasion in preparation for a persuasive effort.

The obvious source of evidence is the library, where books, magazines, newspapers, and bibliographical indexes are available. A place to begin is the *Readers Guide to Periodical Literature*, the card catalogue, and reference books like encyclopedias and information yearbooks. Radio and television also provide a vast amount of current information through news programs, television news magazines such as *"60 Minutes,"* and documentaries.

Most individuals carry about more information than they are aware of, which they have obtained through observation and experience. Persuaders who feel that their experiences are limited should expose themselves to activities that would make their prospective topic meaningful to them. Some suggestions are:

1. Sit in a local emergency room for a day.
2. Volunteer to work at a center for the mentally retarded or a nursing home.
3. Attend a group meeting.
4. Observe a city council meeting.

Personal interviews with community authorities such as police officers, probation officials, and others who have firsthand information concerning crime or juvenile problems provide information that is much more interesting to the persuadee than the same information concerning a distant city. Surveys can also be obtained from local people, and, if they are not available, an individual can conduct his/her own. Pamphlets and brochures are also available at no cost at headquarters or main offices of agencies, political parties, and city offices.

It is advisable to keep a clipping file. A good persuader reads regularly and widely and includes in his/her reading a variety of reliable materials. Be sure to jot down the source of each item.

Persuadee Reception of Evidence

Sometimes evidence means more to the persuadee than other times. Of all the research done in the area of persuasion, there have been less than two dozen studies concerning the effects of evidence. A review by McCroskey (1969) presents the following conclusions concerning the effects of evidence.

1. Including good evidence has little, if any, impact on immediate audience attitude change or source credibility if the source of the message is initially perceived to be highly credible.
2. Including good evidence has little, if any, impact on immediate audience attitude change or source credibility if the message is delivered poorly.
3. Including good evidence has little, if any, impact on immediate audience attitude change or source credibility if the audience is familiar with the evidence prior to exposure to the source's message.
4. Including good evidence may significantly increase immediate audience attitude change and source credibility when the source is initially perceived to have moderate to low credibility, when the message is well delivered, and when the audience has little or no prior familiarity with the evidence included or similar evidence.
5. Including good evidence may significantly increase sustained audience attitude change regardless of the source's initial credibility, the quality of the delivery of the message, or the medium by which the message is transmitted.
6. The medium of transmission of a message has little, if any, effect on the functioning of evidence in persuasive communication. (McCroskey 1969, p. 175)

Evidence makes persuasion interesting, personal, and memorable, but it can also be used supportively as an element in the reasoning process. What is proof, and what is a logical basis for persuasion? What can be determined as reasonable?

A logical basis for persuasion is a basis that permits a person to prove as little as possible and refute as little as possible within the boundaries that the human condition views as reasonable. It is a basis that minimizes differences and maximizes agreement.

REASONING

Evidence is used by a persuader as support for belief statements. But a persuader must also use reasoning in order to redirect the persuadee's perception of the world. Reasoning is the process of establishing the probability of a belief statement—that is, the likelihood that it may be true or false—by linking it to another belief statement. People like to think of themselves as rational. Thus, a persuader who is, or appears to be, rational in the mind of the persuadee should be favorably received, on that level at least.

Interestingly enough, however, receivers do not always judge invalid reasoning correctly. In a recent review of the literature on receiver evaluation of reasoning, Burgoon and Bettinghaus generalize from several studies that the prior attitudes, personalities, and perceived source credibility held by the receivers affect their ability to make validity judgments (Burgoon and Bettinghaus, in Roloff and Miller 1980, pp. 144–45). They also point out that William McGuire (1960) found that in making logical evaluations, people try to maintain attitude consistency. This means that people are more likely to perceive reasoning as valid if it agrees with their attitudes *even though the reasoning itself may be logically invalid.*

Furthermore, personality factors influence judgment of the logical validity of an argument. People who are highly dogmatic make more errors in assessing logical validity than those who are low in dogmatism (Bettinghaus, Miller, and Steinfatt 1970). This study also relates the levels of dogmatism to source credibility and the complexity of the logic.

This information is important to the prospective persuader, for it indicates that belief statements drawn from formal logical structures such as the syllogism or enthymeme or from traditional logical forms may not be perceived as logical. In fact, they may not be understood at all.

Nonetheless, it is useful to know about certain traditional logical forms that rely on evidence as supporting materials for the development of certain belief statements. To reason *from* evidence, sign, or authority, or to establish the causality is helpful. Thus, these time-tested forms are included.

Generalization from Example

When a group of individual examples is reported and a conclusion is drawn from them, this is called generalization from example. The examples selected need to be random examples and not from a single class. Suppose a persuader presented a group of examples of statements from draft-age men and women, stating they were against compulsory military service. If these examples were drawn from college students in the East, the persuadee might silently ask, "But what do students in different economic classes and other parts of the country think?" If the examples had been representative of all classes and geographical areas, the generalization drawn would have been more acceptable.

A sufficient number of examples are necessary to justify the generalization. "My next-door neighbor is seventy-eight years old, and her Social Security check is not sufficient to meet her needs," even though it is a real example, would not be enough to justify change in the Social Security system. Enough examples that would relay that this problem is national in scope would be necessary.

Sign

When a persuader uses a symptom or outward mark to prove existence of a condition, he/she is arguing from sign. For example, where there is smoke, it is a sign of fire. When a flag is flying at half mast, it means that a famous person has died. When a persuader uses argument from sign, he/she must be sure that the sign that is being used to indicate a situation will always at any given time be a sign of that particular condition.

Analogy

Reasoning from analogy consists of providing the recognition of the similarity between two entities as indirect or implied rather than explicit. Because this form of reasoning does not rely on literal resemblance, it may cross the line between species. An example of an analogy might be "Just as an overly protective parent who coddles his child undermines his child's initiative and sense of responsibility, so a nation which coddles its citizens undermines their initiative and sense of responsibility" (McBath 1963, p. 171). The use of analogy is not strong support for a target belief when used exclusively, but is useful for expressing the belief statement in a striking and memorable manner.

Cause-Effect and Method of Residues

Common sense tells us that every event has a cause or several causes. Presenting a series of causes and proving that they are inextricably linked to an effect or effects is a persuasive reasoning process.

The persuader must be sure that the cause is a true cause of a given effect. "I lost my job because Reagan became president" would be a vague cause-effect relationship. The person may have lost his/her job because he/she is incapable or irresponsible. This cause-effect example left too many other alternatives unexplained.

The causes presented must be adequate to produce the alleged effect. "Those three cigarettes she smoked when she was fifteen is the reason she has cancer now at fifty." It would be difficult to persuade a person that only three cigarettes smoked at an early age could be linked to cancer.

The method of residues is another type of cause-effect reasoning. This form of reasoning involves presenting what many would feel were causes of a given event, including the cause that the persuader is claiming to be the valid one. One by one, the persuader shows that each cause is not the reason the event occurred, eliminating all causes except the one that is being claimed. Example: the reason President Carter's presidential term appeared weak was not his youthful staff, Carter's lack of expertise, or a weak secretary of state; therefore, the cause must have been an uncooperative Congress.

Yet, there are other forms of reasoning with an audience that may be effective. What has been labeled "common sense" is really just a way of relating to an audience's beliefs, values, attitudes, and experiences that causes people to say, "That makes sense to me." When reasoning fits the audience's way of seeing things, it does make sense. Consider the following argument against the use of white noise as a mask for loud noise.

Robert Newman, senior vice-president of Bolt, Beranek, and Newman, a Massachusetts company specializing in acoustical engineering, said, "Generating 'white noise' to hide sounds above the annoyance level such as an SST airplane is like using Chanel No. 5 to hide the fact that you haven't bathed for a week" (*Time* May 4, 1970, p. 92). Although acoustics is his business, Newman goes further than to rely on his expertise because he knows his audience *understands* the futility of trying to mask body odors with perfume. Flo Kennedy, a black feminist lawyer, knows how to use evidence in the courtroom. Yet, when addressing women at feminist meetings, she doesn't have to tell them that the proof of inequality isn't in the library: "When you are lying in a ditch with a truck on your ankle, you don't send someone to the library to find out how much the truck weighs. You get someone to get it off" (speech by Flo Kennedy in Fort Worth, Texas, May 1974).

Sometimes common sense has had enormous implications. In 1961, during John F. Kennedy's presidency, there was an international crisis when the secretary-general of the United Nations, Dag Hammarskjöld, was killed in an airplane crash. Instead of following the tradition of appointing another person from a neutral country to replace him, the United Nations seriously considered a proposal from the Soviet Union for a "troika," which is the Russian word for a sled or wagon pulled by three horses. The Russians wanted a triumvirate who would share the responsibilities of the office of secretary-general, one from the Western nations, one from the communist bloc, and one from the emerging Third World nations as a neutral. In reality, the emerging nations were not always neutral, for they were courted with foreign aid from both the power blocs of the world and could sway in either direction. The United States opposed the proposal for fear of two communist-sympathetic leaders against a single Western-affiliated one. For weeks, the United Nations had no secretary-general, and logical reasoning and evidence did nothing to change Russia's mind. Then President Kennedy tried common sense. He invited the Russian ambassador, Andrei Gromyko, to his office, asked him to sit down, and gave him a present! The present was a beautiful parchment copy of the Russian Krylov's fables. The ambassador looked puzzled. The president told him to turn to a certain page and read the fairy tale. It was a story of a troika, but in the story it was a cart that a man hitched to a fish, a swan, and a crab. When he got in and said "Go!" the fish dived into the sea, the swan flew into the sky, and the crab tried to yank it backward. The cart was pulled into a hundred pieces. The ambassador closed the book, thanked the president, and left. The next day, Russia withdrew its troika proposal in favor of a single secretary-general from a neutral nation (Cousins 1971).

In Chapter II, values and group norms were discussed as anchors. They, along with previously held receiver attitudes, can operate as a form of reasoning known as "if . . . then": *if* you value brotherhood (anchor), *then* you should volunteer to help those less fortunate than you (target belief); *if* your group supports fiscal conservatism, *then* you should support candidate X; *if* you like peanut butter, *then* you should also like this candy bar. Because values are so deep-seated and because group norms and attitudes are fairly enduring, they make strong anchors from which to establish a logical connection to a desired target belief. Bem's self-perception theory can also be used in the "if . . . then" reasoning mode. *If* you do something, *then* you must like it.

MOTIVATION

Motivation is the human mobilization of physical and psychological energy in order to fulfill needs, drives, desires, and goals. Hunger is a need, and seeking out food is motivation. The behavior of eating satisfies the hunger need. The direction, intensity, and persistence of a behavioral pattern can often be attributed to our *motives*, which are drives and forces. *Motivational appeals* are persuasive techniques to arouse or appeal to a need, thus creating tension within the receiver if that need is not being met.

Needs, desires, goals, and drives are not necessarily rational, nor are they irrational. They represent how people feel and how they want to be. The advertising industry has for a long time employed motivational researchers who determine prevalent motives of consumers. Most ads appeal to these motives (the need to be sexually attractive, the desire to be recognized, the drive to be successful, or the goal to be rich) but offer a product that they claim—often illogically—will satisfy the need. Neverthe-

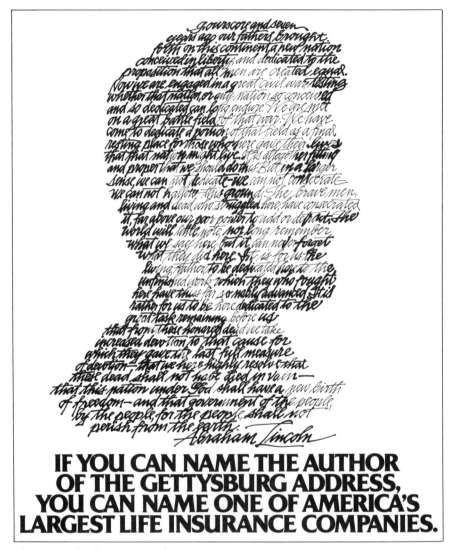

The "If . . . then" reasoning mode. (Time May 11, 1977)

less, many people are motivated to buy these products in the hope of fulfilling their needs.

Needs and drives are common to all cultures. Hunger is common to all people in all societies. The Eskimo may satiate this hunger with blubber, the infant with mashed bananas, and most of us with a hamburger or steak, whichever our pocketbook allows. Ours is a society that teaches us how to fulfill our needs.

Abraham Maslow (1970) developed a theory that suggests that there are two major motivating forces: deficiency and growth. He described people as possessing certain needs, which exist in a hierarchical relationship. He listed the deficiency motives as physiological, safety, belongingness, and esteem. When these motives are satisfied, people are then motivated by the need for growth or self-actualization.

The rank order of the hierarchy is dependent on the satisfaction of each need at the time. This state of satisfaction changes as conditions vary. At one point, for example, a person's need for esteem may outweigh all other needs. It is known that when physical needs such as hunger and fatigue are dominant, a person's thoughts do not turn to other needs such as esteem or self-actualization. Maslow does not believe that these motivations operate in isolation, but that human behavior is multimotivated and reflects his/her integrated wholeness.

Physiological Needs

The physiological needs are food, water, elimination, air, sex, shelter, and sleep. These needs are directly related to self-preservation. None of the other needs will dominate until these needs are satisfied. The term Maslow applied to this priority process is *prepotency*.

Safety Needs

The safety needs consist of a person's desire for order and security. We fear harm or anxiety. Many commercials such as the insurance-company and bank commercials appeal to these needs. The worst riot since the 1960s, which took place in Florida in May 1980, occurred because blacks felt that they no longer had the law and the courts as an avenue for justice. As one of their leaders pointed out, "When people feel that our nation's law no

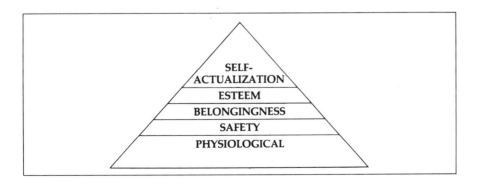

longer protects them, they have lost the last bastion of protection." The promise of intervention by the federal government to see that justice would be done restored some peace to people who believed their safety and security was being threatened.

Belonging and Love Needs

People need to love and be loved. Love includes both romantic love and friendship. A person needs to feel a part of a family and to be accepted as a member of important groups. The important aspect of this need is that it is reciprocal in nature—to love and be loved, to accept and be accepted, and to recognize and be recognized by others.

Esteem Needs

The esteem needs are higher in the hierarchy because they are more active in nature than the comparatively passive belonging needs. Belonging is important, but there comes a time when a person wishes to be singled out and recognized by their family members and group members.

Esteem is twofold in nature. First, it involves the esteem one grants oneself, such as the desire for confidence, independence, and competence. Second, it involves the need for esteem granted to us by others, such as recognition, position of power, and appreciation. Sometimes the two are in conflict.

Self-Actualization

When all other needs are met, an individual is motivated by a need to meet his/her full potential and complete self-fulfillment. There are plateaus and subgoals that one reaches en route to the main goal. Self-actualization for the young is different than it is for the senior citizen. There are many examples of individuals who appear to be actualized. They are competent in their professions and live complete personal lives, and yet, instead of resting on their laurels, they pursue entirely new careers and interests. John Houseman, a famous producer, became an actor at age seventy and gained renewed recognition in the movie and television series *The Paper Chase*.

Maslow lists the desirable characteristics of the self-actualized person or of one who is growing in that direction (Maslow 1970, pp. 153–74, taken from Ross 1974, p. 119):

1. More efficient perception of reality and, consequently, more comfortable relations with it.
2. Increased acceptance of self, of others, and of nature.
3. Spontaneity, simplicity, naturalness.
4. Problem-centered rather than ego-centered.
5. Increased detachment and desire for privacy.
6. Ability to be independent of his/her physical and social environment.
7. Freshness of appreciation and richness of emotional reaction.
8. Higher frequency of "peak," mystic, or transcendent experiences.
9. Increased identification with and feeling for mankind.
10. Deeper, more profound interpersonal relationships.
11. A more democratic character structure.
12. Strongly ethical, clearly distinguishes between means and ends.
13. A philosophical, unhostile sense of humor.
14. A natural, spontaneous creativity.
15. Ability to detach and resist his/her culture.

Maslow's theory is further elaborated by a discussion of eleven of his sixteen motivation propositions (Maslow 1970, pp. 19–38). Ross (1974) states these propositions in the following manner (pp. 121–24):

1. *"The individual is an integrated and organized whole."* (p. 121)

We are motivated as a whole person, not in parts. When our stomachs tell us we are hungry, our feet do not tell us to jog. The whole person becomes involved in the strongest drive at a particular time.

2. *"Using hunger as a paradigm for all other motivations is unsound."* (p. 122)

Hunger, thirst, and other physiological motivations are different from the other motivations because they are identifiable. Other motivations are not so easily identified. When a person sacrifices everything else in life to become a top executive, it is not clear whether the motivation is coming from esteem needs or the need to be important and respected or from belonging needs such as the need to gain approval from a father who never accepted him/her.

3. *"Our desires are usually means to an end rather than ends in themselves."* (p. 122)

Not all goals are conscious ones. It is important, then, to be aware of how one's desires and needs move us toward goals without our awareness. Everyone has said at one time or another, "Now why did I do that?" The answer to that question is not always immediately forthcoming because of the subtlety of how motivations (other than physiological ones) work.

4. *"The ultimate desires of human beings are more alike than their conscious everyday desires."* (p. 122)

The five steps of the hierarchy are shared by all persons. The goals that individuals set to achieve them manifest themselves in different ways. One woman may pursue esteem by maintaining physical beauty while another acquires it by pursuing a Ph.D. Of course, some do both. A man may seek security for himself and his family by purchasing a gun while another may seek security by putting in a burglar alarm system.

5. *"Multiple motivations may exist."* (p. 122)

A talented artist may yearn to go to Europe, engulf himself or herself in the culture, and study art seriously (self-actualization), but may also feel a need to hold a stable job in order to care for his/her mother, the only living relative (love and belonging needs).

6. *"Almost any organismic state of affairs whatsoever is in itself also a motivating state."* (p. 122)

A feeling state acts also as a motivating state. When a person "feels angry," that anger acts as motivation. Motivation underlies every organismic state and, therefore, is constant, never-ending, and fluctuating.

7. *"It is characteristic of the human being that throughout his entire life he is always desiring something."* (p. 122)

Motivational factors are working constantly. When one goal is attained, this means that other needs are relatively satisfied at the moment. Once one goal is satisfied, other motivations become activated. Maslow states, "The human being is never satisfied except in a relative one-step-along-the-path fashion . . . wants seem to arrange themselves in some sort of hierarchy of prepotency" (Maslow 1970, p. 25).

8. *"Atomistic lists of drives or needs are theoretically unsound."* (p. 123)

Atomistic lists of needs imply that they are all equal in potency and probability of appearance. Maslow believes that the probability of one desire emerging to a conscious state is dependent on the satisfaction or dissatisfaction of other desires. All needs are interrelated. One desire may operate as a channel through which another desire is expressed.

9. *"The basis on which any classification of motivational life should be constructed is that of the fundamental goals or needs rather than drives."* (p. 123)

Drives are conscious in nature. Maslow believes that none of the conscious needs and goals is a sound foundation on which to base a motivational life. Rather it is the unconscious goals that provide this foundation.

10. *"The role of cultural determination must be considered, for human motivation rarely actualizes itself in behavior except in relation to the situation and to other people."* (p. 123)

Chapter V addresses itself to this concept. By now we know that all our needs and goals are inextricably linked to the social environment and to those who inhabit it with us.

11. *"We yearn consciously for that which might realistically be attained."* (p. 123)

This phenomenon accounts for the wide variety of goals that exist among individuals, between classes, and between nations. The stereotypic statement "Those people have no desire to better themselves" is indicative of a misunderstanding of this idea. The motivation to become a member of a street gang may be as ultimate a goal in one group as being chairman of the board is to another.

Motivation is an essential ingredient in persuading people to take action. A skillful persuader will (a) appeal to persuadees' motives; (b) remind persuadees that certain needs or goals are unfulfilled; (c) offer a solution in the form of an action that the persuadees are able to take; (d) get some commitment from the persuadees to take action; and (e) show how the desired action can fulfill the needs of the persuadees.

EMOTION

Emotions Are Learned

Associations of feelings with past experiences cause people to have similar feelings in similar situations. Colonel David R. Scott, commander of the Apollo 15 moon mission, describes his feelings when, on the second of three excursions on the lunar surface, he saw the crystalline fragment that has come to be known as Genesis Rock:

I saw the rock perched on a larger rock. In just a few seconds, I observed the parallel grooves that are characteristic of plagioclase, a mineral that is one of the primary components of anorthosite. And anorthosite is thought to be abundant in the ancient lunar highlands and the remnants of the primordial lunar crust. We had hoped to find anorthosite rocks on the moon, such a discovery would help solve a problem about the moon's mass. . . . Thus the discovery of anorthosite was one of our goals, and it was why I radioed to mission control, 'I think we found what we came for.' . . .

I must confess that the sight of that rock, sitting there millions of years waiting for our arrival, set off another wave of excitement for me. It triggered an emotion much like finding the Easter Egg. You know, there are lots of eggs spread across the lawn, but there's only one golden one, and thus it was—The Golden Egg. (*Dallas Morning News*)

The joy Scott felt is the name of a feeling that may have been designated for him by some authority figure. The names for emotions (joy, anger, fear, happiness) were attached to responses that we had at a very early age. A toddler may have been playing on the floor in the kitchen while the mother prepared dinner, when there was a sudden clap of thunder. If the child was startled, the mother may have said, "Don't be afraid." Once learned, the fear of thunder may be a life-long feeling whenever there is a storm.

Emotional responses are brought on by external factors that connect to the individual's inner states. A well-known conceptualization of the determinants of an emotional state is that of S. Schachter, who said that emotion is the joint product of general physiological arousal and situational cues. Interaction of both of these determinants is necessary, according to Schachter, for an emotion to be experienced (Schachter, in Berkowitz 1964). The degree to which the external factors can frustrate or satisfy a need state vary in intensity from a feeling of indifference to a high level of excitement. Different people react differently to the same external stimuli. One person may fear dogs because he/she was bitten by one a long time ago, whereas another person enjoys dogs because he/she happily played with them in the past. Animals, on the other hand, show their reaction in an instinctive and uniform way. Cats all over the world hiss and arch their backs and their hair stands on end when they are afraid. Conversely, humans' emotional reactions have a wide range of demonstration.

There are many classification systems for emotions, but nearly all emotions can be categorized as pleasurable or distressing (Minnick 1968, p. 243).

Importance of Emotion

A persuader needs to understand the importance of the use of emotion in persuasion, and persuadees need to be aware of their own vulnerability to emotional appeals. For most of what is important to an individual is deeply involved in emotion, such as his/her hopes, fears, likes, and ambitions. Emotions are also attached to those qualities that are admired, such as loy-

Fear appeal. (VFW Magazine April 1980)

alty, love, and religion as well as their emotional counterparts. R. W. Rogers and C. W. Deckner stress the importance of the influence of emotions upon attitudes: "The stronger the emotion associated with specific situational cues, the stronger is the attitude toward the source of emotional arousal" (1975, p. 222).

Fear Appeals

Persuadees are exposed to fear appeals daily. The American Lung Association and other health associations use fear appeals that urge listeners to take care of themselves and to contribute funds for further research. Insurance companies tell of emotional consequences for widows and children whose deceased husbands and fathers were not insured. Ministers describe the horrible fate of those who reject salvation.

Fear is associated with mobilizing oneself to avoid or escape danger. Thus, there is a close relationship between the emotion of fear and behavior. For this reason, the effects of fear appeals on both attitudes and

Feelings of love and contentment. (*People* August 4, 1980)

behavior have been carefully studied. Studies reviewed by H. Leventhal (in Berkowitz V 1970) support the generalization that high fear appeals facilitate persuasion. There are other studies, however, that indicate that low fear appeals are more influential in persuasion. These differences could be attributed to the fact that there are variables that are influential other than fear appeals, such as personality type, importance of the topic to the receiver, the situation, and the credibility of the source (Miller 1963).

A fear appeal may be defined as one that claims that harm will befall the persuadee or someone close to him/her if there is failure to adopt the end goal of the persuasion (Burgoon 1974, p. 94). Fear thus motivates protective behavior (Janis, in Berkowitz III 1967). Michael Burgoon summarizes the research on fear appeals (1974, pp. 94–95). A high fear appeal is one that dramatically demonstrates the results. A graphic picture, used by the Right to Life organization, of an unborn fetus after a saline abortion is an example. A high fear appeal is more effective with the use of evidence and when it is aimed at someone important to the persuadee. A low fear appeal states the issue in a passive manner, such as citing a study that includes alarming statistics.

High fear appeals need to be used with discretion because they can sometimes cause a boomerang effect in which the persuadee rejects the whole idea the persuader is trying to present.

Other Emotional Appeals

It is unfortunate that much of the research in emotional appeals has concentrated on fear. It should be possible to assess the usefulness of appeals to happiness, elation, and joy. There is research dealing with cooperative and competitive behavior. but not much of it includes the use of communication, let alone persuasion. As we saw in Chapter IV, people tend to model themselves after those whom they like or admire. Perhaps an admired persuader could appeal to what makes him/her happy, and persuadees might adopt the desired behavior with the end goal of being happy too. There is no research to either substantiate or deny the possibility.

There are studies that support reward as an incentive to behavior change (Rogers 1971). If rewards result in pleasurable emotions, then this would seem to indicate that appeals to rewards would be an effective emotional appeal for behavior change. Remember, however, that rewards for behavior change do not necessarily result in attitude change, whereas non-rewards for behavior do because of dissonance production (see "Cognitive Dissonance," pp. 56–59).

There will probably be communication research that concentrates on the pleasurable emotions. Meanwhile we can only recommend it as an appeal that should seem to be effective as a form of positive reinforcement.

Another means of emotional persuasion is the use of intense language. Language intensity is defined as "the quality of language that indicates the degree to which the speaker's attitude toward a concept deviates from neutrality" (Bowers 1964, p. 416). The emotional state of the receiver at the time the intense language is used has a significant influence on how the intense language affects him/her. When a person is under stress, he/she is more responsive to messages that employ low levels of intensity than to high-intensity language levels. Individuals under stress are more sensitive to overall language differences than those under normal conditions. People on the whole tend to react negatively to language that's extremely intense (Burgoon and King 1974).

Types of Language Intensity

1. Use of qualifiers The use of strong qualifiers is a form of language intensity. The use of "certainly" instead of "probably," "extremely dislike" instead of "don't care for" are examples of making a statement more intense through language choice (Bettinghaus and Burgoon 1980, in Roloff and Miller, 1980, p. 151).

2. Appropriateness People tend to have preconceived ideas about what is appropriate and what is inappropriate. In our culture, persuadees believe that it is appropriate for male persuaders to use intense language but inappropriate for female persuaders (Burgoon and Stewart 1975, in Roloff and Miller 1980, p. 153).

Persuaders who are highly credible sources can be more effective through the use of intense language than those who have low source credibility. We expect those we admire to be forceful just as we expect males to be aggressive, and forceful language is identified with these characteristics (Burgoon 1975, in Roloff and Miller 1980, p. 152).

3. Metaphor Theorists have universally accepted the power of the metaphor. J. W. Bowers conducted a study that proved the power of the metaphor. The author provided four argumentative speeches that were allegedly written by "(1) a well-known college president favoring the raising of college admission standards; (2) a Democratic senator favoring the Peace Corps; (3) a prominent home economist opposing women's fashion change; and (4) a former president of an eastern university opposing progressive education" (1964, p. 416).

Bowers classified a term as metaphorical "whenever it took some effort, however slight, to transfer its denotation from that with which the term was habitually associated to that with which it was associated in the context of the communications" (1964, p. 419). Some of the metaphorical terms used were "plagiarizing" as opposed to "unoriginal" in its design, "stampede" when it describes the actions of women purchasing clothing, and the use of "following the herd" instead of "conforming."

Bowers also revealed that the most powerful metaphors could be broken down into two categories: sex metaphors and death metaphors (1964, p. 419).

Some of the effective sex metaphors were references to fashion publicists as "pimps," students in progressive schools being "raped" by the system, and college admission standards allowing a "perversion" of the goals of education.

Some of the effective death metaphors were the "decay" of American education, the "murder" of traditional education, and the use of the word "ghastly" when referring to women's fashions (Bowers 1964, p. 420).

MESSAGE STRATEGIES

Since successful persuasion usually results in the persuadee feeling that agreement has been given because something has been gained and not because there has been a forced agreement, it is necessary to consider what strategies the persuader might use to enhance interactive cooperation. A *strategy* is defined as a group of techniques toward which potential persuadees tend to respond similarly (Marwell and Schmitt 1967, p. 351). Strategies focus on the characteristics of the persuader or on persuadee outcomes rather than on content of message. Strategies may relate to the persuader's authority, expertise, and admirable qualities or to the consequences that may be reaped by the persuadees if they comply. It is useful for a persuader to have a list of potential strategies from which to choose, but the persuader then has to translate a specific strategy into a specific body of message content. The persuader has certain rhetorical "choices" to make in message preparation. The choices focus on how best to achieve a desired response from the persuadees.

Marwell and Schmitt (1967) have a list of sixteen compliance-gaining techniques which they used with students who were given hypothetical situations and told to determine what they thought were appropriate and effective strategies. The students clustered the sixteen techniques into five groups: expertise, personal commitments, interpersonal commitments, punishing activity, and rewarding activity (pp. 156–58). Miller, Boster, Roloff, and Seibold (1977) extended the use of the sixteen strategies to a diverse group of people and varied the hypothetical situations. Their clusters were all situational and were grouped according to interpersonal, noninterpersonal, short-term consequences, and long-term consequences. They found that their subjects preferred friendly strategies, especially in interpersonal situations.

The following list of strategies is offered to the persuader from which choices can be made. The first sixteen come from Marwell and Schmitt (1967), and the last four come from other research and classroom situations. Note how many strategies utilize the "if . . . then" form of reasoning.

1. promise—If you comply, then I will reward you.
2. threat—If you do not comply, then I will punish you.
3. positive—If you comply, then you will be rewarded because of positive outcomes resulting from the compliance.
4. negative expertise—If you comply, then you will be punished because of negative outcomes resulting from the compliance.
5. liking—The persuader is friendly and helpful, thus putting the persuadee in a good frame of mind.
6. pregiving—The persuader rewards the persuadee before requesting compliance.
7. aversive stimulation—The persuader punishes the persuadee, making cessation contingent on compliance.
8. debt—You owe me compliance because I have done favors for you in the past.
9. moral appeal—If you are moral, then you will comply.
10. positive self-feeling—If you comply, then you will feel better.
11. negative self-feeling—If you do not comply, then you will feel worse about yourself.
12. positive altercasting—A person with good qualities would comply.
13. negative altercasting—Only a person with bad qualities would not comply.
14. altruism—I need your compliance very badly, so do it for me.
15. positive esteem—If you comply, then people you value will think better of you.
16. negative esteem—People you value will think worse of you if you do not comply.
17. conformity—You should comply to be like others with whom you associate.
18. modeling—You should comply in order to be like an admirable or well-liked person.

19. internal refutation—Since you are thinking of reasons not to comply, here are better reasons to answer your objections.
20. foot-in-the-door—Since you complied with a smaller request in the past, you should be able to comply with the present larger request.

Strategies 1, 3, 10, 15, and 18 offer positive outcomes as an end result of compliance. They hold out a promise of some reward, whether from the persuader, the consequences of an act, the self, other people, or identification. Strategies 2, 4, 11, and 16 offer negative outcomes as an end result of noncompliance. They threaten punishment from the persuader, the consequences of an act, the self, or other people. Strategies 5, 6, and 7 work on the persuadee before compliance occurs to put the persuadee in a receptive state, to bribe the persuadee to comply, or to punish until compliance occurs. Strategies 8, 9, 12, 13, and 14 are all value-related and are contingent upon those particular values—paying a debt, exercising morality, wanting to be thought of as "good" and not "bad," and altruism—being sufficiently strong anchors for the persuadees. Strategy 17 is for the persuadee who values group membership, peer affiliation, and conformity. The importance of group membership has already been discussed in Chapter II. Strategy 19 gets into the unspoken objections to compliance, but lets the persuadee know that the objections can be overcome. For example, a persuader might say to a persuadee, "You're probably thinking that that's only one example. Well, let me give you some more" or "You're probably thinking, that would never happen to me. Well, let me show you just how likely it is that it will." Finally, Strategy 20 is one that is based on the persuader having made an earlier request which was much smaller in order to increase the likelihood of the persuadee's compliance with a subsequent larger request. It is the only strategy here that requires exposure to prior persuasion. It needs further explanation.

The foot-in-the-door technique is one that consumers should recognize, for anytime a manufacturer gives away a free sample, it is with the desired end that the sampler become a regular product customer. Trying a free sample is complying with a small request; becoming a regular buyer of the product is complying with a larger request. Freedman and Fraser (1966) report on experiments that substantiate that people who comply with initial small requests are more likely to comply with subsequently larger demands. People who complied with a request by one communicator to put a sign in their yard or sign a petition for keeping the state beautiful were likely to place a large, ugly sign promoting auto safety on their front lawns when asked to do so by a different communicator two weeks later (Roloff and Miller 1980). Keep in mind that it is the second request that is the ultimate desired response. To use this technique, a persuader has to arrange to make an initial request at an earlier time. It would be possible, however, if everyone in a persuader's audience had complied with a smaller request in another situation to utilize this in a single communication. There is another technique that is often discussed along with the foot-in-the-door strategy, although it is different in approach. This is called "door in the face" and refers to a demand for something very large which will presumably be refused. Then, when a second, much smaller request is made, the persuadee is likely to comply. This technique seems to work only in bargaining situations in which mutual concessions can be arrived at interpersonally or in which negotiations are expected to be made.

Finally, some of what is known about attitudes can be used strategically. As was discussed in Chapter III with regard to balance theory, human beings desire and even need psychological balance. When imbalance occurs as the result of cognitive dissonance, incongruity, or conflicting attitudes toward two sources or a source and an idea, subjects will seek a renewed state of homeostasis. As was already discussed at the end of Chapter III, a persuader can deliberately attempt to create imbalance in a persuadee and then offer restoration of balance with the adoption of a new attitude. For example, suppose that a persuadee is an ardent Democrat who also strongly values financial security and social order. If this Democrat felt that the Democratic administration had brought on a recession and had been ineffectual in restoring order to the national and international chaos, he/she may have voted for a Republican president in the 1980 election. When a Democrat votes for a Republican, a state of cognitive dissonance often occurs. A persuader could encourage a positive attitude toward voting Republican by demonstrating the imbalance created when this particular person would support the Democrat and be for conservative fiscal policy at the same time. This may be a more unfortunate imbalance than that which would be created by voting for a Republican while being for fiscal security. If fiscal security were a greater concern for the persuadee than party loyalty, the persuader should point this out.

The choice of strategies as well as evidence, reasoning, emotional appeals, message purpose, and message situation have to be given careful consideration by the persuader when designing a message and by the persuadee when receiving a message.

SUMMARY

The persuasive message is a series of belief statements that link an object to an attribute such as another object, a concept, an event, or a goal. The message includes the content, language, and strategies. The message is facilitated by factors such as the situation, evidence, reasoning, organization, motivation, and strategies.

The persuader needs to know if his/her message is discrepant from the position(s) held by the audience so that he/she might develop a message to reduce or eliminate the discrepancy. It is important for the persuader to be sensitive to persuadee expectations of a persuasive interaction and, certainly, to try to discern persuadee knowledge and philosophy toward the subject matter.

The persuader should determine the message purpose as the response that is desired from the persuadee. This is the target belief statement. Target beliefs need to be supported by evidence, although evidence itself does not guarantee persuadee acceptance of the target belief.

Evidence is data that may be factual or inferential. It takes the form of examples, statistics, and testimony. Evidence is useful to persuasion because it enhances source credibility and learning, audiences expect it to be used, and it enables the audience to perceive things in a new way. Evidence does not, however, compensate for poor delivery and is unaffected by the medium through which the message is sent.

Reasoning, the process of establishing the probability of a belief statement, is used to redirect the persuadee's perception of the world. Yet, other factors such as receiver personality and perceived source credibility influence one's ability to make validity judgments. Both formal reasoning as well as common-sense approaches are useful reasoning modes.

Motivation is relevant to needs, drives, desires, and goals. Thus, a persuader uses motivational appeals to both arouse and satisfy a need. Human needs, according to Maslow, are arranged in a hierarchical pattern, yet they are all interrelated. Motivation is essential in order to get people to act.

Emotions are feeling states that people develop internally as the result of external factors that may stimulate feeling states. Emotions are either pleasurable or distressing. Emotional appeals can be used by a persuader to get persuadees to respond with feeling—sometimes with intense feeling—but should be used with care. It is probably best if emotional appeals are balanced with reasoning and evidence.

Finally, there are twenty strategies for persuasion. They give the persuader certain choices in designing a message. These strategies have to be considered and chosen according to other factors in the overall persuasive situation.

A message is the product of careful design by the persuader. There are many possibilities, but the persuader has to decide on what seems to be the best approach. Persuadees who are exposed to the message can be selectively critical of it if they are aware of what factors go into its design.

KEY WORDS

Message purpose	Analogy
Evidence	Method of residues
Statement of fact	Motivation
Inference	Maslow's hierarchy of human
Use of statistics	motivation
Testimony	Fear appeals
Reasoning	Language intensity
Generalization from example	Strategies
Sign	Foot-in-the-door technique
	Door-in-the-face technique

EXERCISES

1. Select a speech from the periodical *Vital Speeches* on a topic about which you know something. Find an example, statistics, and testimony in the speech, and evaluate the use of evidence.
2. Use the same speech to find examples of reasoning. Identify the kind of reasoning (cause-effect, generalization from example, etc.).
3. Select a story from the front page of your student or local newspaper. Distinguish between statements of fact and statements of inference.
4. Write two short descriptions of a person whom you know well. Use intense language in the first and objective language in the second. Both descriptions should be positive. Read them to the class, and ask for reactions.
5. Give an example from your own experience when a fear appeal affected your judgment. If you had waited to make your decision, would it have been the same?
6. Find five television or magazine advertisements that represent each one of Maslow's hierarchy of needs.
7. Analyze the use of evidence in an advertisement. Is the use of evidence valid?
8. Pretend that you are a political candidate running for a national office. You are to make a sixty-second television commercial with a target audience of lower-to middle-class working people with mortgages and large families who go to church regularly. What persuasive strategies would you use?
9. Start a clipping file of evidence that may be of use to you the next time you give a speech.

READINGS

Janis, I. L. "Effects of Fear Arousal on Attitude Change: Recent Developments in Theory and Experimental Research." In *Advances in Experimental Social*

Psychology, ed. L. Berkowitz, vol. III. New York: Academic Press, 1967.

Leventhal, H. "Findings and Theory in the Study of Fear Communications." In *Advances in Experimental Social Psychology*, ed. L. Berkowitz, vol. V. New York: Academic Press, 1970.

McCroskey, James C. "A Summary on the Effects of Evidence in Persuasive Communication." *Quarterly Journal of Speech* 55 (1969):169–76.

Marwell, G., and **Schmitt, D. R.** "Dimensions of Compliance-gaining Behavior: An Empirical Analysis." *Sociometry* 30 (1967):350–64.

Maslow, Abraham. *Motivation and Personality.* New York: Harper & Row, 1970.

Minnick, Wayne C. *The Art of Persuasion.* Boston: Houghton–Mifflin, 1968.

Roloff, Michael E., and **Miller, Gerald R.,** eds. *Persuasion: New Directions in Theory and Research.* Beverly Hills, Calif.: Sage, 1980.

Schacter, S. "The Interaction of Cognitive and Physiological Determinants of the Emotional State." In *Advances in Experimental Social Psychology*, ed. L. Berkowitz, vol. I. New York: Academic Press, 1964.

8

ORGANIZATION AND LANGUAGE AS FACILITATING FACTORS

OBJECTIVES

Upon completion of this chapter you should be able to:

1. Understand that the act of perception is a method of defining relationships between the self and what is observed.
2. Define *structuralism* and be able to relate it to the organization of speeches.
3. Define and understand the importance of organization in persuasion.
4. Understand how internal and external attention factors are used in persuasive communication.
5. Utilize the principles of organization to facilitate a message.
6. Use language for clarity and interest.
7. Use language to create or reinforce an experience.

As we saw in Chapter I, when a persuader observes reality, he/she does so according to his/her perceptual filters. Observing reality through filters could be thought of as a *method* of perceiving. In fact, every person's method of perceiving contains an inherent bias, which affects what is perceived to a significant degree. A persuader is bound to *create* something of what he/she observes, and, thus, a relationship between the persuader and the observed is established. That relationship subsequently guides the construction of the persuasive message.

Likewise, what the persuadee observes in the persuasive message is also a relationship between the persuadee and the persuader's message. That relationship is created by the persuadee, but it is guided by the persuader's development of the message.

The relationship that is established between the persuader sending a message and the persuadee receiving it is, thus, a relationship between relationships. The concept that is being stressed here is a way of looking at the world and saying that the world is made up of relationships. This way of thinking is called "structuralism." A structuralist defines the relations between sets or subsets of elements that make up the whole.

Structuralists may be found in many fields from mathematics to anthropology. Structuralists such as Claude Lévi-Strauss in anthropology, Roman Jakobson in linguistics, Jean Piaget in psychology, and François Jacob in biology believe that there is in the human being an innate, genetically transmitted, and determined mechanism that acts as a structuring force (Lane 1970, p. 15). Structuralists believe that we have a universal capacity to formulate structure and to submit our own nature to the demands of structuring. Structuralism is, in fact, so much a part of human nature that one could say, as Terence Hawkes has said, "To be human is to be a structuralist" (1977, p. 15).

The human desire for structure is manifest in the way a person spends time, manages money, or drives to work or school. When some semblance of order is apparent, confusion and frustration are avoided (Makay and Sawyer 1973, p. 142). Structure and its resulting organization are necessary for balance and development. Piaget discusses structure as an arrangement of entities that embodies the idea of wholeness—that is, a sense of internal coherence. The individual parts of the whole are not the same as when they were independent parts in a separate existence. As constituent parts of the whole in a special combination, they take on a special character.

Scholars and researchers throughout the history of our discipline have pointed out the importance of organization to message preparation. Organization is important to both the persuader and persuadee. Through organization, the persuader can evaluate the use and placement of evidence and strategies and make decisions about the interrelatedness of ideas and supporting material so that an orderly picture of the whole will emerge. The single piece of evidence takes on a different meaning in relationship to other pieces of evidence and strategies. For the persuadee, organization facilitates an understanding of how the persuader perceives reality. It also aids persuadee retention. Listeners find it difficult to remember evidence and what it relates to unless it is couched in a clear structural pattern. The organization of a message, thus, refers to the relationship of a target belief, supporting beliefs, and evidence in a structure that may appear clear and logical to both the persuader and persuadee. It most accurately reflects the persuader's relationship to the world since he/she is the one who structures the message. Nevertheless, just as message content is gathered with specific persuadees in mind, organization also must be specifically directed to an audience.

It is necessary for the persuader to know where the persuadees are in relation to reality when they come to the persuasive act and where he/she wants them to be at the close of the persuasive message. It is important, therefore, to carefully choose and state the target belief and selected supporting belief statements that the persuader wishes the audience to accept and to phrase them in such a manner that they reflect the audience's beliefs, values, and perceptions of the world.

A well-organized speech should lead the audience through the interactive-dependency philosophy, whereby the audience can see its expectations being met and the persuader makes clear what he/she expects from the audience.

PERSUASIVE EFFECTS OF ORGANIZATION

How does a persuader decide where to put the strongest argument? There have been contradictory findings in studies concerning whether the argument presented first has more effect than the one presented last. F. Lund's (1925) study showed that primacy (first main idea) was the most effective. When this study was replicated by C. I. Hovland and W. Mandell's study (1952), it was contradicted, and recency (last main idea) was shown to be the most effective (in Karlins and Abelson 1970).

In the mid-1960s, R. Lana and R. Rosnow, through a series of studies, discovered that the primacy-recency question was complicated by a vast amount of variables. R. Rosnow and E. Robinson's (1967) conclusions give us the best insight on ordering effects up to this point (in Karlins and Abelson 1970).

Instead of a general law of primacy or recency, there exists an assortment of variables, some of which produce primacy, others of which produce recency, and still others of which produce either primacy or recency, depending on their placement and utilization in a two-sided message. Controversial topics, interesting or nonsalient subject matter, and familiar issues tend to produce primacy. On the other hand, uninteresting subject matter, moderately unfamiliar issues, and salient topics tend to produce recency (Karlins and Abelson 1970, p. 28–29).

If arguments for one side of an issue are perceived to be stronger than arguments for the other side, then, naturally, the arguments perceived to be stronger have the advantage.

Reinforcement can act as a variable as well. If an argument reminds the persuadee of a recent rewarding experience, that argument will take precedence. Conversely, if the argument is associated with a recent punishing event, the argument that is perceived as farther removed in time from the dissatisfying incident will take precedence (Rosnow and Robinson 1967, in Karlins and Abelson 1970, pp. 28–29).

A persuader also must make a decision about whether to present only his/her side of the issue or include the other side of the issue as well. Research indicates that when the audience is favorable, or when the persuader's position is the only one presented, or when immediate, though temporary, opinion change is desired, then a one-sided argument needs to be presented (Karlins and Abelson 1970, p. 22). If, however, the audience is initially unfavorable to the persuader's stance, or if the audience will be later exposed to the opposite side, it is best, then, to present a two-sided argument (Karlins and Abelson 1970, p. 22).

It is often effective to present both sides of the argument because (1) it implies that the persuader is being objective; (2) it impresses audience members with the fact that they are being treated as informed, mature people; and (3) when a persuader presents both sides, it gives him/her the opportunity to anticipate and deal with counterarguments that may exist in the mind of the persuadee (Karlins and Abelson 1970, p. 25).

Disorganization, on the other hand, appears to negatively affect comprehension in written communication, but has doubtful effects one way or the other in oral communication (Beighley 1952).

The conclusion can be drawn that organization—or lack of it—does not "make or break" a persuader. It is how the organization is used to present the material with clarity and interest that makes order in presentation important (Makay and Sawyer 1973, p. 141).

PERSUASIVE USE OF ORGANIZATION

All aspects of organization need to be used for the purpose of creating a direct relationship between the audience and the persuader's stance. A persuasive effort will probably be ineffective if its organization suits only the persuader's needs. Audience preferences must dominate the phrasing of the main idea. The quesion "What is the audience's point of view that must be taken into account if my proposal is to win acceptance?" should dominate the persuader's organization efforts. The persuader then makes choices about ordering ideas strategically. These choices must be dominated by the persuader's anticipation of the audience's responses. What do the persuadees already believe and agree with and what must they agree to accept in order to yield to the persuader's efforts?

A unifying theme that constantly points to the target belief needs to be chosen and woven throughout the fabric of the persuasive act. Martin Luther King's famous speech "I Have a Dream," delivered at the Lincoln Memorial, August 28, 1963, is an effective example of the use of a unifying theme. His speech builds to a climactic use of the "I Have a Dream" theme as he speaks of the plight and the hopes of black Americans:

So, I say to you my friends, that even though we must face the difficulties of today and tomorrow, I still have a dream. It is a dream deeply rooted in the American dream that one day this nation will rise up and live out the true meaning of its creed—we hold these truths to be self-evident, that all men are created equal.

I have a dream that one day on the red hills of Georgia, sons of former slaves and sons of former slave owners will be able to sit down together at the table of brotherhood.

I have a dream that one day even the state of Mississippi, a state sweltering with the heat of oppression, will be transformed into an oasis of freedom and justice.

I have a dream my four little children will one day live in a nation where they will not be judged by the color of their skin but by the content of their character. I have a dream today!

I have a dream that one day down in Alabama, with its vicious racists with its governor having his lips drip with the words of interposition and nullification, that one day, right there in Alabama, little black boys and black girls will be able to join hands with little white boys and white girls as sisters and brothers. I have a dream today!

Efforts should be made to emphasize anchors with which both persuader and persuadee agree. The goal of the organization should be a unified effort aimed at the audience. It helps if the persuader can understand how the persuadee relates to reality.

The main position should be stated in terms of the reaction desired from the audience. A persuader should not say something general like "A sensible diet can reduce stress." Instead, the persuader should be specific and say something like "Unless you take your life in your own hands by avoiding sugar and increasing your intake of fruits, grains, and vegetables, you may subject yourself to stress-related diseases." Then, the main ideas should be stated in such a way as to get the greatest acceptability from the audience, and these ideas should be arranged in an order that leads the audience by easy stages to an acceptance of the proposal. The ideas and evidence should be drawn together with the aid of internal summaries, and the conclusion should point the audience directly toward acceptance of the proposal.

It is important, at this point, to examine how an audience perceives and attends to the elements of a persuasive act. Before looking at ways to organize a speech, let us look at perception and attention.

PERCEPTION

A person's perception of events determines which of those events he/she will attend. Perception is defined as "the assigning of immediate meaning to sensory data by the central nervous system. After perception has been modified, interpreted, or evaluated by extended and complex thought, it becomes a cognition" (Minnick 1968, p. 34). There are two differences between a perception and a cognition: a perception is immediate, a cognition is not; a cognition is also more complex than a perception.

Perception, then, is the process of extracting information from the world outside us as well as from within ourselves. Henry Miller described perception in this way: "The only difference in life is your point of view, how you look at the world. The world does not change, you change. And how do you change? By your different attitude. Whether you see it from down here, like the frog, . . . or up above, like the eagle. Or still higher, like the gods" (Gordon 1971, p. 233).

Each individual possesses his/her own private perceptual field that is unique to him/her. This perceptual field is formed by the influences of values, roles, group norms, and self-image. These factors color the ways in which a person perceives the events around him/her.

The persuader then practices effective communication by being aware that it is "the process by which a speaker manipulates symbols within his perceptual world and, through a complex process of message exchange with a listener, alters the listener's perceptual world in ways the speaker desires" (Hart, Friedrich, and Brooks 1975, p. 61).

So it is, then, that a persuadee must perceive a persuader's efforts before attention can be gained and maintained. If the persuasive effect does not survive the persuadee's perceptual field, then all other efforts are futile.

Perception is strongly influenced by an individual's needs and wants. We hear what we want to hear, see what we want to see, and this is referred to as selective perception. Perception is also influenced by one's physical state. There are times when a person is ill or weary, and perception operates at minimum capacity. Excess worry also influences what we perceive and how we perceive it.

To what degree does attention influence action? It promotes action by determining stimuli to which people will respond. As was learned in Chapter V, individuals perceive their wants in different ways. The following narrative is an excellent example. Saul Alinsky was training his neighborhood organizers in the different ways people perceive:

In Los Angeles four staff members and I were talking in front of the Biltmore Hotel when I demonstrated the point, saying: "Look, I am holding a ten-dollar bill in my hand. I propose to walk around the Biltmore Hotel, a total of four blocks, and try to give it away. This will certainly be outside of everyone's experience. You four walk behind me and watch the faces of the people I'll approach. I am going to go up to them holding out this ten-dollar bill and say, 'Here, take this.' My guess is that everyone will back off, look confused, insulted, or fearful, and want to get away from this nut fast. From their experience when someone approaches them he is either out to ask for instructions or to panhandle—particularly the way I'm dressed, no coat or tie."

I walked around, trying to give the ten-dollar bill away. The reactions were all "within the experiences of the people." About three of them seeing the ten-dollar bill, spoke first—"I'm sorry, I don't have any change." Others hurried past saying, "I'm sorry I don't have any money on me right now," as though I had been trying to get money from them instead of trying to give them money. One young woman flared up, almost screaming, "I'm not that kind of girl and if you don't get away from here, I'll call a cop!" Another woman in her thirties shouted, "I don't come that cheap!" There was one man who stopped and said, "What kind of a con game is this?" and then walked away. Most of the people responded with shock, confusion, and silence, and they quickened their pace and sort of walked around me." (1971, pp. 86–87)

ATTENTION

The model of persuasion in Chapter I emphasizes the passage of the message through the persuadee's perceptual filter. Sometimes the message never reaches the perceptual filter because it fails to capture the attention of the audience. W. J. McGuire (1969) says that many failures at persuasion originate at the initial decoding stage, which includes attention, rather than at the yielding stage. Attention involves methods that facilitate decoding by provoking listeners to attend and listen. *Attention* is defined as the process of selecting a particular stimulus of the many available in one's perceptual field and focusing upon it until it becomes sharp and clear while the others recede to indistinctness or until one's channels are cleared of competing information (Minnick 1968, p. 53).

In order to better understand attention and how to gain it in others, one must be aware of the factors of attention that are both external and internal.

External Factors

External factors come from outside the individual and are physical in nature. The following external attention factors have been adapted from Minnick (1968, pp. 59–60).

1. A phenomenon is *striking and conspicuous*, such as a bright color or a loud noise. The sound of a sonic blast overhead distracts us in the same way as a camera flash in our eyes does.
2. A phenomenon that gains attention in *contrast* with another phenomenon is easily noticed. When the workman's jackhammer outside the window stops during lunch, the silence gains attention. A mother's attention is attracted when toddlers in another room become quiet. Something small is more noticeable when placed next to something large.
3. *Novelty* gains attention. College streakers always gather a crowd. Advertisers have learned that tunes about commodities are successful because viewers find themselves humming the tunes. (Look at how the "Be a Pepper" tune caught on!)
4. *Movement and change* in any aspect of our environment gain attention. An object that is in movement is more exciting than an object that is static. The persuader who *shows* us how exciting exercising can be is going to gain more attention than the persuader who just tells us it is.
5. Just as *repetition* is often an excellent persuasive device to establish clarity and understanding for the persuadee, so it is also an effective attention device. Advertisers know that a single showing of a commercial on television or an ad in only one magazine is ineffective, for it is the repetition that sells the product.

Internal Factors

These come from inside the individual and are activated by one's wants and needs. There are some stimuli that are fairly constant from person to person. These have been adapted from H. Simons (1976, pp. 174–175).

1. The *vital*, the *immediate*, the *tangible*, the *near-at-hand* can be internal attention factors. In the discussion of motivation in the previous chapter, it was learned that some things are so vital to us that, at times, other needs become less important. When one's safety or security is threatened, for example, all attention centers on this fact. That which is personal and close to home commands more attention than that which is impersonal and far away.

2. *Drama, conflict,* and *suspense* have theatrical aspects and, therefore, command attention. Building up to a dénouement is interesting and irresistible.

3. The need for *exploration* and *mastery,* and the *fulfillment of curiosity* are strong motivators for people who will endure a great deal in order to learn, to grow, and to become knowledgeable. That which holds the promise of learning to master something or of answering questions gains attention.

4. In the discussion of balance theory in Chapter III, it was concluded that people need balance as well as closure, with all things fitting together. Therefore, *resolution, completion,* and *rebalancing* gain attention as a result or outgrowth of this need.

5. Another common need shared by all persons is the need for *release, escape,* and *enjoyment.* This is why humor is such a successful attention-getting device as well as anything that helps us escape from worries, upsetting experiences, and anger.

6. People's attention is easily held if it only requires *minimal effort* on their part to attend. An interesting communication requires less attention effort than a dull one.

Why does a person pay attention to some things and not to others? We attend to (1) those things that are so striking that we cannot help but pay attention to them (involuntary); (2) those things that are necessary to our needs and goals (voluntary); and (3) those things for which we are looking (anticipatory).

Involuntary attention factors dominate the perceptual field whether or not one wishes them to. Things like bright lights, loud noises, sudden movements, and anything that is novel are examples.

Since voluntary attention is motivated by needs and drives, a person's background, interests, wants, and goals determine to what stimulus he or she will attend. A study conducted by A. Hastorf and H. Cantril (1954) viewed reactions of Dartmouth and Princeton students to a particularly "rough and dirty" football game between their two schools. The result was that Dartmouth students saw fewer of their team's infractions of the rules than did the Princeton students and saw more of Princeton's infractions than did the Princeton students.

Anticipatory attention occurs when a person is aware of a need and searches the environment for the fulfillment of that need (Minnick 1968, p. 60). When we know what we are looking for, we tend to find it. Navy plane spotters in World War II were able to identify planes as friend or enemy because they were trained to be alert observers—to know what to look for. When a loudspeaker blares "Now hear this," it causes us to anticipate a message.

APPLICATIONS TO PERSUASION

A persuader must seek to serve as a selector of the attention of the persuadee. Psychologist M. D. Vernon says, "Normal consciousness, perception, and thought can be maintained only in a constantly changing environment" (Martin and Andersen 1968, p. 127). The strategy, therefore, must be to provide in delivery a changing milieu and in organization an ever-changing view.

Delivery can gain and sustain attention through actions, gestures, voice, and facial expressions. The use of concrete sensory impressions in the form of vivid descriptions that the persuader can see, hear, or imagine are excellent devices to maintain attention. Harold Nicolson's diary of London in World War II includes a superb description of a 1940 bomb blitz. The description creates concrete sensory impressions bound to gain and maintain attention.

It was a bright, star-filled night, a good English or Maine summer night. I even felt warm as I sat in the car, and the warmth made me sleepy. I guess I had almost fallen asleep when I heard the buzzing, low rumble that all of us, from babies and animals on up (or down) came automatically to identify as a V-I, or flying bomb. The sound was quite clear and it seemed to be growing. I must have started back to sleep despite the warning sound and my now acute sense of self-preservation. Suddenly I sat straight up in the car and began fumbling for the door. The sound that had stirred me before now began to frighten me with its volume and quality. This sound was beginning to go into an unfamiliar new high pitch. It is a sound no man can describe with words, since the words, while they may spell out the sounds cannot become loud or soft on the printed page. Even if they could, I doubt if any words could mushroom to the height of this sound that I was hearing now, sitting there in a tiny auto in the heart of London. . . . With a noise that I hope I shall never hear again, and certainly I never imagined could come into the world, something straight ahead of me began to disintegrate into tiny particles of noise. The explosion was a shaking and rushing of all the air in the world straight at me, and at no other human being. It was a combination of sound and fury that made me think at the moment of a cork on water, the cork having just as much control over its destiny as I had at that fraction of life. I was not in the driver's seat at all. Something big and boisterous was in the driver's seat, pushing me around. (*Saturday Review* August 5, 1967, p. 16)

The use of contrast, movement, and change are devices that provide variety and maintain attention. An example of the use of contrast may be found in a statement by Eugene McCarthy "We have good highways from one slum to another, one polluted stream to another, and one bad educational system to another" (Adler 1969).

An example of movement and change is drawn from a speech on vandalism by Philip C. Ritterbush:

The setting: A typical grade school . . . street lights cast shadows onto the blackboards with their childishly scrawled alphabets barely [distinguishable] in the gloom and books and paper laid away in the night. The stage is silent and still; the absence of the laughing school children can be keenly felt in the way every echo is cushioned and lost in dark corridors. Then a furtive movement is seen in the hall and the door with its Red Cross sticker and child-made calendar swings slowly open and two shadows move slowly into the room. Suddenly the room is filled with flying papers and the sound of silence. The "market" with its toy register, empty soap and food boxes, and make-believe posters which was so carefully closed before the final bell with loving hands meets another kind of caress and goes crashing to the floor. Screams of laughter greet each new exploit and reach a peak as the brand new globe which the PTA had held a special bake sale to buy, flies across the room and shatters against the wall. The shadows leave the room and fade off down the corridor and the stage is once more silent, but for an occasional roar or crash followed by shrill shouts of glee. (Ritterbush 1953–54)

FUNDAMENTALS OF ORGANIZATION

A persuasive speech is divided into three major portions: the introduction, the body, and the conclusion. The three-part division of a speech may not have persuasive impact, but audiences do have expectations that a speech will include each part. They expect to be eased into the speech with an introduction, to be shown the main ideas of the body, and to have a summary at the end. Unlike reading a book, where you can turn back and reread the pages in case you missed something, listening to a speech does not give you that privilege. Therefore, the speaker who builds in initial, internal, and concluding summaries gives the listener an opportunity to pick up material that may have been missed. In fact, one old adage regarding speech organization is: "Tell them what you're going to say; say it; then tell them what you said." Each part of the speech has an important function.

Although you would normally organize the body first so you would know what it is that you are introducing, we shall present the parts in their normal speech order.

Introduction

The introduction should (1) gain the attention and interest of the audience; (2) clarify the persuader's purpose or target belief; (3) orient the audience to the persuader's approach to the topic by providing any information that the audience might need to clearly comprehend the body of the speech; and (4) establish the credibility of the speaker or his/her reason for speaking on the topic. In short, the function of the introduction is to gain attention and sharpen the audience's focus.

In addition, the persuader must give the persuadee a reason for listening. Audiences expect to be given reasons for listening and want to be told for what to listen.

Basically, the introduction should start with the audience and its interests. In effect, the introduction answers the audience's question "Why should I care?" It should establish the relationship between the topic and the audience. A good introduction can make an audience sit up and want to listen to a speech because it arouses a desire to hear more.

One student introduced her speech with a story about her husband, Kenny, when they had just begun dating as young college students:

Kenny and I had a date for dinner on the weekend, but he had spent his last bit of money on his car payment. Not wanting to tell me that we couldn't go out for dinner, he went to the hospital and sold a pint of blood for $20.00. He had to go directly from the hospital to the track field because he was on the track team and it was time to practice. While he was out there on the track field practically killing himself, someone was in the locker room stealing Kenny's blood money. Yes, and the same kind of person stole Laura's persuasion book just a few minutes after she walked out of our classroom without it last week. And the same kind of person took your watch off of your dresser in your room at the dorm. And the same kind of person stole your sweater out of your locker in high school. And the same kind of person steals books and tears pages out of periodicals and steals them from the library.

If she had told the audience from the beginning that she was going to talk about stealing pages from library magazines, the audience might have yawned with boredom. By rousing their indignation over past thefts, she made them feel indignation over thefts from the library, a common problem at the university. She made them realize why they should care.

Another effective form of introduction is to ask the audience direct questions. First, it involves the audience members immediately with the speaker, and, second, their answers can be used to relate to the topic. One student asked three "true-false" questions about how people get venereal disease. There was hesitancy on the part of the students as they were asked, "It is possible to get V.D. from a toilet seat. True? False?" After observing these college students' lack of knowledge about venereal disease on the basis of their mixed and uncertain answers, the speaker told them, "If you were in a seventh-grade sex-education class, you would know all of the answers." This was both embarrassing and motivating for the college audience and put the audience in a state of readiness to hear a speech about the necessity of junior-high-school sex education.

Attention factors are also excellent introductory techniques. One student aroused curiosity and demonstrated novelty when she began her speech by putting her hand in the front pocket of her dress and announcing, "I have something in my pocket that most children are fascinated by and most adults are afraid of. It is often misunderstood and unappreciated. Today, I would like to clear up those misunderstandings and hope that you will, like I have, learn to appreciate it." Then, she pulled a live snake out of her pocket. She had the undivided attention of the audience.

Of course, the introduction should always be relevant to the topic. There are many techniques for gaining attention, but an audience may be turned off if these techniques are used merely to gain attention and do not relate to the topic. What is important is that the introduction be used persuasively to get the audience into a favorable and accepting frame of mind toward the speaker and the topic.

If a unifying theme is being used, it should begin in the introduction. One student told the story of Procrustes from Greek mythology:

Procrustes had two beds in his house, one small, the other large. Offering a night's lodging to travelers, he would lay the short men on the large bed, and rack them out to fit it, put the tall men on the small bed, sawing off as much of their legs as projected beyond it. The American education system treats its students much like Procrustes treated his guests. It shrinks or stretches them to conform to methods which may not truly educate the child.

She then developed her speech on U.S. education, using the "shrinking or stretching" theme.

The introduction should cause the audience to want to hear more, but it is not advisable to baldly tell the audience what you want to persuade it to believe or do. Research on forewarning indicates that telling an audience what a persuader wants it to do reduces the likelihood that the persuader will be successful (Kiesler and Kiesler 1964). There should, however, be a clear statement of what the speech will be about, and then a smooth transition to the body of the speech.

It is also helpful if the persuader reveals his/her qualifications to talk about a particular topic. Recently, in Professor O'Donnell's class, Richard Alexander gave a speech about riding mechanical bulls, a very popular activity in western nightclubs that was influenced by the film, *Urban Cowboy*. Richard began his speech by saying, "I rode the bull at Gilley's Club and then went on to win several cash prizes throughout the summer of 1980." He, thus, established his qualifications to speak on the topic. He further enhanced his target belief (People should not ride mechanical bulls) by adding, "My reward for riding mechanicals bulls was a kidney infection that the doctor said was caused by punishing myself on mechanical bulls."

Body

The body of a persuasive speech consists of (1) supporting belief statements or main points, (2) supporting or amplifying materials, and (3) transitional phrases or sentences. Supporting belief statements or main points need to be stated simply so the persuadee can remember them. All should be interrelated and support the target belief. Most of all, the organization should move toward a conclusion and incorporate persuasive strategies.

Types of Organization   Just as a person needs a road map to reach a given destination or a blueprint to understand the structure of a building, an organizational pattern is needed for the structure of a persuasive message. For this purpose, there are choices of organizational patterns that are available to the persuader. They are (1) chronological order, (2) spatial order, (3) classification or topical order, (4) cause-effect order, and (5) problem-solution order.

1. *Chronological Order*   Chronological order is an organizational pattern arranged according to *time*. For example, "From all apparent signs, this nation could be approaching another depression" could be organized chronologically. Thus, the speech would track the evolution of depression from a certain year up to the present or could go back from the present to the past.
2. *Spatial Order*   Spatial order is used when a persuader wishes to show relationships or phenomena in a territorial manner. A party leader who wishes to persuade workers to be more diligent at soliciting votes may

choose to give them a party status report using the geographical areas (north, south, east, west) of the United States. If an architect wishes to persuade a client to accept certain blueprints, the architect may subdivide the arguments according to sections, rooms, or floors of the prospective home or building.

3. *Classification or Topical Order*   Topical order is organization by topics, categories, or different parts of a whole. For example, if a persuader is advocating the passage of the Equal Rights Amendment, the approach could be structured according to (1) benefits to housewives, (2) benefits to career women, and (3) benefits to minority women. A speech on American government might be divided into (1) executive; (2) legislative; and (3) judicial.

4. *Cause-Effect Order*   This pattern of organization is used to present causes of a given event, problem, or phenomenon. After the causes are actively demonstrated, then the persuader presents the effects of the causes. The order may be reversed so that effects are dealt with initially and the remainder of the persuasive effort is spent discussing the causes. This pattern of reasoning was discussed in the previous chapter.

5. *Problem-Solution Order*   The problem-solution method of organization lends itself to many persuasive topics. In order for an audience to accept a solution, it is necessary to present the problem or to dramatize it in such a way that it leaves no doubt in the mind of the persuadee that a particular solution —the persuader's solution—is the best to solve the given problem.

There are other variations for organizational patterns, but these are the most widely used. Strategically, the persuader should use the best organizational pattern to try to get the audience to accept the purpose of the speech.

Conclusion

In this section of the persuasive speech, a restatement of the target belief, supporting belief statements, and a summary of supporting material is desirable. The final statement should make a lasting impression on the persuadees. A good story or quotation can do this. Robert T. Oliver, a masterful speaker, often ended his speeches with stories. One time, when he was president of the Speech Association of America, he spoke to the newly formed Tennessee Speech Association about the necessity for building the basis of a strong professional organization before attempting to carry out ambitious plans. Dr. Oliver, who had spent much time in Korea as the personal adviser to President Syngman Rhee, used a Korean fable as his conclusion:

Once an old man was walking down the road when a huge and ferocious tiger came out of the bushes. The old man ran away, but the tiger went after him and then took a huge leap at him. The old man flattened himself on the road, thus the tiger sailed right over him. The old man took off in another direction with the tiger close behind. Again and again the tiger leaped, but each time he jumped too far and missed the old man. Finally, the old man ran into a hut, bolted the door, and lay on the floor gasping for breath. Then, he heard a noise outside. Thump. Silence. Thump. Slowly, the old man pulled himself up and looked out the window and this is what he saw. The tiger was practicing smaller leaps!

Thus, the Tennessee Speech Association membership was admonished to take smaller leaps before going on to more ambitious goals lest they miss them altogether. This is what a good conclusion does. It secures the purpose of the speech in an interesting manner. It's the final appeal, the clincher.

Sometimes the conclusion may be a challenge to an audience ("So let's go out and raise three million dollars!"), a quotation ("Old Soldiers never die, they just fade away"), a plea for urgency ("Don't turn your back on those who need you most"), an inspirational statement ("Let us go forth to lead the land we love, asking His blessing and His help, but knowing that here on earth God's work must truly be our own"), or a direct charge ("Tonight, when you go home, lock your door, because if you don't, someday someone might use your killer's description about how easy it was to get into your home").

It is better to end a speech with an explicitly stated conclusion than a suggestion of one. The explicit conclusion appears to affect attitude change (Hovland and Mandell 1952; Biddle 1966). Above all, a speech should not conclude with "Thank you." The audience should thank the speaker, not vice versa.

Transitions

Transition statements act as signposts because they alert the persuadee to what has been said and what is about to be said. "Now that we have seen that, let us look at this." "In contrast to what has been pointed out, we shall discuss the following." "Now that we see what problem exists, let's look for the solution." Transition phrases are necessary, but variety needs to be considered in their usage.

Francis Bacon, in *The Advancement of Learning*, advised speakers to collect and memorize formulaic transitions which can be used where needed. It is helpful to make a collection of phrases and words to be used as transitions.

Each unit of the speech should be joined at the major divisions in order to have cohesion. Transitions provide cement for this cohesion. Sometimes the transition needs to be extended by developing a feature held in common by both sections. For example, in a speech entitled "Challenges of the Twentieth Century," which included the challenge of the nuclear bomb and the challenge of rapid growth in population, the speaker used a common characteristic similar to each challenge in the following example:

Since 1945, our greatest national fear has been the wartime use of the nuclear bomb. We have been preoccupied with it. The feared atomic flash has blinded us, however, from seeing another kind of explosion threatening the civilized world just as severely and perhaps more cruelly . . . more cruelly because its torture of annihilation is measured in years rather than in minutes. The news releases on "the bomb" were analogous to the atomic blast itself—spectacular, blinding. But the other explosion grew slowly—unspectacularly. We did not see its flash, but we can now get a clear view of its mushroom. Its effects will not be as vivid as the picture of Hiroshima, but they will be just as deadly to a continued civilization. The population explosion, although it is ignited by a small fuse, requires the design of a new kind of shelter, and it requires it now.

A transition often summarizes the previous point and introduces the next point. It is a bridge that comfortably leads the listener from one point to another and lends smoothness to the organization of the speech.

LANGUAGE

Meanings do not exist in words themselves but in the minds of the people who interpret them. Consider the following riddle: A man and his son were in an auto accident. The man was killed and the son was rushed to the hospital. The surgeon, upon entering the operating room to perform life-saving surgery, said, "I cannot operate on this boy—he is my son." Who was the doctor? (See below.)

The word "doctor" has no gender. However, if you responded as our students have, you attached gender to the term without realizing it. Language is both a medium of persuasion as well as a facilitating factor. A person can choose how to use language to persuade.

Answer: The mother.

SYMBOLS AND MEANING

Humans are distinguished from animals by their symbol-using ability. We create symbols to identify things and situations. We also use and misuse the language of our own creation. Language is never neutral; it reflects the beliefs, attitudes, and values of the person who uses it. It is within this context that communication has been defined as a process of symbolic interaction (Littlejohn 1978, p. 75). For it is through language that we become human and interact symbolically with others. A person's self-concept is reflected in the language he/she uses, for it is also with language that self-communication occurs. Behaviors are also determined by a person's symbolic definition of the situation. A person sees the self mirrored in the language used in addressing him/her.

Abstraction and Projection   A concept is a common meaning among communicators. Each individual, however, possesses a private meaning that fills in details. This meaning is referred to as a person's conception (Littlejohn 1978, p. 119). This process of generalizing a common concept is referred to as *abstraction*, "the process of leaving out details in perceiving, thinking about, and labeling objects and events" (Littlejohn 1978, p. 121). It is a natural step to move from an actual object or event to a statement about that object or event. The higher the level of abstraction, the more removed from the actual object or event the statement or thought becomes. This is called by general semanticists the vertical form of abstraction. The horizontal form of abstraction pertains to the situation in which two individuals will abstract from the same event in a different manner. This phenomenon occurs as a result of *projection*. Projection is a person perceiving his/her own values as reality and couching an event in those values. "Barbara Tims's statements while visiting her son in Iran were courageous" and "Ms. Tims's statements while visiting her son in Iran were blatantly unpatriotic" are examples of projection.

Time Binding   Through language, knowledge is transmitted from generation to generation. Our ability to span time by using symbols was labeled "time binding" by Alfred Korzybski. He saw the time-binding capacity as a peculiar and characteristic feature of human beings: "Man improves, animals do not; man progresses, animals do not; man invents more and more complicated tools, animals do not; man is a creator of material and spiritual wealth, animals are not; man is a builder of civilization, animals are not" (1921, p. 186).

People can gather and use the experiences of the past as capital for their work in the present. They can accumulate ideas, attitudes, beliefs, values, behaviors, and materials. They can begin where others have left off. Irving Lee, a general semanticist who wrote about Korzybski's ideas, said, "Men can draw from the PAST, in and through the PRESENT, and make ready for the FUTURE. The experience of the race can be accumulated, worked over, magnified, and transmitted" (1941, p. 4).

The time-binding capacity of the human race is a mark of our ability to use symbols to stand for the ideas that are passed on to future generations. Harry Weinberg, another general semanticist, called our symbol-using capacity to time-bind our "most powerful tool and weapon, both useful and dangerous to ourselves and others" (1959, pp. 156–57). Weinberg warned us to be wary of the transmission of false information that could be received and treated as truth.

PERSUASIVE USE OF LANGUAGE

Language is symbolic action. Action is human nature. People can't be moved like a machine but they can act out of their own needs, desires, and wants. People are different and, therefore, separate. As was stated in Chapter VII, people are motivated by different wants, needs, and experiences—properties. Language can resolve (but not eliminate) differences. People can transcend their separateness through identification. Language allows people to act together by sharing common sensations, images, ideas, and attitudes.

Identification requires participation and sharing. Kenneth Burke states, "You persuade a man only insofar as you can talk his language by speech gestures, tonality, order, image, attitude, idea, identifying your ways with his" (1950, p. 579).

Techniques of Identification through Language

Identification may be established through the joining of persuader-persuadee interests. Voluntary attention factors can serve as identification techniques. When Christ said to the vineyard workers "I am the vine and you are the branches," he gained their attention by talking about them and relating their identity to himself.

A persuader may use group norms that already exist as identification factors. This allows persuaders and persuadees to regard one another as equals. The persuader does not ask the persuadee to change so that identification may occur, but makes the persuadee aware that identification already exists. Identification deals with what is, not what should be. It is *being*.

The persuader can share *being* by establishing the fact that "we are students, young, sports lovers" or "we are all searchers for justice, seekers of knowledge, admirers of movie stars."

The use of appropriate language, such as familiar and conversational words, can establish identification. The following excerpt from Richard Nixon's "Checkers Speech," which was delivered on nationwide radio and television on September 23, 1952, is an excellent example for analysis:

I was born in 1913. Our family was one of modest circumstances and most of my early life was spent in a store out in East Whittier. It was a grocery store—one of those family enterprises. The only reason we were able to make it go was because my mother and dad had five boys and we all worked in the store.

I worked my way through college and to a great extent through law school. And then, in 1940, probably the best thing that ever happened to me happened. I married Pat—sitting over here. We had a rather difficult time after we were married, like so many of the young couples who may be listening to us. I practiced law; she continued to teach school. I went into the service.

Let me say that my service record was not a particularly unusual one. I went to the South Pacific. I guess I'm entitled to a couple of battle stars. I got a couple of letters of commendation but I was just there when the bombs were falling and then I returned. I returned to the United States and in 1946 I ran for Congress.

When we came out of the war, Pat and I—Pat during the war had worked as a stenographer and in a bank and as an economist for a Government agency—and when we came out the total of our savings from both my law practice, her teaching and all the time that I was in the war—the total for that entire period was just a little less than $10,000. Every cent of that was, incidentally, in Government bonds.

Nixon based his speech on the assumption that his vast television audience was composed of "regular fellows" from middle-class America. With this audience in mind, he established identification throughout this portion of the speech through many of his statements.

1. He was born in modest circumstances and worked in a family business with his parents and four brothers.
2. He was happily married. Since they were a struggling young couple, his wife worked while he began his practice and later, when he went into the service.
3. He had the "usual" military record. He showed modesty about being where the bombs were falling and receiving battle stars and letters of commendation.
4. He had saved money but had accumulated little, but what he had was invested in government bonds.

Simplicity of language (not simpleness) can establish identification. All people have experienced the frustration that comes from complex language such as the fine print of insurance policies, a physician's interpretation of test results, or academic jargon. President Franklin D. Roosevelt, in a desire for simplicity, changed a sentence one of his speech writers had written from "We are trying to construct a more inclusive society" to "We are going to make a country in which no one is left out."

Ambiguity and vagueness interfere with understanding. So it is necessary to aim for preciseness and clarity. It is difficult to identify with words such as *few, rich, nice, awful,* or *cold*. The term *dog* is more accurate than *animal; sirloin steak* is more accurate than *meat*; and *Harvard* is more accurate than *university*. "John has an IQ of 70" tells us more than "John is dumb."

Meanings need to be considered in terms of the audience. Are the meanings the same for them as for the persuader? There are options from which to choose that can make a difference. These examples from B. Cerf (1948) show various options: "I look younger; you are well-preserved; she had her face lifted." "I am stimulated by talking to successful people; you are a celebrity chaser; he is a snob."

It is also difficult to establish identification when sources of documentation are vague. No one identifies with "they said," "authorities say," or "a magazine article stated." Specific references and qualifications can establish identification with the persuadee.

Concrete language is necessary to paint visual images with which the persuader can identify. The following comparative example shows two versions of the same event—a general treatment and a concrete treatment.

GENERAL:

The giant trees in northern California have been enjoyed by millions of people for many years. The chances are that people in the future are not going to be so lucky. The lumbering interests, well aware of board feet in each tree have reduced the footage significantly between 1909 and 1953. The pace has continued at such a rapid rate that three-quarters of the redwoods are gone. The end of these big trees will surely come soon if some steps are not taken.

SPECIFIC:

Are you one of the fortunate Americans who has seen the magnificent coastal Redwoods in northern California? Your son and daughter may be denied this awe-inspiring experience. These graceful trees, alive two thousand years ago to greet the first Easter, are now over 20 feet in diameter and reach up as much as 350 feet. But even giants must struggle to survive. And they are losing. Persistent lumbermen are hacking away at them. In 1909 one hundred billion board feet of old growth stood against the high Pacific winds; by 1953 the amount had dropped 35 billion board feet. Today three quarters of the Redwoods are gone forever. (Braden 1966, p. 157)

Ralph Waldo Emerson said, concerning concreteness, "Put argument into a concrete shape, into an image, some hard phrase, round and solid as a ball, which . . . the audience can see and handle and carry home with them."

Imagery is capable of reinforcing previous experiences already held by the persuadee. These experiences can be relived through the persuader's effective use of imagery. The following example illustrates how a person responded to visual images, "A vivid picture on the cinema screen presented a boy and a girl pulling down hay from a stack for bedding. I sneezed—from the dust of the hay shown on the screen. On another occasion a colored picture of lilacs—a favorite flower—moved by a gentle breeze, was shown on the screen. I smelled the odor of lilacs distinctly" (Rosett 1967, p. 212).

How do you respond to such words as *decapitate, torn ligament, cancer, charley horse, dry socket,* or *sore throat,* especially if one of these terms is associated with a painful experience that you have had or witnessed?

Emotions such as grief are oftentimes brought to the surface when some symbol of the deceased is heard or seen. A song on the radio can conjure up sad memories of a lost love or happy memories of a better time in one's life.

New experiences can also be created through description, if the description is vivid enough. Let the receiver see, hear, feel, smell, taste, and move with you, the persuader.

Some secrets of description are the use of concreteness, which has already been mentioned, and multisensory words such as *clang, hack, murky, whirlwind, restless, rolling,* and *hurried.* There are special forms of word construction which also enhance description.

Forms of Word Construction

Some forms of word construction are anaphora, metaphor, asyndeton, simile, and alliteration. The *anaphora* contains consecutive clauses or sentences that begin with the same word or series of words. An example of anaphora comes from a speech by George McGovern during the 1972 Presidential campaign:

Our sons have asked for jobs—and we've sent them to an Asian jungle. Our sons have asked for an education—and we've taught them how to kill. Our sons have asked for a full measure of time—and 50,000 of them have been lost before their time.

Another example of anaphora comes from a speech by Vernon Jordan:

Any country that can afford to shovel billions upon billions into the bottomless pit of southeast Asia can afford to keep its own people at work. Any country that can afford to spend a hundred billion dollars a year on weapons and destructive forces can afford to spend a part of that on jobs and constructive forces. And any country that can subsidize its affluent citizenry to the tune of billions of dollars in tax loopholes can afford to subsidize its working people through mass creation of jobs. (Jordon 1975, p. 562)

Alliteration. (*Texas Monthly* August 1980)

A *metaphor* is an implied comparison that is not inappropriate to the context. For example, Jordan compares the black experience to being in the university of survival:

The black experience is such that we are no stranger to hardship and danger. Throughout our history, black people have been honed in hardship and steeped in adversity. We've been educated at the university of survival, and we've worked in the vineyards and tasted bitterness. Yes, we bore the burden in the heat of America's day. Even in times of plenty we've never had enough. Now, although we scrape for the crumbs of society in this dark midnight, we know we're not getting through. (Jordan 1975, p. 562)

A *simile* compares through the use of *like* or *as*. For example, "He had posture like a questionmark."

An *alliteration* involves the use of a series of words that begin with the same letter. Tongue twisters you had fun trying as a child are examples, such as "Peter Piper picked a peck of pickled peppers." The alliteration is used by the poet, but its effect has also been recognized by the advertisers. The peanut-butter commercial where the little boy says "My mom is choosy, but I pick Peter Pan peanut butter" is one example.

Asyndeton is groupings of words or phrases that occur without connectives. A familiar example is Julius Caesar's words "I came—I saw—I conquered." Another example could be "The heart monitor made an erratic sound. A single leap. Then silence."

The figures of speech are just a few devices that can enhance what the persuadee hears with a visual image to accompany it. This combination will make what is said memorable and, it is hoped, persuasive.

SUMMARY

The relationship between the persuader and his/her perception of reality guides the organization of the persuasive message. Likewise, the persuadee forms a relationship to the persuader and his/her message. To speak of persuasion in terms of such relationships is *structuralist* in nature. A structuralist point of view brings a sense of internal coherence to the parts of a whole wherein the individual parts take on a special character because they are part of the whole. Organization is important to the persuader because it gives him/her the opportunity to choose and place the message content in interrelated and strategic ways. For the persuadee, organization may facilitate understanding, retention, and criticism of the message. A well-organized speech can lead an audience through the sequence to a conclusion.

Much research has been conducted on organization variables, but it is difficult to generalize concerning its effects. Much seems to depend on how it is used in given situations. More importantly, organization is the link between speaker and audience that can, if handled strategically, bring them closer together.

A persuader has many avenues to choose from in designing a speech, but it is first useful to understand something about perception and attention. Perception is influenced by an individual's experiences. Thus, not all people perceive things similarly. Yet, perception may lead to attention, which can be aroused by various techniques: external factors, which cause people to attend because they cannot help it, and internal factors, which relate to people's wants and needs.

Most speeches are comprised of an introduction, a body, and a conclusion, each of which has a distinct function. The introduction gets to the audience's interests in order to cause the audience to relate to the speaker and the topic in a favorable manner. The body presents and amplifies the main ideas and the supporting beliefs and evidence. There are also several organizational patterns from which to choose. The conclusion summarizes the content and leaves a memorable impression on the audience.

Language presents a person's symbolic definition of a target belief and its supports. Language is symbolic action and is a major facilitating factor in promoting persuasion. It allows identification between persuader and persuadee. Through language, people can share their perceptions.

There are many techniques of using language to persuade. Language, in general, can reduce ambiguities and vagueness if it is clear and concrete. It can also reinforce previous experiences and create new ones as well. There are various forms of word constructions that can help the persuader put meaning into interesting, if not memorable, forms. These facilitating factors give the persuader and persuadee opportunities to express and receive a message.

KEY WORDS

Structuralist	Chronological order
Law of primacy-recency	Space order
Perception	Cause-effect order
Attention	Topical order
Voluntary attention	Problem-solution order
Involuntary attention	Time binding
Anticipatory attention	Concrete language

EXERCISES

1. Attend a rock concert, a circus, a revival meeting, or a pep rally. Observe the factors of attention. List and identify as many external and internal attention techniques as you can. Notice how and when you pay attention involuntarily. When you attend voluntarily, what inner predispositions cause you to take notice?

2. A television commercial has to gain your attention immediately. Observe several commercials to analyze their attention techniques.

3. Write an introduction to a speech, and use (a) an external attention technique and (b) an internal attention technique.

4. Recall seeing a film or listening to a speech with a friend when you had different perceptions of the same event. Try to explain why your perceptions differed.

5. Read a famous speech from an anthology. Try to make an outline from it. Decide which organization pattern is used. Make a technical plot to identify the speaker's persuasive strategies.

6. Take a descriptive passage from a newspaper, and rewrite it to make it more concrete and vivid.

7. Select an experience that you have had, and write or tell it so that an audience can *see* it, *hear* it, *smell* it, *taste* it, and/or *touch* it. In other words, recreate it.

8. Analyze a speech, a song, a poem, a television program, or a film for its identification techniques.

9. Give an example of an idea that you have acquired through time binding. How can you use that idea to prepare for the future?

10. Start collecting good stories and quotations to use for introductions and conclusions.

READINGS

Braden, Waldo. *Public Speaking: The Essentials.* New York: Harper & Row, 1966.

Hart, R. P.; Friedrich, G. W.; and Brooks, W. D. *Public Communication.* New York: Harper & Row, 1975.

Hawkes, Terence. *Structuralism and Semiotics.* Berkeley, Calif.: University of California Press, 1977.

Hovland, C.; Janis, I.; and Kelley, H. *Communication and Persuasion.* New Haven: Yale University Press, 1953.

Karlins, M., and Abelson, H. *Persuasion: How Opinions and Attitudes Are Changed.* 2d ed. New York: Springer, 1970.

Littlejohn, S. W. *Theories of Human Communication.* Columbus, Ohio: Charles E. Merrill, 1978.

Minnick, Wayne. *The Act of Persuasion.* Boston: Houghton-Mifflin, 1968.

9

PERSUASION IN THE MASS MEDIA

OBJECTIVES

Upon completion of this chapter you should be able to:

1. Define mass media.
2. Understand the persuasive impact of the media.
3. Appreciate the complex relationship among the media, audiences, and society.
4. Understand why the environment in which a film is viewed is important.
5. Appreciate the persuasive potential of film.
6. Understand the pervasiveness of television in American society.
7. Perceive the presence of myths in television programs.
8. Understand the dependency model of mass communication.
9. Know the particular types of circumstances that stimulate aggressive behavior in viewers who watch filmed and televised violence.
10. Understand the reinforcement model of mass communication.
11. Understand the diffusion of innovations.
12. Understand how advertising appeals to consumers' needs and perceptions.

Mass media are omnipresent in the everyday life of the average American. We live in a constant environment of mass communications, which we experience on a daily, if not an hourly, basis. The potential impact of media is mind-boggling. A never-ending flow of events, issues, ideas, objects, and personalities is pushed into the public's attention. Different versions of messages from different media are presented to the public to the point where it is difficult to remember where a specific message was seen or heard.

Mass media can effectively increase knowledge and reinforce prevailing attitudes. Advertising campaigns are effective in persuading individuals to try new products, especially if the individual already feels a need for change. Media researchers are still unable to give straightforward answers to the question of whether or not media have widespread effects on individuals. There are numerous variables related to audience orientation and predispositions and the question of the effects of media. J. Foley, in his overview of mass communication theory and research, says, "It is clear that the mass media have had a major impact on individuals and social systems around the world. It is less clear exactly what the nature of this impact has been, but we are finding disturbing evidence that suggests some of the impacts of the media are harmful" (in Ruben 1978, p. 209).

Mass media are generally considered to be film, television, radio, newspapers, magazines, "popular" books, phonograph records, and the telephone. Much of the research into the mass media has concentrated on television, but mass communication research certainly is not limited to television. Film was the subject of a great deal of research two decades ago, and now it is once again becoming a prominent medium to analyze. Years of research have gone into the subject of aggression and children in both the television and film media. Foley calls our attention to the diversity of topics and media being investigated and mentions a study by M. Sanches concerning the stories in Japanese comic books and a study by I. Pool on the impact of the telephone (in Ruben 1978, p. 211).

We could write a long book instead of a chapter on the mass media. In order to condense the material into a single chapter, we have focused upon the prominent forms of mass media: film and television. Each medium has been examined according to its persuasive impact through a complex interrelationship among the media, audiences, and society.

FILM

Film is a popular entertainment medium, especially with young people. Seventy-four percent of all filmgoers are under the age of thirty-four. This young audience, according to Jack Valenti, president of the Motion Picture Association of America, is also well educated. In a survey sponsored by the MPAA to analyze film audiences, Daniel Yankelovich, Inc. discovered that "thirty percent of the population who have one year or more of college education are frequent movie-goers, attending a minimum of one film per month" (Wuntch 1975, p. 22A). In another study of students who graduated from high school in 1972, researchers compared the number of hours that the students spent watching films to the number of hours that they spent in the classroom. The astonishing results revealed that students spent 7,750 hours from the first through twelfth grades watching films (250 hours watching films in commercial theaters and 7,500 hours watching feature films on television), while they spent only 5,400 hours in classrooms for the first twelve years of their education (McCowan 1972, p. 6).

Film's Environment

Audiences tend to take film naturally, without suspicion, and feel at ease with its conventions. They sit in a comfortable, darkened theater, free from most distractions, giving optimal attention to a flickering image on the screen that is often the only source of light. The dark environment has a tendency to produce a lowered defense reaction and a heightened emotional reaction. Psychologists Gordon Globus and Roy Shulman studied the effects of the darkness on the audience in the movie theater and concluded, "The darkness, immobility, relative lack of distractions, and isolation from objective reality-oriented interpersonal events facilitate an ego regression so that ego boundaries are diffused, affective arousal is enhanced, and more primitive defenses are brought into play" (Evans 1975, p. 141).

Film also engages an audience physiologically, for it surrounds its audience with visual and aural stimuli that flood the senses. A film makes its statement through composition, color, sound, and rhythm. The visual picture and the sound track engulf the eyes, ears, and mind all at once. Research conducted at the Psychological Institute of the University of Rome has revealed that the motion of film provokes kinesthetic responses in the audience such as muscular reflexes, motor impulses, increased pulse rate, and other metabolic behavior (Applbaum and Anatol 1974, p. 20). Movie theater owners have known this without the benefit of experimental research, for when they show horror pictures, they are often asked to increase the amount of air conditioning due to the increased perspiration of the excited viewers.

The Experience of Film

Film's dramatic power of mental and physical stimulation has the capability of bringing the illusion of life as it is lived or the fantasy of how it might be lived directly to its audience. The relationship of audience to film becomes an act of deep-seated communication. It can be a vicarious experience whereby the images on the screen become extensions of the individual personalities of the audience. This is what Rudolf Arnheim, psychologist and film theoretician, means when he refers to film as the "epidermis of reality" (Fell 1975, p. 15), the skin off which our sensations reflect. Through film an audience can see its values personified, renew familiar experiences and feelings, fulfill desires, and find relief from tensions and release from fears.

The Persuasive Potential of Film

The persuasive potential of film can be attributed to the filmmakers, who consciously or unconsciously take sides during the process of planning and shooting their films. To a degree, most commercially distributed films are intended to be persuasive because they are produced to attract large audiences at the box office. To make their films a commercial success, filmmakers must adapt to a variety of audiences and viewing conditions. Thus, filmmakers select elements and events to be dramatized, to be emphasized, or to be ignored. Consequently, this selectivity can result in the manipulation of audiences (Klapper 1960).

This is apparently true in commercial fiction films, but documentary films may also attempt to persuade an audience to act on behalf of some social, political, or economic goal, or to provide information and insight into a dilemma that aids in a decision-making process. Even *cinéma-vérité* (truth cinema) and direct cinema, which record real people and events without script or direction, can be persuasive because they are dependent on the filmmakers' editing decisions regarding what the editors choose to let the audience see. Educational films may attempt to persuade students to learn the presented skills and concepts. Thus, virtually all films are in some respect persuasive. Indeed, Robert Geller, former director of the American Film Institute's Education Division, and Sam Kula, AFI archivist, state that film is persuasive:

Film, however, is a public art both in its creation and its consumption. And since it has a profound effect on not only *how* we see but also on *what* we see, it should be available to all. . . . Unless filmic awareness or literacy becomes widespread, film will continue to affect the quality of life, unchecked by any critical criteria . . . *how* we see will inevitably affect *what* we see and that the passivity of an audience lacking critical criteria for evaluation will permit the quality of life to deteriorate. . . . Film is already widely recognized as one of the most effective communication links between those individuals and groups within society who do not relate to the print forms of the mass media. Film has demonstrated a unique capacity, for example, to teach functional illiterates. Film further has the power to influence, persuade, or condition an audience into accepting a point of view.

Moreover, and more importantly, it actually determines the nature and quality of the environment in which viewpoints are adopted. (1969, pp. 108, 110)

Paul Rotha, British film critic and documentary filmmaker who believes that "cinema is one of the most powerful channels of expression for persuasion and public illumination," gives three reasons for its power: "It possesses: (1) an introduction to the public . . . with a resultant power of mass suggestion, (2) simple powers of explanation and capacities for making statements which, if presented with a craftmanship that takes full advantage of artistic values are capable of persuasive qualities without equal, and (3) virtues of mechanized repeated performance to a million persons, not once but countless times a day, tomorrow and, if the quality is good enough, ten years hence" (1952, p. 58).

Film As Communication

In order to understand the implications of film as persuasive, it must first be examined as communication. Film is communication in which meaning is the result of a relationship between the implication of the filmmakers, the *senders*, and the inference of the audience, the *receivers*. Visual communication in film includes the transmission of signals received primarily through visual receptors. When received, the signals, along with the audio cues, are treated as a *message*.

The filmmakers—that is, the producers, directors, writers, editors, camerapersons, actors, and other technicians and artists—employ selected symbols to communicate a message when they make decisions about the elements that enter into making a film—the script, location, cast, natural sound, dialogue, music, lens, camera setups, staging, composition, and editing. They sort, select, and transmit symbols through the medium of film to the audience with the hope that the audience will receive the message in a way that is similar to what is intended by the senders. The senders seek the *voluntary* cooperation of the receivers through a symbolic interaction with them. In turn, the receivers select and sort the meanings derived from the film through their perceptual-interpretative capabilities and place these meanings into their own system of cognitive feelings with varying degrees of intensity.

The audience's response to a film is part of the significant convergence of sender and receiver that brings a film to realization. Audiences bring to the film many variables—differing values, beliefs, group norms, attitudes, and behavioral patterns—which will affect their responses to it. Filmmakers often calculate the predispositions of the audience in order to produce some behavioral response. The profit motive induces producers to adapt to audience interests in order to promote attendance and increase box-office receipts. One prosperous producer, Dino De Laurentiis, explains, "Success is in isolating certain trends in which the public has a deep emotional interest" (Thomas 1975, p. 4D). Market research is in use at Universal, Columbia, and Twentieth Century Fox, where the plots, possible casting, and advertising of films are pretested. As David Begelman, head of Columbia Studios, says, "We're not about to put a message in a bottle, toss it in the sea and hope that it will reach its destination" (Higham 1975, p. 13). Even Alfred Hitchcock expressed his dependency on relating to audience interests and expectations when making decisions about directing a film: "The art of directing for the commercial market," said Hitchcock, "is to know just how far you can go. In many ways I am freer now to do what I want to do than I was a few years ago. I hope in time to have more freedom still—if audiences will give it to me" (Lindgren 1968, p. 20).

The public, in turn, projects its interests back to the film, and this response can be considered as communicative *feedback*, which could be criticism of a film, recommendations to friends to see it, or multiple viewing. The immediate audience response to a film has no effect on any message adjustment of a specific film after it is released, and, thus, the film, unlike a live performer, remains indifferent to its immediate audience.

How Film Persuades

Yet, the communicative process between a film and an audience may bring about a reinforcement or a change of attitude, belief, or behavior by producing a cognitive restructuring of one's image of the world or of one's frame of reference. A film audience may respond, "I never thought of it that way before" or "I never saw it that way before."

Not all filmmakers consciously attempt to persuade audiences to change attitudes and behaviors, or even to intensify ones that are already in agreement with the messages on the screen. Yet, if we consider persuasion as an attempt to get an audience to accept the persuader's view of reality or fantasy, which is another way of eliciting the "I never thought of it that way before" response, then most films fall under the persuasive domain.

As we know, persuasion is not easily accomplished at any time, for audiences can be resistant to change even when their defenses may be weakened or when they have expectations of only being entertained while viewing a film. Yet, many film theorists believe that film may be the most persuasive of all the media. Bela Balazs said in his introduction to *Theory of Film*, "We all know and admit that film art has a greater influence on the minds of the general public than any other art" (1970, p. 17).

Whether or not filmmakers deliberately intend to persuade is not always clear since the desire to persuade, when present, may be secondary, unconscious, or even deliberately masked. Whatever its intent, however, it can at least be said that film can *function* persuasively for the audience. It is unlikely, however, that a film will persuade all viewers. There will be disagreement over the persuasive effectiveness of film. Nonetheless, there is evidence that film has been a stimulus for both attitudinal and behavioral changes in audiences.

The Effects of Film

Marshall McLuhan relates an interesting example of the effect of American films on the people of another culture. President Sukarno of Indonesia told a large group of Hollywood executives in 1956 that he regarded them as political radicals and revolutionaries who were responsible for political change in the East because what the people of the Orient saw in Hollywood films was a world in which all the ordinary people had cars and electric stoves and refrigerators. Sukarno objected to the exposure of his people to films because he said that the Oriental now regards himself as an ordinary person who has been deprived of the ordinary man's birthright (1964, p. 257).

R. H. Carpenter and R. V. Seltzer present considerable secondary evidence to support their argument that the film *Patton* had a profound effect upon Richard M. Nixon and may have influenced his decision to invade Cambodia in 1970. They claim that the film led the president to believe that the true American spirit followed Patton and not the New Left, a belief on Nixon's part that was "felt by every close advisor who was aware of the President's repeated viewing of the film." They attribute much of the influence to the rhetorical identification that they believe Nixon had with Patton due to "similarities in sensations, ideas, values, and attitudes that are demonstrated symbolically between the parties in a suasory transition such as that between a film and its viewer" (1974, p. 105).

J. P. Mayer offered a series of case studies of British audiences' responses to film and concluded that film often served as a vehicle for making individuals aware of their own personalities (1946, p. 267). F. Fearing, in his review of the effects of film on audiences, says, "Motion pictures achieve their effect because they help the individual to cognize his world" (in McQuail 1972, p. 119). Fearing discusses filmic persuasion as a means of providing a person with interpretative frames of reference that

either reaffirm the norms of his culture or group or reveal previously unsuspected and possibly contrasting alternatives to these norms. He sees how other people behave in a wide variety of situations and is thus provided with patterns of behavior which he may accept or reject. . . . The 'need' is not necessarily consciously experienced by the individual, but is assumed to underline his behavior in seeking the entertainment or amusement provided by the motion picture. It finds expression in the pattern of his acceptances or rejections, approvals or disapprovals, of specific films. (p. 126)

The Payne Fund studies, conducted by a number of sociologists and psychologists and sponsored by the U.S. Motion Picture Research Council, were the first systematic attempt to use experimental techniques to find out the effects of commercial films on specific attitudes and behavior, particularly in the case of children and adolescents (McQuail 1972, pp. 123–24). H. Blumer (1933) found that children imitated the action of film stars and that the films produced heightened emotions of fear, sorrow, and passion. R. C. Peterson and L. L. Thurstone (1933) observed statistically significant shifts in the attitudes of adolescents toward capital punishment, race relations, and Nazism after exposure to films such as *Birth of a Nation, Sons of the Gods*, and *Welcome Danger* which dealt with these subjects. The researchers administered pretests and posttests after a lapse of time. The attitude shifts were in the direction indicated by the film as a result of the exposure to it. In the case of at least one group, the effects persisted in a significant amount for a period of five months. Of the thirteen films viewed, however, only six produced significant attitude changes.

M. Wiese and S. Cole (1946) used a free association technique and had three hundred children answer questions regarding the ideological points in the film *Tomorrow the World* before and after viewing the film. Measurable effects on attitudes in the direction indicated by the film were observed. However, the effects of the film were proportionate to the social, economic, and cultural origins of the individual subjects. This particular study documented an important generalization: the socioeconomic background of the audience determines in large measure what a film means.

M. Keilhacker (1958) investigated the pedagogical effects of film on children and found that children learned values about truth, honesty, and behavior from film long before they went to school. He said that children are not spectators of film but are coactors.

Film and Identification

A person responds to those things in a film that he or she finds significant for him or herself. The story in a film overlaps with the viewer's experiences in life. Life's variety comes not from the duration of an experience, but from its intensity. We seek confirmation of ourselves in film and thus find a reflection of ourselves on the screen.

The dramatic film usually provokes a reaction from the spectator that depends on a projection of his or her character and personality into those of the actor or actress playing in the story. The spectator is also projected into a series of fictional complications and has a vested interest in the outcome. A film can give an aura of reality to notions, situations, and things that may be essentially unreal. Thus, "life" can be worked out as we would like it to be but seldom is. The Russian poet Moravsky expresses the appeal of the dramatic film: "For those whom life has cheated, movies open the electric paradise."

Yet, there has to be a connection between the "paradise" and the world that the audience inhabits, between the characteristics of the characters in the film and the audience. The connection comes through shared experiences, however remote they may be, between the film's characters and events and the personal lives and wishes of the audience. Shared experiences are strong identification factors. In a persuasive speech, a speaker may describe an experience with the hope of gaining an empathic response such as "I know what you mean. Something like that happened to me once." Likewise, in a film, an audience gains meaning and often pleasure by relating to the characters. They share the characters' feelings if they like them, or project negative feelings toward them if they dislike them. These frames of reference are to a body of overt and covert feelings, assumptions, value judgments, that filmmakers expect an audience to share and through which the filmmakers can express feelings *for* the audience. Familiar properties on the screen are extensions of our being. The more familiar they are, the more we become a part of them. Film brings people into the presence of a certain image of themselves. Perhaps this is why Luchino Visconti, the Italian film director, says, "Experience has taught me that the weight, the presence of a man is the only thing that really counts on the screen. . . . I could make a film in front of a blank wall if I was sure of finding the real human elements of the character placed in front of this bare decor" (Durgnat 1971, p. 45).

V. Petric sees the identification power of film as stronger than any other medium, and he believes that identification is a deliberate weapon in persuasion: "Knowing that viewers become psychologically tied to the total illusion on the screen, the filmmaker can easily direct their attention and incite their attitude, injecting into their consciousness certain political concepts; he may trust that —if the audience's identification is complete—three quarters of the viewers will assimilate the ideological standpoint of the hero" (1973, p. 238).

In the film *9 to 5*, Lily Tomlin plays a secretary who has been working in the same office for twelve years training a long chain of young executives, including the one who becomes her boss. When she is passed over for a promotion one more time because her boss has recommended someone else since "the clients would rather deal with a man," we share her rage and her disappointment. When she fantasizes about putting poison in her boss's coffee, we can understand why she feels the way she does.

In another film, *The Elephant Man*, the director causes the audience to develop both curiosity and fear over seeing the face of the man who causes people to run screaming from the freak show. Yet, we have developed sufficient sympathy for him that by the time we see him, we are less horrified. When the film has ended, we have come to like the "elephant man" so very much that it no longer matters what he looks like. We have adopted the point of view of the director rather than the point of view of the historical spectators, who recoiled in disgust from seeing the real John Merrick.

Documentary film, regardless of its claims to objectivity, is also very persuasive. Through its factors of identification, it can sensitize the viewers' perceptions and provide a stimulus that can influence an audience to adopt a point of view or support a solution to a problem. Documentary filmmakers utilize the predispositions and experiences of their audiences to evoke identification with the people and events on the screen. P. Rotha (1952) says, "Documentary relies exclusively on the belief that there is nothing so interesting to ourselves as ourselves. It depends upon the individual's interest in the world around him. It bases its appeal on the community's undeniable zest for getting about the world and, more difficult, on the drama of events that lies at one's own doorstep" (p. 123). The characters and events in a documentary film are familiar to its audience. An idea is explored through a series of experiences that the audience can share, and these experiences form the basic structure of a documentary film.

A good documentary film makes the commonplace as interesting as the exotic. Robert Flaherty went to Hudson Bay to film the emblem of primitive man, *Nanook of the North*. Nanook, an Eskimo, battles the elements of the frozen North in a struggle for survival. Yet, because Flaherty focused on ordinary events—building an igloo, a family sleeping together, children taking medicine, a baby playing with a puppy—audiences have reacted with warmth and humor to people with whom they can identify. Thus, it becomes not a condescending treatment of a primitive, but a compassionate look at human beings, a universal story in which we are all Eskimos. The film is a good documentary because it is a subjective revelation of the human experience, human events portrayed on a human scale.

An Oscar-winning documentary, *The Great American Cowboy*, evoked great identification in a film audience in Denton, Texas, a city surrounded by many small communities that are the home towns of local and national rodeo contestants. The audience, families who had driven to the theater in pickup trucks, dressed in jeans held up by belts with buckles representative of winning rodeo events from junior rodeos to grand championship rodeos, overtly expressed identification when the physical punishment of bull riding, bronc busting, and steer wrestling was depicted in agonizing slow motion. Shouts of recognition were given to cowboys crowded in seedy motel rooms sharing tales of mean bulls. Sleepy contestants traveling all night in old cars, stopping for greasy food in cheap road-side cafés were given instant acknowledgment. Members of the audience groaned when Larry Mahan, the All-Around Champion Cowboy, broke his shoulder, and they murmured understandingly when he took off his cast two weeks early in order to participate in an important rodeo event.

Film, whether dramatic or documentary, can be a powerful instrument of persuasion that can enlarge our experiences and change perceptions of self and the environment so that we can say, "I never thought of it that way before." It is through such interaction, a connection between the viewer's experiences and the film's events, that film has the power to persuade.

Michael Ritchie, in his film *Film: The Art of the Impossible*, shows us how the filmmaker forces the audience to suspend disbelief (1972). He demonstrates how in his film *Downhill Racer* he forced the audience to believe that a skier won a race in an impossible situation. In reality, there was no way that the skier could have crossed over in front of his competitor to beat him to the finish line, yet through the editing process he does. The audience sees this and apparently believes it. Ritchie says, "We see because we want to see." He demonstrates how the subjective camera, editing, and sound together with identification with the audience and a knowledge of the audience's predispositions produce a persuasive impact. Ritchie says that it is not a matter of "seeing is believing," but rather "believing is seeing." He shows us that the viewers willingly accept it not as a record of reality, but as a re-creation of reality dependent on human vision.

Film should be studied as a persuasive force in society because, like other forms of persuasive communication, it, too, has the potential to change attitudes and behavior. One of the most frequent rejoinders one hears after students are asked to analyze film's persuasive techniques is: "Why can't we just view films as pure entertainment?" The answer to the question is related to the purpose of education in a democratic society: "Because you have the right to know what is happening to you." Schillaci (1971) adds to this by reminding us, "Education increasingly means developing the ability to live humanly in the technological culture by changing it. Film is forever spinning out intensifications of the environment which make it visible and livable. . . . An art which creates its own space, and can move time forward or back, can humanize change by conditioning us to live comfortably immersed in its fluctuations" (p. 188).

TELEVISION

Going to the movies is an event that involves planning, anticipation, and expense. Watching television is an everyday occurrence for most Americans. The TV set is a member of the family, and, for most people, watching television is a regular part of the day's activities. More than 95 percent of American homes have television sets which are turned on and watched more than six hours every day (Real 1977, p. 12). Because of television, young people sense the world in ways never sensed before, and, consequently, they have developed an approach to life that is very different from that of their elders (Farson 1969, p. 21). Many psychologists believe that television has had a "hothouse effect" on children that pushes them into maturity earlier than their emotional development can handle it. Ten year olds are stimulated to act like fifteen year olds, fifteen year olds are stimulated to act like twenty year olds. Conversely, because television seems to emphasize youth, it pushes the over thirty year olds to act younger than they are.

For many people, the events on television are perceived as real. A 1975 study found that the young and the poor believe that the drama they see on television accurately portrays reality (Comstock, in Wells 1979, p. 153). R. Primeau (1979) tells the story about a family out for a ride with six children in the car. In a sudden downpour of rain, they get a flat tire and the father braves the storm to change it. Inside the car, the children are fighting and the babies are screaming. The nine year old shouts a solution to his father and gets the following answer: "But this isn't TV; this is really happening. We can't change the channel" (pp. vii–viii).

Television not only provides the public with broadcasting, but, with the advent of cable systems, it brings "narrowcasting" into our homes. We also play games on our television sets, and now, with two-way systems in some cities, people can even talk back to their television sets. It would appear that television, like Cleopatra in Shakespeare's *Antony and Cleopatra*, satisfies where most it makes hungry.

G. Gerbner feels that the "public-making" significance of television lies in its ability to create publics, define issues, provide common terms of reference, and thus allocate attention and power (in Dance 1967, p. 45). Marshall McLuhan says that television (electronic technology) has brought the world back to a tribal or a global village wherein rapid delivery of information forces "us to reconsider and reevaluate practically every thought, every action, and every institution formerly taken for granted" (1964, p. 7).

Flow

Television programs do not exist in and unto themselves. They are surrounded by commercials, station breaks, announcements, and other programs. This has the effect on the viewer of staying with television on and on through an endless flow. *Flow* is the term that Raymond Williams has used to describe the uninterrupted following of one thing by another, a characteristic that is central to the television experience (Williams 1975, p. 95). According to R. Adler, "One result of this flow is a powerful tendency to blur the contents of television together. To some degree, this tendency is encouraged by the network and station planners, who design their schedules specifically so that one program leads effortlessly into the next. We frequently will tune into television at an arbitrary time, watch for awhile, then tune out again at an equally arbitrary time. The goal of the programmer is to persuade us to stay tuned in for as long as possible" (1976, p. 7).

Flow tends to confuse the viewer about the specific source of the content of television. We've all said, at one time or another, "I saw it on television, but I cannot remember which program." This worked in Jimmy Carter's favor during the 1976 presidential compaign. Gerald Rafshoon resurrected the five-minute commercial for Carter's campaign in Florida in the early months of 1976. A few days after the first five-minute ads were shown on the air, Joseph Lelyveld, a *New York Times* correspondent, discovered while interviewing people in Orlando, Florida, that "TV viewers, even attentive TV viewers, often found it difficult to distinguish between what they had seen in political ads and what they had seen on network news programs":

A number of viewers, for instance, did not seem to recognize Carter's five-minute commercials as advertising, despite the disclaimer at the end of the ads, always following a pitch for a vote. A barber named Rolla Balzier told me he had seen a "15-minute special" on Jimmy Carter. It was plainly one of the ads. "He had to work to get where he is," the barber said, repeating the copy. "He comes across as a human being, not a machine." Carolyn Allen, a student nurse, described in detail a news report she said she had seen on Carter. Again, it was an ad. Her neighbor, Virginia Sharpe, said she had become aware of Carter "just when he came on TV." When I asked what she liked about him, she also paraphrased an ad, remarking that he was "more for the working people" because he had worked with his hands. (1976, p. 70)

The blurring of television advertising and television news is a product of flow. Yet, television critics, who should be examining such phenomena, tend to overlook this significant aspect of television. David Littlejohn surveyed the writings of television critics who work for the twenty-five leading newspapers in America, and he also examined the critics' applications of critical methodology from other media. He found that the critics tend to look for novelty, quality, controversy, and the new and the different in television programs, discussing single episodes as one-time-only happenings (in Adler 1976, pp. 149–50). These leading critics ignore flow and thus ignore essential characteristics—that most television shows are of a recurring nature, part of continuing series, and that they interact with other things around them.

Another important result of flow is that the average viewers look to television for familiar faces, for reassuring sameness. Viewers anticipate well-recognized characters and situations. The impact of flow on the viewer reinforces R. Williams's notion that "one of the innovating forms of television is television itself" (1975, p. 77). Television is highly structured, and, indeed, the viewer structures his or her viewing behavior accordingly. It also structures viewer responses, for viewers know that a show will reach some sort of dénouement before the half hour or hour or two is over.

MYTH MAKING IN TELEVISION

The familiar characters of television and how they fit into television's flow are an important part of television's message. While it is important to study television's audience, it is also important to study the content of the medium. Socrates warned us that the stories that are told shape the minds of children. Modern anthropologists also tell us that our culture is shaped by the stories we are told.

One way of analyzing the "stories" of television is myth analysis. The myth of the rescuer, a mysterious stranger coming from nowhere, asking nothing in return, and saving those in distress, bringing happiness to the kingdom and restoring justice, can be found in every culture. Robert Jewett and John Lawrence, two philosophers, have written a book called *The American Monomyth* (1977) in which they say that television has secularized the Judeo-Christian dramas with supersaviors in pop culture functioning as replacements for the Christ figure. Their version of the television myth is the American monomyth:

A community in a harmonious paradise is threatened by evil: normal institutions fail to contend with this threat: a selfless superhero emerges to renounce temptations and carry out the redemptive task: aided by fate, his decisive victory restores the community to its paradisal condition: the superhero then recedes into obscurity (p. xx).

From "Star Trek" to "The Incredible Hulk," from "The Six Million Dollar Man" to the "Little House on the Prairie," from "Mork and Mindy" to "Charlie's Angels," superheroes act out their redemptive tasks, restoring peace and order before the final commercial and announcement about next week's show at the end of the hour. G. Gerbner and L. Gross (1975), after studying the content of television, found that people under thirty show far greater readiness to accept the hero concept as an answer to all problems. Their perception of the real world has been shaped by the monomythic paradigm (in Jewett and Lawrence, pp. 200–201).

Myths are abundant in other types of television formats as well. The myth of finding the treasure is the core of the game show. Like the Ancient Mariner, game shows tell their tales again and again, offering fame and fortune to a public eager to dress up in silly costumes or perform ridiculous acts to get them.

The myth formula is also transmitted in our news programs. Robert R. Smith, in his study of "Fictive Elements in Television News" (1978), found that television news is cast in traditional mythic forms. Using Carl Jung's archetypes, he found that the actors in the news were cast as Trickster, Wise Man, Nurturing Woman, Decisive Man, and Villain. The narrative themes of the news were cast into Armageddon, injustice, corruption, brotherhood, progress, nature, patriotism, hero rescues, and tests of strength. He concluded that television shaped social reality by creating stories primarily about omnipotent political leaders, beyond both marketplace and law, struggling with each other to determine the rules under which the rest of us must live. Like the Greek gods on Mount Olympus, government leaders are portrayed as remote and powerful.

If myths are the stories we tell ourselves about ourselves, outer revelations of our inner experiences, feelings, and thoughts, then television, with its mythic representation of reality, may be a mirror of reality, not shaping its public, but reflecting its beliefs and values. For many, television is the only mirror of the world at large, and, some would say, it is a funhouse mirror, shrinking, elongating, widening, narrowing, and exaggerating what stands before it.

THE IMPACT OF MASS COMMUNICATION

There are many theories and models that attempt to account for the uses of, effects of, and experiences with television and other forms of media. One of the more important models is the DeFleur and Ball-Rokeach dependency model. It proposes an integral relationship among audiences, media, and the larger social system. The model assumes an interactive-dependency among media, audiences, and society (Fig. 9.1 on page 208).

Dependency Model

At the center of the DeFleur and Ball-Rokeach model is the concept that people depend on media information to meet needs and attain goals. There are numerous ways in which people are dependent on media to satisfy information needs. One way is based on the need to *understand* one's social world. Another way arises from the need to *act* meaningfully and effectively

THE INFLUENCE
OF
TELEVISION

LECTURE # 1.

(*TV Guide* August 16, 1980)

in that world. A third way is based on the need for *fantasy-escape* from the problems of everyday life. DeFleur and Ball-Rokeach say, "The greater the need and consequently the stronger the dependency in such matters, the greater the likelihood that the information supplied will alter various forms of audience cognitions, feelings, and behavior" (DeFleur and Ball-Rokeach 1975, p. 262).

The dependency need is also affected by social stability, for dependency is heightened when a relatively high degree of change and conflict is present within a society. Change and conflict cause established institutions, beliefs, and practices to be challenged and force people to make reevaluations and choices. At such times, reliance on the media for information increases.

In stressing the tripartite relationship among media, audience, and society, DeFleur and Ball-Rokeach state, "Altering audience cognitive, affective, and behavioral conditions can feed back in turn to alter both society and the media" (p. 263). Their model attempts to predict certain types of cognitive effects:

1. Events in the media often create *ambiguities*, leading to a need for clarifying information. However, the media themselves often create ambiguity. Whenever ambiguity is present, dependency on media increases and the power of mediated messages to structure understanding or define situ-

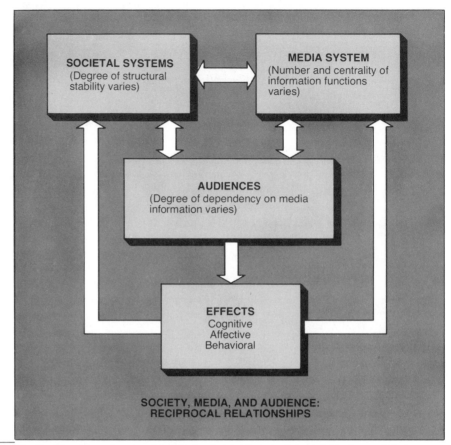

SOCIETAL SYSTEMS
(Degree of structural
stability varies)

MEDIA SYSTEM
(Number and centrality of
information functions
varies)

AUDIENCES
(Degree of dependency on media
information varies)

EFFECTS
Cognitive
Affective
Behavioral

SOCIETY, MEDIA, AND AUDIENCE:
RECIPROCAL RELATIONSHIPS

**FIGURE
9.1**

The De Fleur Dependency and Ball-Rokeach Model of Audience-Media-Society Relations (De Fleur and Ball-Rokeach 1975, p. 264)

ations may be very great. When ambiguity is lessened, this effect is reduced (pp. 264–66).

2. Because audiences rely heavily on media information, their *attitudes may be formulated* accordingly. Publics have formed new attitudes about speed limits, environmental problems, specific wars, captured Americans, and political misdeeds. Attitudes toward public figures are also formed as new people appear in the media. Even new objects become the focus of attitude formation as the public becomes aware of new technologies, birth-control devices, life-saving drugs, and various gadgets. Of course, DeFleur and Ball-Rokeach remind us that the media are not monolithic in their influence on such attitudes. There is a certain amount of selectivity exercised by people and their opinion leaders. (More on opinion leadership in the section on the reinforcement model.)

3. Media communications create *agenda-setting* when people use the media to decide what the important issues are and to determine what they should be concerned about. This does not mean that the media tell the people what to think, but rather they tell them what to think about. By focusing upon certain issues over time, the importance of the issues is emphasized. Vietnam was a place that very few Americans had heard about in 1960, but by 1968 it was a place that very few Americans had not heard about due to the media coverage of the Vietnam war and the public reaction to the war as it was monitored by the media. Agenda-setting also determines the world view that the public holds. By repetition of given themes (violence, sex, and socially defined roles), situations, dramatic resolution, and so forth, people's views of the world are shaped and set. Maxwell McCombs (1977) relates the agenda-setting function of the media to public-relations campaigns, showing that agenda-setting directs attention to the early stages of knowledge about an issue as it emerges in the media.

DeFleur and Ball-Rokeach point out that individual differences and social categories affect an individual's concern with issues. "Specific individuals will set their personal agendas in relation to their unique background of prior socialization, experience, and personality structure" (p. 268). There are broad strata of people, however, who have sufficient uniformity of social circumstances to enable them to share many problems and concerns in spite of individual differences. The public sorts out its interest and concern with the information presented on the media and assigns differential levels of importance.

4. A fourth cognitive effect is *expansion of the belief system*. Information presented on the media may broaden beliefs within categories such as politics or economics, and it may also increase a person's number of categories of beliefs.

5. Mass-mediated information plays an important part in *value clarification*. The media can facilitate value clarification by bringing values into conflict within audience members. The environmentalist movement has received wide media coverage and has heightened the conflict between economic values and survival and aesthetic values. Once the value conflicts are posed, people are moved to examine their own value positions. This often forces a painful choice. Thus, value priorities become clarified.

Affective effects are emotional responses that may be aroused by media. Feeling states such as fear, anxiety, or alienation can be produced or intensified by television coverage of the news or its depiction of places and groups of people. People who live in rural or suburban areas often fear the city because of the emphasis in the media on crime and violence in the cities. As media messages about ethnic groups or women or nationality groups change, it appears that members of those groups experience heightened feelings about themselves (DeFleur and Ball-Rokeach 1975, p. 273).

Finally, behavior may be affected by information received over the media. People may initiate new behavior (join a car pool) or cease an old behavior (stop eating sugar) as a result of media exposure. General patterns of behavior may be affected also. DeFleur and Ball-Rokeach cite a 1971 study that suggests that subjects who watch "Mister Rogers," a children's television show, increased their level of cooperative activity over several weeks of exposure to the program (DeFleur and Ball-Rokeach 1975, p. 274). Years of research have gone into the question of whether or not media violence affects aggression levels in people, especially children.

Media Violence and Aggression

L. Berkowitz, who has been testing adolescents and young adults, and A. Bandura, who has been testing children, have, for more than a decade, engaged in very careful, piece-by-piece experimental research on the causal relationship between filmed and televised aggression and subsequent behavior. Although both Berkowitz and Bandura and their colleagues were very careful to state that they make no claim to any situation outside of the laboratory, they found that film and television violence can incite violent behavior in viewers. Berkowitz said that "filmed violence may well increase the probability that someone in the audience will behave aggressively in a later situation [if] the fastasy situation appears socially justified" (Berkowitz, Corwin, and Heironimus 1963, p. 229). He also indicated that repeated exposure to violence increases the probability of subsequent aggressive acts for some members of the audience, but other factors also determine what may happen—how aggressive the subject is, how hostile the film makes him or her, how much he or she associates the story in the film with situations in which he or she learned hostile behavior, and the intensity of guilt and/or aggression anxiety aroused by the exposure to the film (Berkowitz 1962). Bandura also found that children, under certain conditions, are apt to reproduce aggressive action after observing adults exhibit novel and aggressive action on the screen (Bandura, Ross, and Ross 1963). Reviews of their extensive research lead us to the conclusion that sometimes media violence may be persuasively effective with the attitude changes consisting more often of modifications than of conversions. With respect to behavior changes, it can be generalized that some types of depicted violence will be found to have some types of effects on the aggression levels of some types of children under some types of conditions.

One of the most interesting aspects of the experimental evidence concerning the relationship between the media and behavior change is that subjects tend to be influenced by film and television characters that they perceive to be similar to themselves. Berkowitz uses the rhetorical term "identification" when he talks about implicit role taking on the part of the subjects (Turner and Berkowitz 1972), and he, along with William J. McGuire (in Lindzey and Aronson 1969, pp. 180–87), P. H. Tannenbaum and E. P. Geer (1965), and Walter Hess (in Lindzey and Aronson 1969, pp. 77–195), has found that viewer identification is the central concept in the interpretation of film and television effects. The extent to which viewers rated themselves as similar to particular characters influenced their reactions to the aggressors in the media.

Reinforcement Model

The DeFleur and Ball-Rokeach theory states that media messages will affect people only to the degree that the people are dependent on media information. J. T. Klapper (1960) found that the media messages reinforced rather than created attitudes and behavior. He said that the media function among and through a nexus of mediating factors and influences, which are (1) individual differences that cause selective exposure, selective perception, and selective retention and (2) group norms and group interaction. Within social interaction, people seek advice and confirmation of attitudes. Certain members of these groups have important functions within the group, and, thus, they are designated as *opinion leaders*. These people are the ones that the other members of the group turn to for advice on specific matters and, thus, formulate opinions.

Opinion Leaders

Research on opinion leadership has been generated from two major traditions. Sociologists studying the election of 1940 found that voters were seldom affected by the media. Instead, P. F. Lazarsfeld, B. Berelson, and H. Gaudet (1968) discovered the existence of what they termed "opinion leaders." Opinion leaders were generally found to be peers, more interested in the election than others, and voluntarily exposed to more media than the nonopinion leaders. The involvement of interpersonal communication via the opinion leader led Lazarsfeld and his associates to formulate what is known as the *two-step flow hypothesis*: information flows from the mass media to certain opinion leaders in the community who facilitate communication effects through discussions with their peers.

While Lazarsfeld, Berelson, and Gaudet were analyzing presidential elections, rural sociologists were studying the adoption of hybrid corn by Iowa farmers. Among their findings were data that argued that the advice and influence of neighbors became increasingly important in later stages of the adoption process. It was generally conversations with homophilous neighbors that were the key to adoption for the majority of the farmers surveyed.

The concept of homophily/heterophily is basic to the concept of opinion leadership. E. M. Rogers and F. F. Shoemaker define homophily as the "degree to which pairs or individuals who interact are similar in certain attributes, such as beliefs, values, education, social status, and the like" (1971, p. 210). They articulate two "rules" that are basic to opinion leadership: (1) communication is generally seen as being homophilous, and (2) opinion leaders are generally perceived as being of slightly higher competence or knowledge than others. The main point in all of this is that the opinion leader is seen as being imbedded in a group.

Other researchers have defined other characteristics of opinion leadership. H. F. Lionberger (1953), E. A. Wilkening (1952), and C. P. Marsh and A. L. Coleman (1954) all found that the opinion leader shows a high degree of conformity to group norms. R. K. Merton (1957), E. M. Rogers and L. Svenning (1969), H. Menzel and E. Katz (1956), and E. M. Rogers (1961) all have found that the opinion leader tends to be more of a cosmopolite than nonopinion leaders, who tend to be localites. Lazarsfeld, Berelson, and Gaudet (1968), Lionberger (1953), and Katz and Lazarsfeld (1964) further defined the opinion leader as a person who tends to be actively involved in social organizations. Finally, opinion leaders tend to be sought out for their advice in specific matters. In other words, the opinion leader sought out for advice on which candidate to vote for in an election would probably not be the same opinion leader selected for advice on how to fix a leaky roof. The perceived "expertise" of the opinion leader may, however, affect related areas. The opinion leader who gives advice on roof repair might also be asked about home repairs in general.

As researchers studied the opinion leader concept further, they began to modify the original two-step flow model. The first modification was in the form of the "multistep flow" model. According to this model, people are seen as obtaining ideas and information from the media directly, but still going to the opinion leader for confirmation and attitude formation. A later modification introduced the concept of saliency. According to this model, people will only seek out an opinion leader for advice on ideas and information that they receive from the media when the ideas and information are considered very important. For example, a person not interested in football who hears on television that the Pittsburgh Steelers are the best team might accept that appraisal without "checking it out" with an opinion leader. Research has shown that the ultimate number of relays between the media and final receivers is highly variable. In the adoption of an innovation, for example, some people will hear of the innovation directly from the media, while others are many steps removed.

Diffusion of Innovations

Other research in rural agriculture has contributed to our understanding of the spread of media influence. Diffusion of innovations occurs when an idea spreads from a point of origination to surrounding geographical areas or from person to person within a single area. Rogers and Shoemaker (1969) relate diffusion of innovations to the process of social change in general. Social change includes invention, diffusion or communication, and consequences. Change can occur internally from within a group or externally through contact with outside change agents, in which case contact may occur spontaneously or accidentally, or it may result from planning on the part of outside agencies. Diffusion is a time-consuming process, but once established, an innovation will have significant consequences. An innovation is any new idea in a social system. The diffusion process occurs through both mass and interpersonal communication channels.

Gatekeeping

Information does not diffuse throughout a system in random fashion, but is channeled through certain decision points or *gates*. Kurt Lewin (1951) has been credited as being one of the first to apply the term *gatekeeping*. His study dealt with the distribution of food and other consumer goods during the Second World War. D. M. White (1950) was one of the first to take the gatekeeping model and apply it to the mass media. His study was focused upon the decisions made by a wire-service editor in selecting stories to send over the wire. In both cases, the question asked was: "What materials or information are allowed to flow along given channels to the consumer?"

Donohue *et al.* (in Kline and Tichenor 1972, pp. 41–69) have done much to broaden the concept of gatekeeping to include more of a systems approach. They are concerned with how gatekeeping functions in the mass communication process, where it functions, and what the consequences of its functioning are. They do not assume that the only function of gatekeeping is social control, but that all communication processes have control functions that are either *manifest*, such as editors' decisions concerning what stories will be published in the newspaper and their length and placement in a given section on a given page, or *latent*, such as the limitations of a given medium.

In keeping with their perspective that gatekeeping is a control function occurring within the mass communication process, Donohue *et al.* define gatekeeping as "including all forms of information control that may arise in decisions about message encoding, such as selection, shaping, display, timing, withholding, or repetition of entire messages or message components" (in Kline and Tichenor 1972, p. 43). Overall, their definition and conceptualization of gatekeeping is that it is a function that occurs during the mass communication process, with the emphasis placed upon the social systems and subsystems involved.

It would appear, then, that the mass media, especially television in its prevalence, organize, mediate, and comment on significant aspects of social and cultural experience. The 1970s marked a time when media activists attempted to reform the medium. Action for Children's Television succeeded in obtaining legislation to govern children's programming and advertisements aimed at selling children's products. In 1972, a report by the U.S. Surgeon General established a causal link between violence on television and violent behavior in children. Concern about violence on television led the Federal Communications Commission chairman, Richard E. Wiley, to institute a plan in 1975 to restrict depiction of rapes and murders until after 8:00 P.M.

In a landmark courtroom trial in Florida, a defense attorney argued that his client, a shy teen-aged boy, killed an elderly neighbor because the youth had been conditioned by years of exposure to violent television shows. A jury found the boy guilty nonetheless. It is very difficult to "prove" that television influences individual actions, but that does not stop a great many people from thinking that it does.

Television probably does not have a great deal of political power. McCombs, in his survey of mass communication in political persuasion, tells us, "There are few documented instances of real political or ideological conversion" (in Kline and Tichenor 1972, p. 170). He believes that television may crystallize and reinforce more than it converts.

There are many other influences upon voting behavior, notably social groups, fellow workers, formal associations, and party affiliation. Many times the effects of media will disappear when the full set of other variables that influence voting behavior are examined. McCombs discusses the "law of minimal consequences" as an answer to those who expect sweeping attitudinal and behavioral changes when individuals are exposed to political persuasion on television (Kline and Tichenor 1972, p 177). C. Atkin says that the degree of influence is related to the level of involvement of the voter. A person who is highly involved will respond to media political persuasion by receiving, recalling, evaluating, forming attitudes, and taking action. A low involvement person will be passive in responding to certain stimuli. Such a person may be aware but will not bother to evaluate critically the content or form an opinion (in Roloff and Miller 1980, p. 287).

Television has reached a stage in its development where it now satirizes itself. In programs such as "Second City Television Network" and "NBC's Saturday Night Live," the subject of television itself has become dominant. The most potent medium attack, however, came from the film *Network*, released in 1976, which scathingly condemned the power of television. Ironically, the film was written by Paddy Chayefsky, a veteran of television's golden age of drama.

ADVERTISING IN THE MASS MEDIA

Because of the preponderance of the mass media, Americans are daily exposed to as many as 1,600 advertisements. Since this satiated audience may be inclined to try to escape the overwhelming number of ads in the media, the advertisers have to get to the audience quickly before the audience tunes out. Advertisers employ scientific techniques of motivational research, but their work is also based on a mixture of intuition, hunches, and a background of theory of advertising which varies from one agency to the next (Brown 1968, p. 185). One general technique that seems to prevail, however, is an appeal to psychological satisfaction. As Vance Packard pointed out in *The Hidden Persuaders* (1957), the motivational analysts add depth to the selling of ideas and products and offer the consumer much more than the actual item involved. He quotes a Milwaukee advertising executive who comments on what it is that the consumers believe they are buying: "The cosmetic manufacturers are not selling lanolin, they are selling hope. . . . We no longer buy oranges, we buy vitality. We do not buy just an auto, we buy prestige" (p. 5).

An interesting study was conducted with brand cigarette smokers. Donald Armstrong gave Rorschach tests to eighty smokers to determine their personality traits and then predicted to which brand of cigarette each subject had a strong loyalty. His predictions were over 90-percent accurate. He said, "Just looking at the test results you knew immediately the brand the poor devil had to smoke" (Brown 1968, p. 180).

A basic formula that advertisers use to create their ads is (1) they must gain the attention of the audience as quickly as possible. Many of their techniques are patterned after the attention-getting factors discussed in Chapter VIII. Novelty, contrast, something striking and conspicuous, movement and change, and clever slogans or catchwords are often used. The jingle, according to Harry Wayne McMahan, a twenty-five-year veteran of the advertising industry and monthly columnist for *Advertising Age*, is found in 42 percent of today's money-making commercials (Wright 1979, pp. 314–15). (2) The presence of a familiar personality in very close proximity to the product is frequently used as an attention-getting device. Thirty-three percent of the commercials use this technique.

Another attention-getting technique is to appeal to a common need or desire or some widespread fear or anxiety. People worry about bad breath, unattractiveness, sociability, health, and cleanliness. This need or lack of fulfillment is then related in the second stage of the commercial to the product. A bridge of visual and verbal symbols is used to make a transition from fact to dream and from the dream to the illusion of the product. Satisfaction is suggested, rarely guaranteed. Because of the subtle use of suggestion, today's advertising more closely resembles propaganda than it does persuasion. In fact, advertising may well be the most widespread use of propaganda operating in America. While most advertising agencies utilize retention testing to see if consumers or prospective consumers can remember the contents of the advertisement, media researchers have found that buying behavior is influenced by advertising (Day 1971, Wright 1979).

SUMMARY

The mass media are prevalent in the life of the average American. Film, which is enjoyed and seen more by young Americans than by older people, has a strong capacity to persuade. Film is communication that can fulfill the interactive-dependency needs of the filmmakers and the viewers. The identification power of film is stronger than that of any other medium, and most filmmakers know this.

Television viewing is a part of everyday life for most Americans. The young and the poor believe that what they see on television is real. Television can create publics, define issues, and allocate power.

The "flow" of television confuses the viewer about the origins of content. Flow also gives a reassuring sameness to the television experience. Familiar faces and types reappear in many programs, which not only make them popular, but also provide the substance of myths which reflect the beliefs and values of the audience.

There are many theories and models to account for the impact of mass communication. The dependency model of DeFleur and Ball-Rokeach stresses the fact that people depend on the media to meet needs and attain goals. Reliance on the media increases during times of social conflict and change. Media dependency can result in new attitudes being formulated, agenda-setting, expansion of belief systems, value clarification, heightened emotional responses, and behavior changes.

Studies that have focused on media violence and aggressive levels in viewers, especially the young, conclude that some types of depicted violence will be found to have some types of effects on the aggression levels of some types of children under some types of conditions.

The reinforcement model states that audience attitudes are

reinforced rather than changed. Opinion leaders facilitate media communication effects through interpersonal communication. The two-step flow theory says that information from the media flows through opinion leaders in the community.

The multistep flow theory shows people going to the media directly, then going to opinion leaders for confirmation. The number of relays between the media and final receiver is highly variable.

Media are also contributing factors to the diffusion of innovations. Whenever social change occurs, it is diffused through the media and interpersonal channels with significant consequences.

Gatekeeping is the decision-making function of media personnel to allow certain information to be communicated in the media. It is a form of information control.

Many groups of people outside the media attempt to control media content and programming also. Of particular concern to these groups is television violence, sex, and advertising.

Advertising is predominant in the media. It plays upon the consumers' needs and anxieties. It is a form of propaganda.

KEY WORDS

Mass media
Identification
Flow
Myth making
Dependency model
Agenda-setting
Reinforcement model

Opinion leaders
Two-step flow theory
Multistep flow theory
Diffusion of innovations
Gatekeeping
Law of minimal
   consequences

EXERCISES

1. Go to see a "message" film, and analyze the persuasive elements in it. During the film, analyze it much like you would a persuasive speech, and in an essay describe what you found. Consider the following elements as you find them in the film:
   a. What is the purpose of the film—that is, what is the film's message?
   b. What anchors are apparent in the film (values we seem to share, goals, basic beliefs, attitudes—things we believed in before seeing the film or things that the filmmaker in his/her view of society thinks we believe in)?

c. Is cognitive dissonance produced by a violation of basic beliefs, attitudes, or values? How is this done in film?

d. Does acceptance of the "message" alleviate the dissonance? Do you feel differently about anything after seeing the film? Do you think that your behavior might change?

e. If you already believe in the central message of the film, consider the ways in which your belief is reinforced.

f. What devices are used to focus your attention, external or internal, upon that which the filmmaker wants to emphasize? (Notice the use of music as an attention-getting factor.)

g. What basic needs (of Maslow's) are appealed to?

h. How does the film produce an emotional response in you? Are you motivated to accept the "message" because of your emotional response? When you experience a "feeling-response," do you participate vicariously in the situation on the screen?

i. To what extent can you identify with the characters in the film? What attempts are made to gain audience involvement? Can you remain aloof from the action? Are there any recognizable traits of yourself in the characters on the screen? How do you feel if you recognize yourself?

j. Are there any group appeals made in the film? Do you identify with any of the groups? If so, do you feel pressured to accept the message because of the group identity? Analyze your feelings about negative reference groups, if they are used.

k. What have the filmmakers used as symbols of their message? Look for objects, scenery, lighting, shots, color, film speed, and, of course, the characters whom the actors portray. Identify what the symbols represent.

l. Discuss the visual images of the film. How do they determine your frame of reference, alter your perception, or put you in a state of readiness to respond?

m. Does the film provide you with an awareness that you didn't have before viewing it? Does it make you say, "I never thought of it that way before"?

2. Take a character from myth (the Savior-Hero, the Trickster, and so forth), and locate this character in a dramatic program, a comedy show, and the news on television.

3. Can you think of any new attitudes or behavior that you have formed as the result of watching television?

4. Who are your community's opinion leaders? Do you consult them about issues in or from the media?

5. Analyze your decision to vote in the last major election. How did the media and opinion leaders affect that decision?

6. Watch television news every day for one to three weeks. Can you notice agenda-setting? What new issues become prominent topics as the result of repetition on the media?

7. Analyze a television commercial. How does it get your attention, arouse a need or an anxiety, offer to fulfill your desires with a product, and promise satisfaction?

READINGS

Adler, R. *Television As a Cultural Force.* New York: Praeger, 1976.

DeFleur, M. L., and **Ball-Rokeach, S.** *Theories of Mass Communication.* New York: David McKay, 1975.

Jewett, R., and **Lawrence, J.** *The American Monomyth.* Garden City, N.Y.: Anchor Press/Doubleday, 1977.

Klapper, J. T. *The Effects of Mass Communication.* Glencoe, Ill.: The Free Press, 1960.

Kline, F. G., and **Tichenor, P. J.,** eds. *Current Perspectives in Mass Communication Research.* Beverly Hills, Calif.: Sage, 1972.

O'Donnell, V. "Analysis of Film As Communication." In *Mass Communication in Education and Society,* ed. R. E. Davis. Austin, Texas: SCA Summer Conference, 1975.

Petric, V. "Film in the Battle of Ideas." *Arts in Society* 10 (1973):231–40.

Rogers, E. M., and **Shoemaker, F. F.** *Communication of Innovations.* New York: Holt, Rinehart and Winston, 1969.

10

RESISTANCE TO PERSUASION

OBJECTIVES

Upon completion of this chapter you should be able to:

1. Understand the background of resistance to persuasion research.
2. Induce resistance through inoculation pretreatment.
3. Understand the process of building resistance through bolstering or changing belief structures.
4. Understand how anchoring to values, important beliefs, and highly valued groups or sources can increase resistance.
5. See how aggressiveness, high self-esteem, anxiety, and psychological reactance can be inhibitors of persuasion.
6. Discern how sex and sex-role type can induce resistance.
7. Understand impression management theory.

n each historical period, there seems to arise a need to prepare people to resist persuasive efforts from formidable enemies. During wartime, efforts were made to make the members of the military immune to propaganda and brainwashing. At present, it is difficult to thumb through a popular magazine or tune in to a talk show without hearing or reading the pathetic story of a parent whose child has joined a cult group such as the Moonies, Hare Krishna, or the Church of Scientology. It is known that these groups do an excellent job of preparing the members to resist persuasive attempts by parents to leave the cult or to even see their families.

Certainly, the majority of people live their lives without being subjected to brainwashing by a national enemy or cult leaders, but, as was seen in the previous chapters, we are subjected on a daily basis to a multitude of exposures to mass media and a variety of other persons. One sociologist-psychologist recognizes that "we are all—except for the catatonic schizophrenic—susceptible to some degree to peer-group pressure or to a mass media barrage" (McGuire 1970, p. 30).

Concern over the business of human manipulation has prompted scholars to seek and find deterrents to behavior control. Skill in resisting persuasion can be that deterrent. In this discussion of resistance, students should not perceive it as playing "the flip side of the record" of persuasion, but, as G. Miller and M. Burgoon suggest, "the process of inducing resistance is best viewed as an extension of the persuasion process" (1973, p. 19). So the creation of resistance is not the opposite of the persuasive process, but is an extension of it. Also, the persuader needs to be aware that outer signs that make a persuader believe that his/her efforts have been successful are sometimes just that—outer signs. In certain situations, the persuadee feels that it is socially appropriate to appear to be persuaded. Resistance to persuasion can occur both intentionally and accidentally.

Throughout the literature, a variety of ways are presented to induce persuasion resistance. We shall first present a chronological overview of this literature and then develop eight of the prevalent concepts.

OVERVIEW OF RESISTANCE LITERATURE

This overview and the subsequent development of concepts should provide the persuader with some choices. W. C. Minnick stated, "Common sense would call upon the speaker to attempt a variety of ways of increasing resistance, not just one" (1979, p. 202). The persuader, then, uses judgment to decide which method would be most successful for him/her in a given situation.

One of the major figures in the study of resistance to persuasion is psychologist William J. McGuire. His work on "inoculation" as a defense against persuasion is considered a milestone in the research literature. McGuire (in Berkowitz I 1964, 192–231) reviews the area of inducing resistance by discussing the following five approaches: (1) the behavioral-commitment approach, (2) anchoring the beliefs to other cognitions, (3) inducing resistant cognitive states, (4) prior training in resisting persuasive attempts, and (5) his own inoculation theory.

Leon Festinger and Nathan Macoby (1964) examined resistance to persuasion and provided some insight into the nature of the possible effects of distraction. When J. L. Vohs and R. L. Garrett (1968) attempted to replicate the findings of Festinger and Macoby, they discovered two additional variables—(1) involvement and (2) familiarity with counterarguments. The Festinger-Macoby and Vohs-Garrett studies provide information that relates to the relevance of Festinger's (1957) cognitive dissonance theory to the resistance to persuasion.

Kenneth E. Andersen (1971) explores self-persuasion, which can be likened to resistance to persuasion. A parallel in purpose can be recognized through his classifications of reinforcement, commitment, and cognitive balance as patterns of self-persuasion.

Miller and Burgoon (1973) first deal with individual differences of the persuadee. Individuals differ, they imply, in degrees of self-esteem, in feelings of anxiety and hostility, and in levels of education. Miller and Burgoon also offer the following resistance-generating strategies: (1) changing internal belief structures; (2) reducing cognitive inconsistency; and (3) inoculation.

W. Thompson (1975), in generally discussing persuasibility, attends to commitment, anchoring, resistant cognitive states, forewarning, inoculation, and selective exposure as methods of inducing resistance.

In their most recent social psychology text, R. Baron and D. Byrne (1977) outline psychological reactance and inoculation as the two major factors of resistance to persuasion.

The most current literature, representing a foundational approach to this subject, has been produced by Burgoon *et al.* (1978). These empiricists searched for a model of resistance to persuasion, considering a variety of variables, and found two conditions to be mediators of resistance: (1) induced critical response set and (2) the target of the criticism.

All of the above theoretical approaches are grouped into eight general sections for discussion and clarification.

INOCULATION

The most widely acknowledged technique of inducing resistance is inoculation. It is a strategy analogous to physical immunization. An individual can develop belief resistance in people in the same manner that disease resistance is developed biologically in man or animal. Inoculation theory was formulated and furthered by McGuire (McGuire, in Berkowitz I 1964).

His inoculation experiments were based on beliefs he referred to as "cultural truisms." He defined cultural truisms as those beliefs one holds "that are so widely shared within the person's social milieu that he would not have heard them attacked, and indeed, would doubt that an attack were possible" (McGuire, in Berkowitz I 1964, p. 201). An example of a truism from his experiments is "The effects of penicillin have been, almost without exception, of great benefit to mankind" (McGuire, in Berkowitz I 1964, p. 201).

Providing Counterarguments

In order to prepare a person for subsequent attacks on such a truism, one is faced with two obstacles. First of all, the person lacks practice in defending the belief, and, second, he/she lacks motivation to prepare or practice a defense of the belief, because a challenge of it appears so remote.

It is necessary, then, for the pretreatment process to motivate the persuadee to develop a defense. An effective means of motivation is to threaten the belief with a mild form of attack argument. Since the persuadee has probably never practiced bolstering a belief, he/she needs careful instruction in developing defensive data.

There are two types of pretreatment defenses: supportive and refutational. The supportive defense strategy, which is nonthreatening in nature, consists of providing the person with various arguments in support of the truism or belief. The refutational defense strategy, which is more threatening in nature, provides arguments that attack the belief and proceed by refuting those attacks.

Suppose an instructor had a bright student who was being tempted to drop out of school to take a position that paid a high salary. The instructor might adapt the truism "Everyone should pursue goals commensurate with his/her talent and potential."

Supportive defense strategies might be: "You are too bright to settle for the future you would have without a degree"; "Even though the job would be gratifying now, you would feel frustrated in later years because promotions would be unavailable to you."

A refutational defense strategy might be: "Take advantage of a good opportunity to earn a high salary, and forget long-range goals." An attack on such an argument might be: "If you get your bachelor's degree, you can earn even more money. Don't settle for less."

There is a tendency on the part of the persuadee to lose motivation to assimilate the defenses adequately enough to endure a future attack. This is especially true in the supportive defense situation. The defenses can then be strengthened if the person receives a forewarning of an attack on the truism before the defenses are presented (McGuire and Papageorgis 1962).

The innoculation process, then, involves providing counterarguments and identifying the weaknesses in those arguments. A forewarning that one's beliefs will be attacked can motivate the person to see the importance of defense preparation. A forewarning is not enough motivation to make it happen (Hass and Grady 1975). Also, the potential persuadee's active participation in the defense-building process makes inoculation more successful.

The most successful counterarguments are those that are internally generated. The fact that they are the persuadee's "own" makes them more congruent and meaningful to his/her belief system (Roberts and Macoby 1973, p. 302).

D. F. Roberts and N. Macoby also suggest, "Given motivation to resist a persuasive appeal, receivers will interpret their own counterarguments—give them meaning—in terms of how they will refute points in the attacking message. Resistance, *per se*, then, will be a function of how successfully the receiver perceives himself to have refuted the attack" (Roberts and Macoby in Clark 1973, p. 302).

BOLSTERING OR CHANGING BELIEF STRUCTURES

Bolstering or changing belief structures is another major category of resistance technique. This classification encompasses commitment and anchoring. Commitment to a belief can be exhibited in the form of a private decision, a public announcement of one's belief, active participation on the basis of the belief, or external commitment. These subclasses are McGuire's, although the underlying ideas are supported by the research of other scholars (Miller and Burgoon 1973, pp. 27–31).

1. Private Decision

The weakest form of belief commitment is a private admission on the part of the person that he/she does hold the belief. This private decision provides more resistance than when making no decision at all, but will not withstand persuasive efforts in all situations. Every student has been in the situation in which the private decision was made to spend all evening studying for the following day's exam only to see that private commitment go by the wayside when someone suggested that relaxing with a beer and pizza would make the study session "easier."

2. Public Announcement of One's Belief

Kurt Lewin suggested that a public announcement of one's belief tended to induce a firmer commitment than a private decision. Another study confirmed that the public announcements did provide resistance to peer conformity pressures (In Fisher, Rubenstein, and Freeman 1956).

Research evidence points to the fact that forcing a person to make a public declaration can be an effective means of building resistance to future persuasive appeals (Miller and Burgoon 1973, p. 28).

3. Active Participation on the Basis of the Belief

After achieving success in persuading someone to state his/her belief publicly, resistance can be increased by persuading him/her to engage in some action that supports the belief. Political parties, cults, and various organizations persuade people to pass out pamphlets, collect money door to door, or make speeches to groups. After performing these tasks, these people are more committed than those who only made a private commitment such as sending a check. When the person complies with the suggested action, it is certain to increase resistance if (a) there were other alternatives from which to choose and (b) there was little pressure on them to comply (Festinger 1957).

4. External Commitment

External commitment involves reporting to the subject that other persons think that he/she holds the belief. The persuadee is then presented with arguments that attack the belief. M. E. Rosenbaum's studies show that persuadees who are subjected to this form of pretreatment are more resistant to subsequent opposition than those who have not been externally committed (Rosenbaum and Franc 1960; Rosenbaum and Zimmerman 1959).

ANCHORING

Additionally classed by McGuire (1964) are three anchoring approaches, which differ regarding the type of cognitions to which a given belief is linked. A belief can be anchored (and, therefore, resistant to change or persuasion) by linkage to accepted values that are important to the individual, by linkage to other beliefs of a highly salient value to the individual, or by linkage to an individual, group, or source that the listerner holds in high esteem. To change the belief would mean a change in the value, the other belief, or the person or group held in high esteem.

Linkage to Accepted Values

This form of anchoring involves linking the belief to be immunized to specific values or goals held by the persuader. C. E. Nelson's study (1968) indicated that the amount, activity, and difficulty of anchoring beliefs to values created a significant amount of resistance to persuasion. It was found that active participation in prior anchoring created a significant amount of resistance (p. 329). In other words, when a persuadee can establish a link between belief and values, resistance will be strengthened. If, also, you can convince the persuadee that he/she must hold the belief in order to achieve an important goal, resistance will be strengthened in this situation as well. If, for example, parents of a college-bound student were worried about his/her having disciplined study habits and knew that being a leader among his/her peers was valued by him/her, the parents might try to establish a link between studying and gaining recognition in the college scene. "Being captain of the football team and president of the student body is more important than academic achievement in high schoool, but academic achievement in one's chosen field is what brings recognition and respect in college." This argument might cause the student to resist suggestions to put off studying made by students who are not seeking recognition.

Linkage to Related Important Beliefs

This immunization method involves pointing out to the persuadee that his/her particular belief is logically and inextricably tied to other important beliefs and if the one belief is changed, it would create imbalance with the linking beliefs. McGuire suggests that by "merely asking the person to rehearse the related beliefs which he already possesses makes more salient these linkages to the given belief, and thereby confers enhanced resistance to subsequent attacks—at least to the extent that such attacks will introduce inconsistencies into his belief system" (McGuire, in Berkowitz I 1964, p. 196–97).

Linkage to a Highly Valued Group or Source

The purpose here is to convince the persuadee that individuals and group members whom the persuadee values hold the same belief (that the persuadee wants to retain), thereby increasing resistance. To change the belief would place the persuadee at odds with significant others, which, in turn, creates psychological discomfort. Anticipating this psychologically uncomfortable dilemma creates resistance. Even nonspecific groups can have the same effect—"Everybody believes that . . ." or "Reliable sources contend that . . ."

COGNITIVE STATES

In the previous section, a threat of psychological discomfort was mentioned as a factor that creates resistance. So it is, then, that cognitive consistency, as opposed to cognitive inconsistency, imbalance, or dissonance, is desirable for resisting persuasive attempts. Festinger (1957) suggests that when a person is in a state of cognitive imbalance, he/she is prone to change. If one can maintain cognitive balance or consistency, then, there exists a condition of "no threat" and no need for change in attitude. Reducing cognitive inconsistency obviously is a strengthening factor against persuasion.

PREDISPOSITIONS TO RESISTANCE

There are certain personality, motivational, or ideological states that are correlated with resistance to the pressures of social influence. In other words, an individual can theoretically be predispositioned to be unsusceptible to issues. This predispositioning can be accomplished through inducing anxiety, inducing aggressiveness, and raising a person's self-esteem.

Inducing Anxiety

One motivational state that can significantly heighten resistance is anxiety. A 1959 study concluded that there is a direct correlation between anxiety level and resistance (Nunnally and Bobren 1959). The anxiety must be chronic in nature rather than situational. Persons who are low in chronic anxiety are likely to be persuaded by irrelevant fear appeals, whereas those who have chronic high anxiety have their resistance increased by irrelevant fear appeals (Miller and Burgoon 1973, p. 25).

Inducing Aggressiveness

Chronic aggressiveness can induce resistance, but only to certain types of messages. One study indicated that when a persuadee had been subjected to abrasive treatment in the past he/she is resistant to benign arguments that are harsh in nature (Weiss and Fine 1956). Miller and Burgoon conclude that because agressiveness causes one to dislike his or her fellow humans, he/she is more receptive to antihuman and/or society messages and is less receptive to messages that express good or neutral ideas or actions (Miller and Burgoon 1973, p. 24).

Raising Self-Esteem

If the persuadee can be exposed to a successful experience, it can increase his/her resistance. This is a fact, even if the experience is unrelated to the subsequent message. The resistance is further increased if the persuadee witnesses the source of the subsequent message having an unsuccessful experience. Also, when the subsequent message is complex, better message receptivity is achieved by the persuadee. Increased reception can then lower resistance. So, it is safe to say that raising self-esteem is an effective way to build resistance to simple suggestions and bold conformity appeals. On the other hand, it is not possible to predict conclusively the effect of self-esteem in building resistance to complex messages (Miller and Burgoon 1973, pp. 22–23).

PSYCHOLOGICAL REACTANCE

The process of psychological reactance (Brehm 1972) involves an individual's natural reaction to a freedom threat. Most people are strongly motivated "to maintain their freedom of action" (Baron and Byrne 1977, p. 129).

When a freedom threat occurs as a result of influence from others, people strive to maintain it. The result is that people totally reject the persuasive appeals and sometimes completely change and favor the opposite stance (Baron and Byrne 1977, p. 129). The desire to maintain one's freedom is so strong in some people that they respond negatively even when the persuader's stance is similar to the persuadee's own opinion.

A 1973 study (by Heller, Pallak, and Picik) indicated that just hearing about a possible attempt to persuade can create the same reaction. In this study, a group of college students was divided into three groups. One group overheard a comment that another person was going to exert persuasive influence on the subjects concerning a particular issue. The comment was made by a confederate of the experimenters. The second group's information did not indicate such an attempt. The third group heard nothing at all prior to the persuasive attempt. Later, the subjects received a note. The first group was ordered to write an essay supporting a particular side of an issue; the second group received only a suggestion that the subjects do so; and the third group received no message at all. The next step involved all subjects expressing their opinions on the issue.

The results were that those students who felt that their freedom was being threatened shifted attitudes in the opposite direction of the one the accomplice recommended. This also happens when a person is exposed to hard-sell techniques (Baron and Byrne 1977, p. 129–130). How many times has one of your friends said to you, "I think I ought to warn you that Bill is going to try to talk you into . . ." Your response was probably "Thanks a lot! Now I can be prepared." You know someone is planning to invade your freedom, and resistance usually occurs.

ANDROGYNY

A recent study (Montgomery and Burgoon 1980) sought to integrate knowledge about the effects of sex and sex role into the resistance model proposed by Burgoon and associates (Burgoon *et al.* 1978). There exists an abundance of literature concerning the effect of sex differences in persuasion and attitude change. The results of these studies point to the fact that we all tend to have strong and lasting expectations of the differing sex roles attributed to males and females. The new research, however, instead of dealing with *gender* differences, has begun to classify *individuals* according to traditionally sex-typed and nontraditionally sex-typed individuals based on both sex and masculinity/femininity (Montgomery and Burgoon 1980, p. 59). Traditional sex-types consist of what society would view as feminine females and masculine males. Nontraditional sex-types (*androgynous* individuals) exhibit either feminine or masculine behaviors determined by the social situation (Montgomery and Burgoon 1980, p. 59).

The subjects in this study (an equal number of male and female graduate students) were asked to make a decision about where a group of orphans should be taken on a field trip. They were given two options. One suggestion was to take them to a homecoming football game. The other was to take them to a community arts and crafts show. These situations were selected because a traditional male would probably advocate a football game, and the nontraditional male would probably favor the arts and crafts show.

The message was attributed to one of two sources, both of which were male. The traditional male was identified as a physical-education major, construction worker, and member of the track team. The nontraditional male was identified as a male nurse, member of the artisans' guild, one who worked with small children, and one who enjoyed cooking.

The groups heard the traditional male's delivery of the traditional message, the nontraditional male's delivery of the nontraditional message, and vice versa.

The results indicated that gender alone had no main effects. On the other hand, negative violations of receivers' expectations definitely inhibited compliance. The conclusion indicated that individuals develop expectations about how others will communicate that are based on the information these individuals have concerning the persuader's sex type. Also, the sex type of the persuadee will determine in part how he/she will react to violations of expectations concerning appropriate communicative behavior.

This study, then, can enable us to predict resistance to persuasion. Communication from a sex-typed source can violate the expectations of some persuadees while fulfilling expectations of others. When the expectancy is fulfilled, persuasion is enhanced; when the expectancy is violated, more threat is present and resistance is enhanced. When the persuadee feels threatened, the motivation to counterargue is increased. Increased counterarguing increases resistance to persuasion (Montgomery and Burgoon 1980, p. 67).

IMPRESSION MANAGEMENT

The preceding pages give us insights about how resistance can be intentionally established in the persuadee. There are times, however, when resistance occurs that only indirectly involves the persuader or does not involve him or her at all. The persuader, however, needs to be aware of resistance that may occur outside of his/her realm of influence.

There are social factors that exist in many persuasive situations which cause the persuadee to resist influence. Impression management theory indicates that persuadees in certain situations will appear to be persuaded if it means fulfilling the expectations of others. Fulfilling others' expectations often supersedes keeping a persuadee's private beliefs consistent (Tedeschi 1972). This theory applies to those persons who are overly concerned or even apprehensive about how others perceive them. This social phenomenon is situational in nature. Where a persuasive effort on a one-to-one basis may be successful, this same effort may be unsuccessful if performed in the presence of others.

A 1974 study (by Cialdini, Braver, and Lewis) indicates that individuals believe that yielding to persuasive attempts causes them to be perceived as lower in intelligence than if they show resistance (p. 636). Again, what others might think creates resistance. Another impression management study (Kalle, Riess, and Tedeschi 1981), based on the bogus pipeline approach (Jones and Sigall 1971 in Kalle, et al. 1981), presents a different aspect. Impression management theory means that a person, after performing a counterattitudinal behavior such as writing an essay on "Toothbrushing Is Harmful," will modify attitudes on paper-and-pencil tests to the extent that there will be more consistency between the behavior (the essay) and his/her true attitude. In the bogus pipeline studies, subjects were informed that they would later be attached to a lie-detector device in order to check the consistency of their answers. When subjects believed they would not be monitored or checked, they moderated their attitudes so there would be more concurrence between their counterattitudinal behavior and their attitude.

In essence, then, impression management studies tell us that we will moderate our attitudes to coincide with counterattitudinal behavior unless we believe we will be discovered. The persuader, then, may believe he/she has been successful when in reality moderation has occurred in the persuadee for one of the above reasons.

SUMMARY

Since it is desirable to develop resistance to some persuasive efforts, various means of doing so have been developed. Several approaches for resistance to persuasion were offered as ways to prevent persuasion from taking place.

Inoculation theory is an approach that develops resistance in the same manner that shots provide immunization against disease. A person can be inoculated against future persuasive exposures by providing counterarguments, which can be both supportive and refutational in nature.

Bolstering or changing belief structures involves commitment and anchoring. Degrees of commitment can be attained by (1) private decision, (2) public announcement of one's belief, (3) active participation on the basis of the belief, and (4) external commitment. Anchoring occurs by linking the resistance efforts to accepted values, linking to highly salient beliefs, and linking to persons or groups held in high esteem.

Cognitive states play an important role in resistance theory. By showing when the target person does not resist future persuasive efforts, inconsistency or psychological unpleasantness will occur.

Certain personality, motivational, or ideological states are correlated with resistance to social influence. A person can then develop predispositions to be unsusceptible to issues by inducing anxiety, appealing to aggressiveness, and raising one's self-esteem.

Psychological reactance involves a person's response to a freedom threat. This can cause resistance, especially to hard-sell persuasive techniques.

Recent research involving androgyny indicates that sex-role influences resistance to persuasion if audience expectations are not met.

Resistance can sometimes occur by accident or from forces not under the control of the persuader. Due to the social pressures to appear favorably in the eyes of others, people will appear to be persuaded when they actually are not. In general, people feel that yielding to persuasion is unacceptable to others.

The bogus pipeline studies support other impression management theories by showing that when individuals engage in counterattitudinal behavior, they will modify their attitudes on paper-and-pencil tests to decrease the difference between the two. If, however, they are told later they will be subjected to some lie-detector device, they tend to express their real attitudes.

To study persuasion is to study influence attempts from the perspective of both the persuader, who desires to influence, and the persuadee, who may be willing or unwilling to change. If the persuadee is unwilling to change then it would be helpful for him/her to learn to resist persuasion.

KEY WORDS

Behavioral-commitment approach
Anchoring
Inoculation
Pretreatment defense strategy
External commitment
Inducing anxiety

Inducing aggressiveness
Raising self-esteem
Psychological reactance
Androgyny
Impression management
 theory

EXERCISES

1. Select something that you are being strongly tempted to believe or do. Get a small group together, and tell the members about your temptation. Ask them to assume the role of tempter and to attack your position, which is to maintain the status quo. Come to your own defense by refuting their arguments and designing counterarguments to defend your position.

2. Make a public statement about your position (against the temptation), and say that you intend to maintain your position.
3. Take action that supports and reinforces your position.
4. Locate the key values, beliefs, and groups or a highly valued source that substantiate and support your position.
5. Share your temptation with a group of classmates, and ask them to help you raise your self-esteem in order to resist.

READINGS

Burgoon, M.; Cohen M.; Miller, M.; and **Montgomery, C. L.** "An Empirical Test of a Model of Resistance to Persuasion." *Human Communication Research* 5 (1978):27–39.

Festinger, L., and **Macoby, Nathan**. "On Resistance to Persuasive Communication." *Journal of Abnormal and Social Psychology* 68 (1964):359–66.

Kalle, R.; Riess, M.; and **Tedeschi, J.** "The Bogus Pipeline and Attitude Moderation Following Forced Compliance: Misattribution of Dissonance Arousal or Impression Management Inhibition." *Journal of Social Psychology* in press.

McGuire, W. J. "Inducing Resistance to Persuasion: Some Contemporary Approaches. " In *Advances in Experimental Social Psychology*, Leornard Berkowitz, ed. vol. 1. New York: Academic Press, 1964, pp. 192–227.

Miller, G., and **Burgoon M.** *New Techniques of Persuasion*. New York: Harper & Row, 1973.

Montgomery, C. L., and **Burgoon, M.** "The Effects of Androgyny and Message Expectations on Resistance to Persuasive Communication." *Communication Monographs* 47 (1980):56–67.

APPENDIX
THE PREPARATION OF A PERSUASIVE SPEECH

One afternoon a Roman emperor was entertaining himself at the Colosseum by feeding Christians to the lions. Several Christians were sacrificed, and the crowd screamed for more.

The next martyr said something to the lion, and the beast slunk away. Then a second lion; same result. And a third. The amazed throng began to shift its sympathies to the Christian. The emperor announced that the Christian's life would be spared. He insisted, however, that the martyr appear before him.

"I am sparing your life," said the emperor, "but before I release you, I demand to know what it was that you said to those lions."

"I merely said to each one," he replied, "that after dinner, of course, you'll be expected to say a few words."

Giving a speech need not be a dreaded experience. Like any other important activity, it requires careful planning and preparation. Think of people who have impressed you while giving a speech. Chances are that they were people who spoke directly to the audience without reading word for word from a manuscript, who were enthusiastic and sincere, and who probably spoke after long and careful preparation.

During the national Democratic convention of 1976, two prominent Democrats appeared on the platform during the same evening. The first speaker was John Glenn, the astronaut. The second speaker was Barbara Jordan, congresswoman from Texas and member of the House Judiciary Committee which had investigated Nixon and the Watergate scandals. Most platform speeches during conventions include similar content and vary little. Few of these speeches are considered significant and are seldom remembered, unless, of course, they are given by the party's choice for president and vice-president. John Glenn's speech faded into the usual oblivion, but Barbara Jordan electrified the immediate as well as the mass audience on television, just as she had done when she made her famous speech during the Nixon impeachment hearing. Jordan's speaking expertise has singled her out from the mainstream of the late twentieth century's speakers.

It is useful to make an outline of the speech. It is not recommended to write a speech out in manuscript form. A speech read to an audience can become what James Winans, a speech professor noted for his books on the psychology of attention and delivery, called "an essay on its hind legs." An outline gives a speech structure without locking into place the actual words used to deliver it. This allows the speaker to design and know a structure for a speech and be able to deliver it naturally and conversationally with few or no notes.

OUTLINING

Outlining serves the persuader as a working procedure that indicates his/her intentions during the presentation. It should have built-in flexibility to aid the persuader in being adaptable to the audience. The outline provides opportunity to test and analyze the effects of the forthcoming persuasive effort. Outlining eventually allows the persuader to "forget" the speech because the structure is permanently embedded in the thought processes. Outlining on the part of the persuader is also important to the persuadee because of the need to hear the presentation in some sequence.

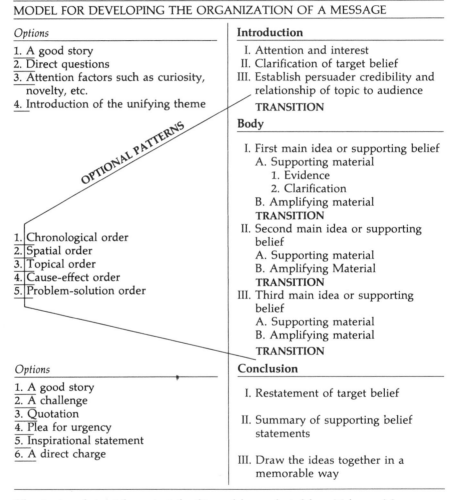

MODEL FOR DEVELOPING THE ORGANIZATION OF A MESSAGE

Options	**Introduction**
1. A good story	I. Attention and interest
2. Direct questions	II. Clarification of target belief
3. Attention factors such as curiosity, novelty, etc.	III. Establish persuader credibility and relationship of topic to audience
4. Introduction of the unifying theme	**TRANSITION**

OPTIONAL PATTERNS

Body

I. First main idea or supporting belief
  A. Supporting material
    1. Evidence
    2. Clarification
  B. Amplifying material
  TRANSITION
II. Second main idea or supporting belief
  A. Supporting material
  B. Amplifying Material
  TRANSITION
III. Third main idea or supporting belief
  A. Supporting material
  B. Amplifying material
  TRANSITION

1. Chronological order
2. Spatial order
3. Topical order
4. Cause-effect order
5. Problem-solution order

Options	**Conclusion**
1. A good story	I. Restatement of target belief
2. A challenge	
3. Quotation	II. Summary of supporting belief statements
4. Plea for urgency	
5. Inspirational statement	III. Draw the ideas together in a memorable way
6. A direct charge	

(The structure, but not the content, for this model was adapted from Makay and Sawyer 1973, p. 162.)

Once this outline is completed, the persuader can evaluate the total picture and add or delete information to make the presentation more acceptable to audience needs.

There are two types of outlines: (1) a complete-sentence outline and (2) a word or phrase outline. The complete-sentence outline is one that is detailed and includes all of the information that will be in the persuasive speech. Each target belief statement and supporting belief statement is phrased in a complete declarative sentence.

The second form of outlining is the key-word or phrase outline. It can be drawn from the complete outline but only includes words or phrases that serve as reminders to the persuader, who must have the details well cemented in his/her mind. The use of either or both of these methods will eliminate rambling, the loss of balance, or the omission of important aspects of the flow.

The following is a model for both the organization and outlining of a speech. It shows the basic structure of an outline with options for the three parts of the organization. Usually a brief speech (five to eight minutes) should have no more than three main points in the body in order to allow enough time to develop each one. It would not be difficult to adapt either a complete-sentence or word or phrase outline to this model.

Regardless of the type of outline utilized, it is helpful to include a technical plot in the left-hand margin of the outline. The technical plot is an indication of the various strategies, methods, and techniques being used, such as anchors, belief appeals, forms of support, creation of cognitive imbalance, forms of reasoning, and other message techniques designed for the audience (Oliver, Zelko, and Holtzman 1962, p. 131). The technical plot, together with the outline, is the by-product of your preparatory analysis and synthesis of your ideas and materials. It is especially useful in persuasion because it links the message content reflected in the outline to the interactive-dependency between the persuader and persuadee.

The following outline was done in Professor O'Donnell's persuasion class by LaVerne Perkins. It includes many of the persuasive techniques discussed in this book. The techniques are listed in the technical plot opposite the simple but adequate complete-sentence outline.

The technical plot, which highlights the selected persuasive techniques, serves as a stream of consciousness for the persuader. It also focuses on a persuasive justification for every part of the outline. Unnecessary or irrelevant points can be eliminated if they cannot be justified in the technical plot.

DELIVERY

Delivery of the persuasive speech is important. Although delivery cannot be persuasive by itself, it helps if a persuader appears to be confident, enthusiastic, and prepared.

Delivery is defined as the added perceptual dimension that is cre-

OPEN YOUR DOOR—AND DIE!

Technical Plot

Gain attention from the audience while identifying with them

Specific example (shock element)

Relate example to audience
Emphasis on the central idea of the speech
Leading question—transition

First main idea established

Proof by examples (probably familiar but not in the context of this central idea until now—hope to get reaction: "I never thought of it that way!" This should begin to create dissonance.)

Anchors:
Reinforce attitudes: murder is wrong; people should not act without thinking of consequences.
Convincing details through descriptive language.
Direct quotation of murderer and his victim.

Use belief (self-preservation, aversion to murder, protection) to secure belief that we shouldn't let strangers in our houses.

Transition

Second main idea stated

Outline
Introduction

I. This incident happened a few years ago, on a street much like yours and mine.
   A. A housewife was almost assaulted by a cosmetics "saleslady," who was a man in disguise.
   B. This should make you realize how easily someone might gain entrance into your house. How many times have you let some salesperson into your home?

Body

I. People should learn to know whom they let into their homes.
   A. Examples of people who let a stranger into their homes were given in the detailed confession of the Boston Strangler when he told how easily he gained entry to his victims' homes.

      1. He told Anna Slesser he had to repair a leak—and she let him in.
      2. He used the same approach at Evelyn Corbin's.
      3. At Helen Blake's he said, "I got to do some work on the apartment." She said, "Well, it's about time."
   B. He attacked and strangled to death eleven women using variations of this approach.

But sometimes criminals don't even have to knock on doors.

II. Because people do not keep their doors locked even though they should.

Proof by specific examples (familiar)

Use belief (protection, repulsion, to terror and murder) to secure belief that we should keep our doors locked.

Personal experiences and involvement

Summarize and relate to the audience; also a transition to conclusion

A. Remember the multiple murders in Kansas of the Clutter family.
B. Corazon Amurao, the only survivor of the student nurses attacked by Richard Speck in Chicago, couldn't remember if their door had been locked or not.
C. I thought my door was locked a couple of weeks ago.

It could happen to anyone, anywhere.

Conclusion

Central idea re-stated (The audience should accept this new attitude and behavior because it alleviates the dissonance)

Plant the idea in a memorable way—let the audience carry it home with them. (Just in case enough dissonance wasn't created before, this should do it!) This will also cause the audience to identify with the problem rather strongly.

I. It takes only a few minutes to lock your door and to think twice before letting a stranger into your home.

II. Someday, someone might use *your* killer's detailed confession in a speech similar to this one.

ated through the effective use of the body and the voice (Makay and Sawyer 1973, p. 165). Delivery, to be effective, must be fused with all other variables in the persuasive message, such as the message itself, its structure, its content, and the source credibility of the speaker. Delivery must be adapted to all these variables.

Good delivery eliminates many elements that can distract from the message. Research indicates that good delivery enhances comprehension, retention, attitude change, and source credibility. E. Bettinghaus, in his study, discovered that "effectiveness in delivery contributes not only to the source credibility of the speaker, but also to the persuasiveness of the speaker in achieving acceptance of his message" (1961, in Thompson 1967, p. 142). Good delivery in J. L. Vohs's study produced high retention scores and increased the capacity to handle information on the part of the subjects (1964, p. 360).

A good style of delivery is that which is spontaneous, direct, and void of distractions. In order to better understand what leads to successful delivery, the vocal and other nonverbal elements will be discussed.

Vocal Elements

Vocal elements are those physical aspects related to the voice that an individual uses to present the prepared message. It is the general conclusion of researchers that persons associate some personality stereotypes with certain vocal characteristics (Cronkhite 1978, p. 289). For example, a breathy female voice can cause a listener to perceive the speaker to be feminine, pretty, petite, or effervescent. Throatiness in a male voice may cause the speaker to be perceived as mature, realistic, sophisticated, and well adjusted. One has to be cautious about attributing personality characteristics to vocal qualities because such associations are not very accurate.

Vocal characteristics that can convey more accurate impressions to the persuadee are rate, volume, pitch, and quality.

Rate   Rate can have a major influence on message reception and comprehension. Extremely fast rate can interfere with correct pronunciation and proper stress on key words, which can ultimately prevent comprehension. Speech rate that is very rapid can indicate excess nervousness on the part of the persuader. It can also be an indication that the persuader is not in control. On the other hand, if the rate pattern is very slow, the speaker could bore the audience or appear to be bored him/herself.

Volume   Volume refers to the qualities of loudness and softness of the voice. An adequate level of volume is necessary in any communication situation. Volume can range from a whisper to a loud roar, so the volume level must be adjusted to the situation and the thrust of the message. Some military commanders are most effective while performing on the drill field, but are unable to resist being sergeants in interpersonal or public-speaking situations.

It is important that a persuasive speaker be heard without effort on the part of the persuadee. A person must be aware of the environment in which persuasive communication occurs, for in an environment there exist problems of space (or lack of it) and distractions of many kinds to which one's volume must be adapted.

Pitch   Pitch refers to the range of levels that the voice possesses. The range of pitch or normal pitch level is not the same for everyone because of the difference in the size of the vocal bands. Each person, however, does have the capacity for a pleasant pitch range. When this capacity is not utilized, the result is a monotone. Pitch levels can clarify meanings, but when delivery is monotonic, all words are conveyed as equal and with no difference in meaning or importance. Women often have voices that are very high-pitched and tend to make them sound young and nonauthoritative. There are ways to lower one's pitch, if necessary, for a pleasant and authoritative speaking voice.

Quality Good voice quality is produced through the effective use of variety in rate, volume, and pitch. A comprehendable rate, adequate volume, and pleasant pitch, and variety in each, are necessary, but not enough in themselves. The use of variety in rate, volume, and pitch is an effective means by which to accent, punctuate, and color words according to meaning.

These vocal skills or lack of them can create a status image of the persuader in the mind of the persuadee (Ellis 1967). A strong factor that contributes to the perception of status is dialect. When speakers have obvious regional dialects, they are generally judged to be of lower status than persons who speak Standard American English (Cronkhite, 1978, p. 289). This dialect is the one that national network news announcers usually speak. On the other hand, one's accent may be a significant part of his/her personality that should not be changed.

Vocal qualities are faciliting factors that can aid the persuader by making listening a pleasant and comfortable experience.

One of the most prevalent problems in communication is the use of too many nonfluencies. Nonfluencies are the audible sounds (not verbal in nature) that people use to fill gaps. Examples of nonfluencies are *ah, uh,* and *ahem. You know,* even though it is verbal, functions also as a nonfluency.

Nonverbal Elements

The nonverbal elements of delivery include body and facial movements that contradict or enhance the message. These nonverbal behaviors carry significant social meanings, even more so than verbal behaviors (Mehrabian and Ferris 1967). Our nonverbal behavior also affects how we are perceived as persuaders. A. Mehrabian and M. Williams (1969) concluded in their study that the degree of perceived persuasiveness of a message is correlated with the level of nonverbal activity exhibited by the persuader such as the increased use of volume, rate, facial expressions, and gestures.

Appearance In the chapter on source credibility, attractiveness proved to be an important asset. Whether a person likes it or not, he/she is initially judged by physical appearance. It is not suggested here that there is a single image that is considered "attractive" in a persuasive situation. A person's

(By Berke Breathed, *The Daily Texan* 1980)

appearance must be adapted to the persuadees, the situation, and the persuader's perception of his/her own role in relation to to the persuadees. Scholars have concluded that people who are perceived as attractive have more persuasive impact than people who are perceived as unattractive (Widgery and Webster 1969). Judson Mills and E. Aronson discovered that persuadees respond positively when an attractive persuader reveals an intent to persuade them, but respond negatively when an unattractive persuader reveals the same intent (in Cronkhite 1978, p. 282). Obviously, it is also evident that political persuaders attempt to emphasize attractiveness by their concern over clothing, make-up, and hair length before appearing on television.

Clothing is of importance insofar as it is appropriate to the situation and the audience's expectations. While campaigning for Frances Farenthold for governor in 1972, Professor O'Donnell appeared before the Democratic Women's Club on a hot June night wearing a simple cotton dress that had little style but was cool. The woman who spoke for Farenthold's opponent was stylishly dressed in a raw silk dress that was beautiful and costly. After their speeches, the president of the club came up to Professor O'Donnell and complimented her on her speech and then said, "Not only did we like what you said, but we liked the way you look. You look like we do."

Posture and Movement

A person's approach to and departure from the podium or an interpersonal encounter can create a permanent impression on the persuadee. Try to recall your posture of reluctance as you walk toward the dentist's chair as compared to the manner in which you approach a stage to receive a coveted award. When one approaches the podium, the body posture can say, "I have something important to say and I'm looking forward to it" or "I don't want to do this, but I guess I have to."

Also, a persuader's posture can contradict the verbal message no matter how well it is articulated. Shifting weight from one foot to the other can say, "I'm not committed to what I am saying." Standing still throughout the speech becomes visually monotonous. Motivated moves on transitions can alert the persuadee to the fact that the persuader is moving to another unit of the speech. The word "motivated" is important, for unmotivated moves, such as pacing, detract from the important purpose, which is the message.

Mehrabian's study revealed that close physical proximity, good eye contact, and a forward lean, rather than a backward lean, toward the persuadee communicate positive attitudes toward the persuadee on the part of the persuader (1970, p. 249). Another interesting finding of this study was that persuadees attribute higher status to the more relaxed persuasive speaker.

A person's body movements can indicate both physical problems such as pain or fatigue and emotional states such as tenseness, depression, or pleasure. Self-confident people move about easily, hold up their heads, and stand up straight while shy people tend to do just the opposite (Barker 1968, p. 337).

Facial Expressions and Eye Contact   Facial expressions are powerful enhancers of the persuasive message and communicate what type of emotion the persuader is feeling. The intensity of that emotion is evidenced in body movements (Ekman 1964; Ekman and Friesen 1967). Mehrabian states that when there is a conflict between verbal expression and facial expressions, the facial expressions have more impact (1971, p. 43).

Eye contact, on the other hand, not only conveys information, but receives it as well. For it is through eye contact that we can evaluate feedback and tell if communication channels are open or closed. The lack of eye contact shuts out the persuadee and makes the persuader appear evasive.

Gestures Gestures are the movements of hands and arms that convey specific meanings. Gestures are more specific than other nonverbal behaviors and do not exist at as low a level of awareness. They can work to create a visual image and clarify the verbal meaning, such as indicating quantity, size, or shape, and can lend emphasis to important statements. They should, however, be natural to the persuader and not artificial or distracting.

Nonverbal communication works below the level of awareness. Ekman and Friesen (1967; in Cronkhite 1978) offer five types of nonverbal behaviors and indications as to the level of awareness of each. These five behaviors are (1) emblems, (2) illustrators,(3) affect displays, (4) regulators, and (5) adaptors.

Emblems are forms of nonverbal behavior that leave no doubt about their meanings. When the Romans made a fist and pointed their thumbs down, there was no doubt about the fate of the doomed Christian in the arena. *Illustrators* are those gestures used to clarify meaning and have no significance without the verbal message. The salesman who uses his hands to show how small his computer is is an example. When a person's emotional states are betrayed by his/her facial expressions, these expressions are referred to as *affect displays*. When someone calls to break a dinner date, a person's face reveals the emotion of disappointment whether anyone else is in the room or not. It is difficult for a person to keep his/her face from revealing his/her true emotion. *Regulators* are those nonverbal behaviors we use to encourage or alienate other people's communicative efforts. We have all experienced being ignored by a professor in a classroom or stared down when he/she disapproved of our behavior. *Adaptors* are nonverbal behaviors in which we engage without awareness, usually as an indication of discomfort. Crossing one's leg and shaking a foot would be an example. Adaptors and affect dispays are at a lower level of awareness than the other three types of nonverbal behavior.

GUIDELINES FOR CONFIDENCE IN PERSUASIVE SPEAKING

Nearly all speakers experience a stomach full of butterflies or the fear of a blank mind. These symptoms should be recognized as signs of strength rather than of weakness. All good speakers have them and, in fact, should worry when they do not. These symptoms are not true fear or anxiety, but rather they are signs of emotional excitement, which can add to an enthusiastic delivery of a speech. Speakers who lack emotional excitement come across as dull and drab. Just as the adrenaline levels increase in an athlete before he/she goes out to play a game, so does the speaker experience that additional energy necessary for an important communication situation.

If a speaker has allowed sufficient preparation time, made an adequate outline, has practiced sufficiently, and, perhaps most important of all, cares about the speech itself, all should go well. It helps to remember that no one knows your speech but yourself; therefore, if you do forget, no one will know unless you tell him or her. A conversational and natural delivery will allow you to keep talking, and eventually you will get back on the track without anyone ever suspecting that you forgot.

It helps if a speaker talks about the topic in conversations prior to the speech. Without revealing that the topic is for a speech, the prospective speaker can gain confidence by merely discussing the issues in order to become articulate and experienced in talking about them. This can also generate valuable informal feedback, which may be useful when the speech is actually delivered.

SUMMARY

Preparing a persuasive speech is sometimes intimidating to people, but, if done systematically, it can be a pleasant and fulfilling preparation step. It helps to make an outline, either complete-sentence or key word, from which to practice a speech. In this way, a speaker can have the outline in his or her mind and not have to worry about memorizing every word of a manuscript. Outlining not only helps a speaker, but has a tendency to help the members of the audience as well. It gives the audience a systematic approach to a topic that may help them remember the ideas too.

The delivery of a speech is not persuasive in itself. If delivery is fused with other persuasive variables, it may enhance the message. Delivery is an added perceptual dimension that is created through the use of the body and the voice.

Vocal characteristics may create certain personality stereotypes whether or not they exist in reality. Certain vocal characteristics can create status images in the minds of the persuadees.

Nonverbal factors are sometimes apparent to persuadees, whereas others exist below the level of awareness. Certain nonverbal behaviors have been associated with an increasing intent to persuade.

Practice along with good preparation activities may help a speaker build confidence. It is also helpful if the speaker feels a sense of commitment to and enthusiasm for the topic and the audience's response.

KEY WORDS

Delivery   Posture
Complete-sentence outline   Gestures
Key-word outline   Affect displays
Technical plot   Emblems
Rate   Illustrators
Volume   Regulators
Pitch   Adaptors
Vocal quality   Non-fluencies

EXERCISES

1. Select a speaker whom you found to be stimulating and memorable. Make a list of his/her delivery characteristics.
2. Select another speaker whom you found to be dull and forgettable. Make a list of his/her delivery characteristics.
3. What do you consider to be your strengths and weaknesses in delivery? How can you reduce the weaknesses?
4. Get a friend to listen to you practice a speech. Ask your friend to constructively criticize your delivery.
5. How do you convey messages nonverbally?
6. Learn to interpret feedback to your speaking. The next time you give a speech, ask some of your classmates if your interpretation of their nonverbal feedback was correct.
7. The next time you prepare a speech, try conversing about the topic with others as a form of practice.

READINGS

Cronkhite, G. *Public Speaking and Critical Listening.* Menlo Park, Calif.: Cummings, 1978.

Ekman, P. "Body Position, Facial Expression, and Verbal Behavior during Interviews." *Journal of Abnormal and Social Psychology* 68 (1964): 295–301.

Ekman, P. and W. Friesen. "Head and Body Cues in the Judgment of Emotion." *Perceptual and Motor Skills* 24 (1967): 711–724.

Mehrabian, A. and Ferris, S. R. "Inference of Attitudes from Nonverbal Communication in Two Channels." *Journal of Consulting Psychology* 31 (1967):248–252.

Mehrabian, A. and Williams, M. "Nonverbal Concomitants of Perceived and Intended Persuasiveness." *Journal of Personality and Social Psychology* 13 (1969), 37–58.

BIBLIOGRAPHY

Acock, A. C., and **DeFleur, M. L.** "A Configurational Approach to Contingent Consistency in the Attitude-Behavior Relationship." *American Sociological Review* 37 (1972):714–26.

Adler, Bill, ed. *The McCarthy Wit.* Greenwich, Conn.: Fawcett, 1969.

Adler, R. *Television As a Cultural Force.* New York: Praeger, 1976.

———. *Research on the Effects of Television Advertising on Children.* Washington, D.C.: U.S. Government Printing Office, 1977.

Alinsky, S. D. *Rules for Radicals: A Practical Primer for Realistic Radicals.* New York: Random House, 1971.

Allen, L. "The Jury Selection Game." *Dallas Morning News,* August 17, 1975, p. F1.

Altman, I. *The Environment and Social Behavior.* Monterey, Calif.: Brooks/Cole, 1975.

Andersen, K. E. "An Experimental Study of the Interaction of Artistic and Non-Artistic Ethos in Persuasion." Ph.D. diss., University of Wisconsin, 1961.

———. *Persuasion: Theory and Practice.* Boston: Allyn & Bacon, 1971.

Applbaum, R. F., and **Anatol, K. W. E.** *Strategies for Persuasive Communication.* Columbus, Ohio: Charles E. Merrill, 1974.

———. "The Factor Structure of Source Credibility As a Function of the Speaking Situation." *Speech Monographs* 39 (1972):216–22.

Appleyard, D. "Environment As a Social Symbol: Within a Theory of Environmental Action and Perception." *American Planners Association Journal* 45 (1979):143–53.

Argyle, M., and **Dean, J.** "Eye Contact: Distance and Affiliation." *Sociometry* 28 (1965):289–304.

Bandura, A. *Principles of Behavior Modification.* New York: Holt, Rinehart and Winston, 1969.

———. *Social Learning Theory.* Englewood Cliffs, N.J.: Prentice-Hall, 1977.

Bandura, A., and **Barab, P. G.** "Conditions Governing Nonreinforced Imitations." *Developmental Psychology* 5 (1971):244–55.

Bandura, A.; Grusec, J. E.; and **Menlove, F. L.** "Observational Learning As a Function of Symbolization and Incentive Set." *Child Development* 37 (1966):499–530.

Bandura, A., and **Jeffrey, R.** "Role of Symbolic Coding and Rehearsal Processes in Observational Learning." *Journal of Personality and Social Psychology* 26 (1973):122–30.

Bandura, A.; Jeffrey, R.; and **Bachicha, D. L.** "Analysis of Memory Codes and Cumulative Rehearsal in Observational Learning." *Journal of Research in Personality* 7 (1974):295–305.

Bandura, A.; Ross, D.; and **Ross, F.** "Imitation of Film-mediated Aggressive Models." *Journal of Abnormal Psychology* 66 (1963):3–11.

Barker, R. G. *Ecological Psychology: Concepts and Methods for Studying the Environment and Behavior.* Stanford, Calif.: Stanford University Press, 1968.

Baron, R., and **Byrne, D.** *Social Psychology.* Boston: Allyn & Bacon, 1977.

Barton, S. "Don't Let Your Kids Go down the Tube." *Dallas Morning News,* October 19, 1979, pp. 22–23.

Baseheart, J. R., and **Bostrom, R. N.** "Credibility of Source and Self in Attitude Change." *Journalism Quarterly* 49 (1972):742–45.

Becker, E. *The Birth and Death of Meaning.* Glencoe, Ill.: The Free Press, 1962.

Beighley, K. C. "An Experimental Study of the Effect of Four Speech Variables on Listener Comprehension." *Speech Monographs* 19 (1952):249–58.

————. "A Summary of Experimental Studies Dealing with the Effect of Organization and of Skill of Speaker on Comprehension." *Communication Journal* 2 (1952):58–65.

Belazs, B. *Theory of Film.* New York: Dover, 1970.

Bem, D. J. "An Experimental Analysis of Self-Persuasion." *Journal of Experimental Social Psychology* 1 (1965):199–218.

————. *Beliefs, Attitudes, and Human Affairs.* Belmont, Calif.: Brooks/Cole, 1970.

Berkowitz, L., ed. *Aggression: A Social Psychological Analysis.* New York: McGraw-Hill, 1962.

————. *Advances in Experimental Social Psychology.* Vols. I–V. New York: Academic Press, 1964–1970.

————. "The Contagion of Violence: An S-R Mediational Analysis of Some Effects of Observed Aggression." *Nebraska Symposium on Motivation* 18 (1970):95–135.

Berkowitz, L.; Corwin, R.; and Heironimus, M. "Film Violence and Subsequent Aggressive Tendencies." *Public Opinion Quarterly* 27 (1963):229.

Berkowitz, L., and Rawlings, E. "Effects of Film Violence on Inhibitions against Subsequent Aggression." *Journal of Abnormal and Social Psychology* 66 (1963):405–12.

Berlo, D. K.; Lemert, J. B.; and Mertz, R. J. "Dimensions for Evaluating the Acceptability of Message Sources." *Public Opinion Quarterly* 33 (1969–70):563–76.

Bettinghaus, E. "The Operation of Congruity in an Oral Communication Situation." *Speech Monographs* 28 (1961):131–42.

Bettinghaus, E.; Miller, G.; and Steinfatt, T. "Source Evaluation, Syllogistic Content, and Judgments of Logical Validity by High and Low Dogmatic Persons." *Journal of Personality and Social Psychology* 16 (1970):238–44.

Biddle, P. R. "An Experimental Study of Ethos and Appeal for Overt Behavior in Persuasion." Ph.D. diss., University of Illinois, 1966.

Birdwhistle, R. *Kinesics and Context.* Philadelphia: University of Pennsylvania, 1970.

Blumer, H. *Movies and Conduct.* New York: Macmillan, 1933.

Blumer, H., and Hauser, P. *Movies, Delinquency, and Crime.* New York: Macmillan, 1933.

Bogardus, E. S. "Measuring Social Distance." *Journal of Applied Sociology* 9 (1925):299–308.

Bowers, J. W. "Some Correlates of Language Intensity." *Quarterly Journal of Speech* 50 (1964):415–20.

Bowers, J. W., and Ochs, D. J. *The Rhetoric of Agitation and Control.* Menlo Park, Calif.: Addison-Wesley, 1971.

Braden, W. *Public Speaking: The Essentials.* New York: Harper & Row, 1966.

Brehm, J. W. *Responses to the Loss of Freedom: A Theory of Psychological Reactance.* Morristown, N.J.: General Learning Press, 1972.

Brooks, W. D. *Speech Communication.* Dubuque, Iowa: William C. Brown, 1978.

Brown, J. A. C. *Techniques of Persuasion from Propaganda to Brainwashing.* Middlesex, Eng.: Penguin, 1968.

Burgoon, M. *Approaching Speech Communication.* New York: Holt, Rinehart and Winston, 1974.

———. "Empirical Investigations of Language Intensity: III. The Effect of Source Credibility and Language Intensity on Attitude Change and Person Perception." *Human Communication Research* 1 (1975):251–54.

Burgoon, M., and King, L. B. "The Mediation of Resistance to Persuasion Strategies by Language Variables and Active-Passive Participation." *Human Communication Research* 1 (1974):30–41.

Burgoon, M.; Cohen, M.; Miller, M.; and Montgomery, C. L. "An Empirical Test of a Model of Resistance to Persuasion." *Human Communication Research* 5 (1978):27–39.

Burke, K. *Counter-Statement*. New York: Harcourt, Brace, 1931.

———. *Permanence and Change*. New York: New Republic, 1935.

———. *Attitudes toward History*. New York: New Republic, 1937.

———. *The Philosophy of Literary Form*. Baton Rouge: Louisiana State University Press, 1941.

———. *A Grammar of Motives*. New York: Prentice-Hall, 1945.

———. *A Rhetoric of Motives*. New York: Prentice-Hall, 1950.

———. *A Rhetoric of Religion*. Boston: Beacon Press, 1961.

———. *Language As Symbolic Action*. Berkeley: University of California Press, 1966.

Byker, D., and Anderson, L. J. *Communication As Identification*. New York: Harper & Row, 1975.

Byrne, D. *The Attraction Paradigm*. New York: Academic Press, 1971.

Cantor, J. R.; Alfonso, H.; and Zillman, D. "The Persuasive Effectiveness of the Peer Appeal and a Communicator's First-Hand Experience." *Human Communication Research* 3 (1976):293–309.

Carpenter, R. H., and Seltzer, R. V. "Nixon, Patton, and a Silent Majority Sentiment about the Viet Nam War: The Cinematographic Bases of a Rhetorical Stance." *Central States Speech Journal* 25 (1974):105–10.

Cathcart, R. S. "An Experimental Study of the Relative Effectiveness of Four Methods of Presenting Evidence." *Speech Monographs* 22 (1955):227–33.

Cerf, Bennett. *Saturday Review of Literature*. September 4, 1948, p. 4.

Cialdini, R.; Braver, S.; and Lewis, S. "Attributional Bias and the Easily Persuaded Other." *Journal of Personality and Social Psychology* 35 (1974):631–37.

Clark, P. *New Models for Mass Communication Research*. Beverly Hills, Calif.: Sage, 1973.

Clements, D. A., and Frandsen, K. D. "On Conceptual and Empirical Treatments of Feedback in Human Communication." *Communication Monographs* 43 (1976):11–28.

Collins, B. E.; Martin, J. C.; Ashmore, R. D.; and Ross, L. "Some Dimensions of Internal-External Metaphor in Theories of Personality." *Journal of Personality* 41 (1973):471–92.

Cooper, Lane, trans. *The Rhetoric of Aristotle*. New York: Appleton-Century-Crofts, 1960.

Cousins, Norman. "President Kennedy and the Russian Fable." *Saturday Review*, January 9, 1971, pp. 20–21.

Cronkhite, Gary. *Persuasion: Speech and Behavioral Change*. New York: Bobbs-Merrill, 1969.

———. *Public Speaking and Critical Listening*. Menlo Park, Calif.: Cummings, 1978.

Dance, F. E. X. *Human Communication Theory.* New York: Holt, Rinehart and Winston, 1967.

Day, G. S. "Attitude Change, Media, and Word of Mouth." *Journal of Advertising Research* 11 (1971):31–40.

Deabler, H. "Colors and Mood Tones." *Journal of Applied Psychology* 41 (1957):279–83.

De Fleur, M. L., and **Ball-Rokeach, S.** *Theories of Mass Communication.* New York: David McKay, 1975.

Delia, J. G. "A Constructivist Analysis of the Concept of Credibility." *Quarterly Journal of Speech* 62 (1976):361–75.

Dresser, W. R. "Effects of 'Satisfactory' and 'Unsatisfactory' Evidence in a Speech of Advocacy." *Speech Monographs* 30 (1963):302–06.

Duncan, H. D. *Communication and Social Order.* New York: Oxford University Press, 1962.

————. *Symbols in Society.* New York: Oxford University Press, 1968.

Durgnat, R. *Films and Feeling.* Cambridge, Mass.: MIT Press, 1971.

Eagley, A. H., and **Chaiken, S.** "An Attribution Analysis of the Effect of Communicator Characteristics on Opinion Change: The Case for Communicator Attractiveness." *Journal of Personality and Social Psychology* 32 (1975):136–44.

Edwards, W. "The Theory of Decision Making." *Psychological Bulletin* 51 (1954):380–417.

Ehrlich, D.; Guttman, I.; Schonback, P.; and **Mills, J.** "Post-decision Exposure to Relevant Information." *Journal of Abnormal and Social Psychology* 54 (1956):98–102.

Ekman, P. "Body Position, Facial Expression, and Verbal Behavior during Interviews." *Journal of Abnormal and Social Psychology* 68 (1964):295–301.

Ekman, P., and **Friesen, W.** "Head and Body Cues in the Judgment of Emotion: A Reformulation." *Perceptual and Motor Skills* 24 (1967):711–24.

Ellis, D. S. "Speech and Social Status in America." *Social Forces* 45 (1967):43–451.

Epstein, S. "The Self-Concept Revisited or a Theory of a Theory." *American Psychologist* 28 (1973):404–16.

"The Electoral Numbers Game." *Newsweek,* October 13, 1980, p. 39.

Evans, Walter. "Monster Movies and Rites of Intiation." *Journal of Popular Film* 4 (1975):140–46.

Evans, R., and **Novak, R.** "The Last Republican Hope." *Washington Post,* November 1, 1978.

Farson, R. "How Could Anything That Feels So Bad Be So Good?" *Saturday Review,* September 6, 1969, pp. 20–21, 48.

Fell, J. L. *Film: An Introduction.* New York: Praeger, 1975.

Festinger, L. *A Theory of Cognitive Dissonance.* Stanford, Calif.: Stanford University Press, 1957.

Festinger, L., and **Macoby, N.** "On Resistance to Persuasive Communication." *Journal of Abnormal and Social Psychology* 68 (1964):359–66.

Film: The Art of the Impossible. New York: Learning Corporation of America, 1972.

Fishbein, M. *Readings in Attitude Theory and Measurement.* New York: Wiley, 1967.

Fishbein, M., and **Ajzen, I.** *Beliefs, Attitudes, Intentions and Behavior: An Introduction to Theory and Research.* Reading, Mass.: Addison-Wesley, 1975.

Fisher, S.; Rubenstein, I.; and Freeman, R. W. "Intertrial Effects of Immediate Self-Committal in a Continuous Social Influence Situation." *Journal of Abnormal Psychology* 52 (1956):200–7.

Freedman, J. L., and Fraser, S. C. "Compliance without Pressure: The Foot-in-the-Door Technique." *Journal of Personality and Social Psychology* 4 (1966):195–202.

Geller, Robert, and Kula, Sam. "Toward Filmic Literacy: The Role of the American Film Institute." *Journal of Aesthetic Education* 3 (1969):98–110.

Gilham, J., and Woelfel, J. "The Galileo System of Measurement: Preliminary Evidence for Precision, Stability, and Equivalence to Traditional Measures." *Human Communication Research* 3 (1977):222–34.

Goffman, E. *Interaction Ritual: Essays in Face-to-Face Behavior.* Chicago: Aldine, 1967.

Gordon, G. *Persuasion: The Theory and Practice of Manipulative Communication.* New York: Hastings House, 1971.

Greenstein, T. "Behavior Change through Value Self Confrontation." *Journal of Personality and Social Psychology* 34 (1976):254–62.

Griffitt, W. "Personality Similarity and Self-Concept As Determinants of Interpersonal Attraction." *Journal of Social Psychology* 78 (1969):137–46.

Guttman, R., ed. *People and Buildings.* New York: Basic Books, 1972.

Hall, C. S., and Lindzey, G. "Lewin's Field Theory." In *Theories of Personality.* New York: Wiley, 1970.

Hall, E. T. *The Hidden Dimension.* Garden City, N.Y.: Doubleday, 1966.

———. *Beyond Culture.* Garden City, N.Y.: Anchor Press/Doubleday, 1976.

Hart, R. P.; Friedrich, G. W.; and Brooks, W. D. *Public Communication.* New York: Harper & Row, 1975.

Hass, R. G., and Grady, K. "Temporal Delay, Type of Forewarning, and Resistance to Influence." *Journal of Experimental Social Psychology* 11 (1975):459–69.

Hastorf, A. H., and Cantril, H. "They Saw a Game." *Journal of Abnormal and Social Psychology* 49 (January, 1954):130–32.

Hawkes, Terence. *Structuralism and Semiotics.* Berkeley: University of California Press, 1977.

Heider, Fritz. "Attitudes and Cognitive Organization." *Journal of Psychology* 21 (1946):107–12.

Heller, J. F.; Pallak, M. S.; and Picik, J. M. "The Interactive Effects of Intent and Threat on Boomerang Attitude Change." *Journal of Personality and Social Psychology* 26 (1973):273–79.

Hertzler, Joyce O. *A Sociology of Language.* New York: Random House, 1965.

Higham, Charles. "Wy Stix Nix Big Pix." *The New York Times,* October, 1975, p. 13.

Holman, P. A. "Validation of an Attitude Scale As a Device for Predicting Behavior." *Journal of Applied Psychology* 40 (1956):347–49.

Holtzman, P. D. *The Psychology of Speakers' Audiences.* Glenview, Illinois: Scott, Foresman, 1970.

Horton, D., and Dixon, T., eds. *Verbal Behavior and S-R Behavior Theory.* New York: Prentice-Hall, 1968.

Hovland, C. I.; Janis, I. L.; and Kelley, H. H. *Communication and Persuasion.* New Haven, Conn.: Yale University Press, 1953.

Hovland, C. I., and Mandell, W. "An Experimental Comparison of Conclusion

Drawing by the Communicator and by the Audience." *Journal of Abnormal and Social Psychology* 47 (1952):581–88.

Hovland, C. I., and **Rosenberg, M. J.,** eds. *Attitude Organization and Change.* New Haven: Yale University Press, 1960.

Infante, D. A. "The Function of Perceptions of Consequences on Attitude Formation and Communicator Image Formation." *Central States Speech Journal* 23 (1972):174–80.

———. "Forewarnings in Persuasion: Effects of Opinionated Language and Forewarner and Speaker Authoritativeness." *Western Speech* 37 (1973):185–95.

———. "Differential Functions of Desirable and Undesirable Consequences in Predicting Attitude and Attitude Change toward Proposals." *Speech Monographs* 42 (1975):115–34.

Insko, C. *Theories of Attitude Change.* New York: Appleton-Century-Crofts, 1967.

Ittelson, W. H.; **Proshansky, H. M.; Rivlin, L. G.;** and **Winkel, G. H.** *An Introduction to Environmental Psychology.* New York: Holt, Rinehart and Winston, 1974.

Izard, C. E. "Personality Similarity and Friendship." *Journal of Abnormal Psychology* 61 (1960):47–51.

Jaccard, J. G.; **King, C. W.;** and **Pomozal, R.** "Attitudes and Behavior: An Analysis of Specificity of Attitudinal Predictors." *Human Relations* 30 (1977):817–24.

Jewett, R., and **Lawrence, J.** *The American Monomyth.* Garden City, N.Y.: Anchor Press/Doubleday, 1977.

Jones, E. E.; **Kanouse, D. E.; Kelley, H. H.; Nisbett, R. E.; Valens, S.;** and **Weiner, B.,** eds. *Attribution: Perceiving the Causes of Behavior.* Morristown, N.J.: General Learning Corp., 1972.

Jones, E. E., and **Sigall, H.** "The Bogus Pipeline: A New Paradigm for Measuring Affect and Attitudes." *Psychological Bulletin* 76 (1971):349–64.

Jordan, V. E., Jr. "Special Problems Facing Black Graduates and Institutions." Speech delivered at Morehouse College, Atlanta, Georgia, May 18, 1975. In *Vital Speeches* (1975):561-63.

Kalle, R.; **Riess, M.;** and **Tedeschi, J.** "The Bogus Pipeline and Attitude Moderation Following Forced Compliance: Misattribution of Dissonance Arousal or Impression Management Inhibition." *Journal of Social Psychology* in press.

Karlins, M., and **Abelson, H. I.** *Persuasion: How Opinions and Attitudes Are Changed.* 2d ed. New York: Springer, 1970.

Katz, D. "The Functional Approach to the Study of Attitudes." *Public Opinion Quarterly* 24 (1960):163–204.

Katz, E., and **Lazarsfeld, P. F.** *Personal Influence.* New York: The Free Press, 1964.

Katz, J. S. *Perspectives on the Study of Film.* Boston: Little, Brown, 1971.

Keilhacker, M. "Results of Recent Psychological and Pedagogical Research on the Protection of Youth and the Cinema" (in German). In *Jugend und Film.* Munich: 1958.

Kelley, H. "The Processes of Causal Attribution." *American Psychologist* 28 (1973):107–27.

Kelley, H., and **Woodruff, C. L.** "Member Reactions to Apparent Group Approval of a Counter-Norm Communication." *Journal of Abnormal and Social Psychology* 42 (1956):67–74.

Kelman, H. D. "Compliance, Identification, and Internalization through Processes of Opinion Change." *Journal of Conflict Resolution* 2 (1958):51–60.

Kiesler, C.; Collins, B. E.; and Miller, N. *Attitude Change: A Critical Analysis of Theoretical Approaches.* New York: Wiley, 1969.

Kiesler, C. A., and Kiesler, S. B. "Role of Forewarning in Persuasive Communications." *Journal of Abnormal and Social Psychology* 67 (1964):547–49.

King, M. L. *I Have a Dream.* Speech delivered at the Lincoln Memorial, Washington, D.C., August 28, 1963.

Klapper, J. T. *The Effects of Mass Communication.* Glencoe, Ill.: The Free Press, 1960.

Kline, F. G., and Tichenor, P. J., eds. *Current Perspectives in Mass Communication Research.* Beverly Hills, Calif.: Sage, 1972.

Knapp, M. L. *Nonverbal Communication in Human Interaction.* New York: Holt, Rinehart and Winston, 1972.

————. *Nonverbal Communication in Human Interaction.* New York: Holt, Rinehart and Winston, 1978 (2d ed.).

Korzybski, A. *Manhood of Humanity.* New York: Dutton, 1921.

KQV-AM News. Pittsburgh, Pa.: June 17, 1976.

Kraut, R. E. "Effect of Social Labeling on Giving to a Charity." *Journal of Experimental Social Psychology* 9 (1973):551–62.

Lane, M., ed. *Introduction to Structuralism.* New York: Basic Books, 1970.

Lazarsfeld, P. F.; Berelson, B.; and Gaudet, H. *The People's Choice.* New York: Columbia University Press, 1968.

Leavett, H. J. "Some Effects of Certain Communication Patterns on Group Performances." *Journal of Abnormal Social Psychology* 46 (1951):38–50.

Lee, I. *Language Habits in Human Affairs: An Introduction to General Semantics.* New York: Harper & Row, 1941.

Lelyveld, J. "The Selling of a Candidate." *New York Times Magazine*, March 28, 1976, pp. 16–17, 65–71.

Leppaluoto, J. R. "Resistance to Persuasion As a Function of Time and Issue Familiarity." *Proceedings of the Annual Convention of the American Psychological Association* 7 (1972):169–70.

Lewin, K. *Field Theory in Social Sciences.* New York: Harper & Row, 1951.

Likert, R. "A Technique for the Measurement of Attitudes." *Archives of Psychology* 140 (1932).

Linden, G. W. *Reflections on the Screen.* Belmont, Calif.: Wadsworth, 1970.

Lindgren, E. *The Art of the Film.* New York: Macmillan, 1968.

Lindzey, G., and Aronson, E., eds. *Handbook of Social Psychology.* Vol. V. Reading, Mass.: Addison-Wesley, 1969.

Linkugel, W. A.; Allen, R. R.; and Johannesen, R. L. *Contemporary American Speeches.* 3d ed. Belmont, Calif.: Wadsworth, 1972.

Lionberger, H. F. "Some Characteristics of Farm Operators Sought As Sources of Farm Information in a Missouri Community." *Rural Sociology* 18 (1953):327–38.

Littlejohn, S. W. *Theories of Human Communication.* Columbus, Ohio: Charles E. Merrill, 1978.

"Louder, Please." *Time*, May 4, 1970, p. 92.

Lund, F. "The Psychology of Belief." *Journal of Abnormal and Social Psychology* 20 (1925):174–96.

Lutz, R. J. "Cognitive Change and Attitude Change, A Validation Study." Ph.D. diss., University of Illinois, 1973.

Lynes, R. "Catalysts of Taste." *Architectural Digest* (March 1980), pp. 36–40.

McBath, J. H., ed. *Argumentation and Debate, Principles and Practices.* New York: Holt, Rinehart and Winston, 1963.

McCombs, M. "Agenda-setting Function of Mass Media." *Public Relations Review* 3 (1977):89–95.

McCowan, Clark. *It's Only a Movie.* Englewood Cliffs, N.J.: Prentice Hall, 1972.

McCroskey, J. C. "A Summary on the Effects of Evidence in Persuasive Communication." *Quarterly Journal of Speech* 55 (1969):169–76.

McCroskey, J. C.; Holdridge, W.; and Toomb, J. K. "An Instrument for Measuring the Source Credibility of Basic Speech Communication Instructors." *Speech Teacher* 23 (1974):26–33.

McCroskey, J. C.; Jensen, T.; and Todd, C. "The Generalizability of Source Credibility Scales for Public Figures." Paper presented at the annual convention of the Speech Communication Association, Chicago 1972.

McCroskey, J. C.; Jensen, T.; and Valencia, C. "Measurement of the Credibility of Mass Media Sources." Paper presented at the annual convention of the Western Speech Communication Association, 1973.

———. "Measurement of the Credibility of Peers and Spouses." Paper presented at the annual convention of the International Communication Association, Montreal, 1973.

McCroskey, J. C.; Scott, M. D.; and Young, T. J. "The Dimensions of Source Credibility for Spouses and Peers." Paper presented at the annual convention of the Western Speech Communication Association, Portland, 1971.

McCroskey, J. C., and Young, T. J. "Ethos and Credibility: The Construct and Its Measurement after Three Decades." Unpublished paper, 1977.

McGovern, G. *Dallas Morning News,* October 11, 1972.

McGuire, W. J. "Persistance of the Resistance to Persuasion Induced by Various Types of Prior Belief Defenses." *Journal of Abnormal and Social Psychology* 64 (1962):241–48.

———. "The Nature of Attitudes and Attitude Change." In *The Handbook of Social Psychology.* Reading, Mass.: Addison–Wesley, 1969.

———. "A Vaccine for Brainwash." *Psychology Today* 5 (1970):30–36.

McGuire, W. J., and Papageorgis, D. "Effectiveness of Forewarning in Developing Resistance to Persuasion." *Public Opinion Quarterly* 26 (1962):24–34.

McLuhan, M. *Understanding Media.* New York: Signet, 1964.

McQuail, D., ed. *Sociology of Mass Communication.* Middlesex, Eng.: Penguin, 1972.

Makay, J. J., and Sawyer, T. C. *Speech Communication Now: An Introduction to Rhetorical Influences.* Columbus, Ohio: Charles E. Merrill, 1973.

Marsh, C. P., and Coleman, A. L. "Farmer's Practice-Adoption Rates in Relation to Adoption Rates of 'Leaders.'" *Rural Sociology* 19 (1954):180–81.

Martin, H. H., and Andersen, K. E. *Speech Communication.* Boston: Allyn & Bacon, 1968.

Marwell, G., and **Schmitt, D. R.** "Dimensions of Compliance-gaining Behavior: An Empirical Analysis." *Sociometry* 30 (1967):350–64.

Maslow, A. H. *Motivation and Personality.* New York: Harper & Row, 1970.

Mayer, J. P. *Sociology of Film.* London: Faber & Faber, 1946.

Meerloo, J. *The Rape of the Mind.* New York: World, 1956.

Mehrabian, A. "A Semantic Space for Nonverbal Behavior." *Journal of Consulting and Clinical Psychology* 35,2 (1970):248–57.

————. *Public Places and Private Spaces, the Psychology of Work, Play and Living Environments.* New York: Basic Books, 1976.

Mehrabian, A., and **Ferris, S. R.** "Inference of Attitudes from Nonverbal Communication in Two Channels." *Journal of Consulting Psychology* 31 (1967):248–52.

Mehrabian, A., and **Williams, M.** "Nonverbal Concomitants of Perceived and Intended Persuasiveness." *Journal of Personality and Social Psychology* 13 (1969):37–58.

Menzel, H., and **Katz, E.** "Social Relations and Innovations in the Medical Profession: The Epidiology of a New Drug." *Public Opinion Quarterly* 19 (1956):337–52.

Merrill, J. C., and **Lowenstein, R. L.** *Media, Messages, and Men.* New York: David McKay, 1967.

Merton, R. K. *Social Theory and Social Structure.* New York: The Free Press, 1957.

Miller G. "Studies in the Use of Fear Appeals: A Summary and Analysis." *Central States Speech Journal* 14 (1963):117–25.

Miller, G.; Boster, F.; Roloff, M.; and **Seibold, D.** "Compliance-gaining Message Strategies: A Typology and Some Findings Concerning Effects of Situational Differences." *Communication Monographs* 44 (1977):37–50.

Miller, G. R., and **Burgoon, M.** *New Techniques of Persuasion.* New York: Harper & Row, 1973.

————, and————. "Persuasion Review and Commentary." *Communication Yearbook 2.* B. D. Ruben, ed. New Brunswick, N.J.: International Association, 1978.

Mills, J., and **Aronson, E.** "Opinion Change As a Function of the Communicator's Attractiveness and Desire to Influence." *Journal of Personality and Social Psychology* 1 (1965):73–77.

Mills, Karren. "Could Willie's Twang Cause More Drinking?" *Dallas Morning News,* February 1980, p. 3.

Minnick, W. C. *The Art of Persuasion.* Boston: Houghton-Mifflin, 1968.

————. *Public Speaking.* Boston: Houghton-Mifflin, 1979.

Montgomery, C. L., and **Burgoon, M.** "The Effects of Androgyny and Message Expectations on Resistance to Persuasive Communication." *Communication Monographs* 47 (1980):56–67.

"Murder on Television and the Fourteen Year Old." *Saturday Review,* January 8, 1972.

Nader, R. *Unsafe at Any Speed.* New York: Grossman, 1965.

National Public Radio News. KERA-FM. Dallas, Texas. January 15, 1978.

————. KERA-FM. Dallas, Texas. December 4, 1980.

Nelson, C. E. "Anchoring to Accepted Values As a Technique for Immunizing Beliefs against Persuasion." *Journal of Personality and Social Psychology* 9,4 (1968):329–34.

Newcomb, H. "Toward Television History." *Journal of the University Film Association* 30 (1978):9–14.

———, ed. *Television: The Critical View.* 2d ed. New York: Oxford University Press, 1979.

Nixon, R. "Checkers" speech. Delivered on radio and television, September 23, 1952.

North Texan, May 30, 1980, p. 9.

Norton, R. W., and **Pettigrew, L. S.** "Communicator Style As an Effective Determinant of Attraction." *Communication Research* 4 (1977):257–82.

Nunnally, J. C., and **Bobren, H. M.** "Variables Influencing the Willingness to Receive Communications on Mental Health." *Journal of Personality* 27 (1959):38–46.

Oliver, R. T. *The Psychology of Persuasive Speech.* New York: David McKay, 1957.

Oliver, R. T.; Zelko, H. P.; and **Holtzman, P. D.** *Communicative Speech.* New York: Holt, Rinehart and Winston, 1962.

Osgood, C. E., and **Tannenbaum, P. H.** "The Principles of Congruity in the Production of Attitude Change." *Psychological Review* 62 (1955):42–55.

Packard, Vance. *The Hidden Persuaders.* New York: David McKay, 1957.

Park, R. E., and **Burgess, E. W.,** eds. *Introduction to the Science of Sociology.* Chicago: University of Chicago Press, 1921.

"People, etc." *Dallas Times Herald,* May 25, 1980.

Peterson, R. C., and **Thurstone, L. L.** *Motion Pictures and the Social Attitudes of Children.* New York: Macmillan, 1933.

Petric, V. "Film in the Battle of Ideas." *Arts in Society* 10 (1973):234–41.

Primeau, R. *The Rhetoric of Television.* New York: Longman, 1979.

Pryor, T. D. "The Persuasive Environment of the Dallas Loew's Anatole Hotel." Unpublished paper, 1979.

Real, M. R. *Mass-mediated Culture.* Englewood Cliffs, N.J.: Prentice-Hall, 1977.

Rhine, R. J., and **Severance, L. J.** "Ego-Involvement, Discrepancy, Source Credibility, and Attitude Change." *Journal of Personality and Social Psychology* 16 (1970):175–90.

Ritterbush, P. C. "Vandalism and Juvenile Delinquency." *Vital Speeches* 20 (1953–54):302–3.

Rogers, C. R. "Toward a Modern Approach to Values." *Journal of Abnormal and Social Psychology* 68 (1964):160–67.

Rogers, E. M. "Characteristics of Agricultural Innovators and Other Adopter Categories." Wooster Ohio Agricultural Experimental Station Circular No. 94 (1961).

———. "Incentives in the Diffusion of Family Planning Innovations." *Studies in Family Planning* 2 (1971):241–48.

Rogers, E. M., and **Shoemaker, F. F.** *Communication of Innovations.* New York: Holt, Rinehart and Winston, 1971.

Rogers, E. M., and **Svenning, L.** *Modernization among Peasants.* New York: Holt, Rinehart and Winston, 1969.

Rogers, R. W., and Deckner, C. W. "Effects of Fear Appeals and Physiological Arousal upon Emotion, Attitudes, and Cigarette Smoking." *Journal of Personality and Social Psychology* 32 (1975):222–30.

Rokeach, M. *The Open and Closed Mind.* New York: Basic Books, 1960.

———. *Beliefs, Attitudes, and Values: A Theory of Organization and Change.* San Francisco: Jossey-Bass, 1969.

———. *The Nature of Human Values.* New York: The Free Press, 1973.

———. *Understanding Human Values.* New York: The Free Press, 1979.

Rokeach, M., and Kliejunas, P. "Behavior As a Function of Attitude-toward-Object and Attitude-toward-Situation." *Journal of Personality and Social Psychology* 22 (1972):194–201.

Roloff, M. E., and Miller, G. R., eds. *Persuasion: New Directions in Theory and Research.* Beverly Hills, Calif.: Sage, 1980.

Rosenbaum, M. E., and Franc, D. E. "Opinion Change As a Function of External Commitment and Amount of Discrepancy from the Opinion of Another." *Journal of Abnormal and Social Psychology* 61 (1960):15–20.

Rosenbaum, M. E., and Zimmerman, I. M. "The Effect of External Commitment on Responses to an Attempt to Change Opinions." *Public Opinion Quarterly* 23 (1959):247–54.

Rosett, J. *The Mechanism of Thought, Imagery, and Hallucination.* New York: Academic Press, 1967.

Rosnow, R., and Robinson, E., eds. *Experiments in Persuasion.* New York: Academic Press, 1967.

Ross, R. S. *Persuasion: Communication and Interpersonal Relations.* Englewood Cliffs, N.J.: Prentice-Hall, 1974.

Rotha, P. *Documentary Film.* London: Faber & Faber, 1952.

Ruben, B. D., ed. *Communication Yearbook 2.* New Brunswick, N.J.: International Communication Association, 1978.

Schillaci, Anthony. "Films as Environment." In *Perspectives on the Study of Film.* John S. Katz, ed. Boston: Little, Brown, 1971.

Scott, D. R. "Man's Boundless Curiosity Goes Past Moon." *Dallas Morning News,* August 13, 1971, p. 5A.

Seamon, D. *A Geography of the Lifeworld: Movement, Rest, and Encounter.* New York: St. Martin's Press, 1979.

Sears, S. O., and Freedman, J. I. "Selective Exposure to Information: A Critical Review." *Public Opinion Quarterly* 31 (1967).

Sherif, C., and Sherif, M. *Attitude, Ego-Involvement and Change.* New York: Wiley, 1967.

Sherif, M., and Sherif, C. W. *Social Psychology.* New York: Harper & Row, 1969.

Simons, H. W. *Persuasion: Understanding, Practice, and Analysis.* Reading, Mass.: Addison-Wesley, 1976.

Simons, S. B.; Howe, L. W.; and Kirschenbaum, H. *Social Psychology.* New York: Harper & Row, 1969.

———. *Values Clarification.* New York: Hart, 1972.

Smith, R. R. *Beyond the Wasteland.* Falls Church, Va.: Speech Communication Association, 1976.

———. "Fictive Elements in Television News." Paper presented at the annual convention of the Eastern Communication Association, Boston, 1978.

Snyder, M. "Self-Monitoring of Expressive Behavior." *Journal of Personality and Social Psychology* 30 (1974):526–37.

Sommer, R. *Personal Space, the Behavioral Basis of Design.* Englewood Cliffs, N.J.: Prentice-Hall, 1969.

————. *Design Awareness.* San Francisco: Rinehart, 1972.

Spillman, B. "The Impact of Value and Self-Esteem Messages in Persuasion." *Central States Speech Journal* 30 (1979):67–74.

Steele, E., and Redding, W. C. "The American Value System." *Western Speech* 26 (1962):83–91.

Steiner, I. D., and Rogers, E. D. "Alternative Responses to Dissonance." *Journal of Abnormal and Social Psychology* 68 (1963):38–44.

Steinfatt, T., and Infante, D. "Attitude-Behavior Relationships in Communication Research." *Quarterly Journal of Speech* 62 (1976):267–78.

Sternthal, B.; Phillips, L. W.; and Dholakia, Ruby D. "The Persuasive Effect of Source Credibility: A Situational Analysis." *Public Opinion Quarterly* 43 (1978):285–314.

Strodtbeck, F. L., and Hook, L. H. "Social Dimensions of a Twelve Man Jury Table." *Sociometry* 24 (1961):297–415.

Stuart, Charlotte. "Architecture in Nazi Germany: A Rhetorical Perspective." *Western Speech* 37 (1973):253–63.

Swanson, G.; Newcomb, T.; and Hartley, E., eds. *Readings in Social Psychology.* 3d ed. New York: Holt, Rinehart and Winston, 1958.

Tannenbaum, P. H., and Geer, E. P. "Mood Change As a Function of Stress of Protagonist and Degree of Identification in a Film-viewing Situation." *Journal of Personality and Social Psychology* 2 (1965):612–16.

Tedeschi, J., ed. *The Social Influence Process.* Chicago: Aldine, 1972.

Thomas, Bob. "de Laurentiis Plans 10 Movies in 1976," *Dallas Morning News,* August 25, 1975, p. 4D.

Thompson, W. *The Process of Persuasion: Principles and Readings.* New York: Harper & Row, 1975.

Thompson, Wayne. *Quantitative Research in Public Address and Communication.* New York: Random House, 1967.

Thurstone, L. L. "The Measurement of Attitudes." *Psychological Review* 26 (1931):249–69.

Tobin, R. L. "When Dynamite Rains from the Sky." *Saturday Review,* August 5, 1967, pp. 18–19.

Triandis, H. C. *Attitude and Attitude Change.* New York: Wiley, 1971.

————. *Interpersonal Behavior.* Monterey, Calif.: Brooks/Cole, 1977.

Trudeau, G. B. *Doonesbury's Greatest Hits.* New York: Holt, Rinehart, and Winston, 1978.

Turner, C. W., and Berkowitz, L. "Identification with Film Aggressor (Covert Role Taking) and Reactions to Film Violence." *Journal of Personality and Social Psychology* 21 (1972):256–64.

Turner, R. "Role-taking, Role Standpoint, and Reference Group Behavior." *American Journal of Sociology* 56 (1956):316–28.

United Nations Educational, Scientific, and Cultural Organization. "Reports and

Papers on Mass Communication." In *The Influence of the Cinema on Children and Adolescents*. Paris: UNESCO, 1961.

Valins, S. "Cognitive Effects of False Heart-Rate Feedback." *Journal of Personality and Social Psychology* 4 (1966):400–8.

Vohs, J. L. "An Empirical Approach to the Concept of Attention." *Speech Monographs* 31 (1964):355–60.

Vohs, J. L., and **Garrett, R. L.** "Resistance to Persuasion: An Integrative Framework." *Public Opinion Quarterly* 32 (1968):445–52.

Weinberg, H. *Levels of Knowing and Existence*. New York: Harper & Row, 1959.

Weiss, W., and **Fine, B. J.** "The Effect of Induced Aggressiveness on Opinion Change." *Journal of Abnormal and Social Psychology* 52 (1956):109–14.

Wells, A. *Mass Media and Society*. Palo Alto, Calif.: Mayfield, 1979.

White, D. M. "The Gatekeeper: A Case Study in the Selection of News." *Journalism Quarterly* 27 (1950):383–90.

Wicker, A. W. "Processes Which Mediate Behavior Environment." *Behavioral Science* 17 (1972):265–77.

Widgery, R. N., and **Webster, B.** "The Effects of Physical Attractiveness upon Perceived Credibility." *Michigan Speech Journal* 4 (1969):9–15.

Wiese, M., and **Cole, S.** "A Study of Children's Attitudes and the Influence of a Commercial Motion Picture." *Journal of Psychology* 21 (1946):151–71.

Wilkening, E. A. "Informal Leaders and Innovators in Farm Practices." *Rural Sociology* 17 (1952):272–75.

Williams, R. *Television: Technology and Cultural Form*. New York: Schocken, 1975.

Winans, J. A. *Public Speaking*. New York: Century, 1915.

Wolfgang, M., and **Ferraciti, F.** *The Sub-Culture of Violence: Towards an Integrated Theory in Criminology*. London: Tavistock, 1967.

Woolbert, C. H. *The Fundamentals of Speech: A Behavioristic Study of the Underlying Principals of Speaking and Reading*. New York: Harper & Brothers, 1920.

Wright, C. R. "Functional Analysis and Mass Communication." *Public Opinion Quarterly* 24 (1960):605–20.

Wright, J. W., ed. *The Commercial: Advertising and the American Mass Media*. New York: Delta, 1979.

Wuntch, Philip. "Valenti: A Man for ALL Movies." *Dallas Morning News*, January 29, 1975, p. 22A.

Zajonc, R. "Attitudinal Effects of Mere Exposure." *Journal of Personality and Social Psychology* 9 (1968):1–27.

Zimbardo, P. G. "Involvement and Communication Discrepancy in Determinants of Opinion Conformity." *Journal of Abnormal and Social Psychology* 60 (1960):86–94.

INDEX

Victoria O'Donnell is Professor of Speech Communication at North Texas State University. Graduated from the Pennsylvania State University, she received her Ph.D. from the same university. The recipient of numerous research grants and honors including being named Honor Professor at North Texas State University in 1976, Victoria O'Donnell has been a Danforth Foundation Associate and a Summer Scholar of the National Endowment for the Humanities. In addition, she has served on the Board of Directors of the University Film Association as well as on the Advisory Board of the University Film Foundation. At present she is Director, Division of Interpersonal and Public Communication, in the Department of Speech Communication and Drama. Victoria O'Donnell has published numerous articles and is the coauthor of a book in progress, *Persuasion and Propaganda*, to be published by Sage Publications in the fall of 1982.

June Kable is a Professor in the Department of Communication and Theatre at Midwestern State University, Texas. Graduated from Baylor University, she received a Ed.D. from North Texas State University. A past President of the Texas Speech Association, June Kable was also a Danforth Foundation Associate and has served as Chairperson of the Communication and Theatre Department at Midwestern State. Although she has published articles about her primary areas of concern, *Persuasion: An Interactive-Dependency Approach* represents her first book.